The New Media Invasion

The New Media Invasion

Digital Technologies and the World They Unmake

JOHN DAVID EBERT

McFarland & Company, Inc., Publishers
Jefferson, North Carolina, and London

LIBRARY OF CONGRESS CATALOGUING-IN-PUBLICATION DATA

Ebert, John David, 1968–
    The new media invasion : digital technologies and the world
they unmake / John David Ebert.
        p.   cm.
    Includes bibliographical references and index.

    ISBN 978-0-7864-6560-6
    softcover : 50# alkaline paper ∞

    1. Information technology — Social aspects.   2. Digital —
media — Social aspects.   3. Internet — Social aspects.
4. Technology and civilization.   5. Civilization, Modern —
21st century.   I. Title.
HM851.E25   2011
303.48'33 — dc23   2011034854

BRITISH LIBRARY CATALOGUING DATA ARE AVAILABLE

On the cover: *St. Jerome in His Study* (oil on linen paper on panel) by
Jan van Eyck (c. 1390–1441) (attr. to). Detroit Institute of Arts/City of
Detroit Purchase/Bridgeman Art Library

Manufactured in the United States of America

McFarland & Company, Inc., Publishers
  Box 611, Jefferson, North Carolina 28640
  www.mcfarlandpub.com

For my brother Tom Ebert

Acknowledgments

Firstly, I would like to thank, as always, John Lobell and William Irwin Thompson for taking the time to read through the manuscript and offer thoughtful criticisms and suggestions for improvement.

In addition, I would also like to thank those who have read portions of the manuscript and offered their support and enthusiasm for the project as a whole: Lawrence Phillip Pearce, Jeremy Johnson, Ptolemy Tompkins, Benton Rooks, Jacques de Beaufort, Kheir Fakhreldin, Rachmael Pendragon, Jeremy Ray Twiss, Ray Grasse, Emily Kischell and Heidemarie Berken.

Thanks for reading, guys.

Table of Contents

Incipit

In Jan van Eyck's 1435 painting of Saint Jerome (on the cover), we see the scholar in his study, lion at his feet. The patron saint of libraries, scholars and archives; the first to translate the Bible into Latin. In Van Eyck's painting, he is conflated with the Renaissance scholar surrounded by stacks of books, the edges of their pages already yellowing. His lion has been miniaturized to the size of a domestic cat; later, the lion — Jerome's *vahana*— will be placed at the thresholds and entrances of libraries in his honor. He has been placed at the entrance to this book for similar reasons.

Traditionally speaking, one always invoked gods of media at the start of any literary undertaking: in India, the reciter of tales begins with an homage to Ganesha, the breaker of paths through the forests of adversity; in antiquity, the poets began with the Muses. Admittedly, I'm not a poet, but it can't hurt to cover your tracks.

Actually, what fascinates me about this painting is how Jerome needs the light spilling in through the window above him in order to see his text, presumably some Greek or Roman classic recently translated and brought over to Europe from Constantinople — the historical Jerome dates back to the fourth century, but in Van Eyck's painting, he actually exists in two timelines simultaneously, for he is both fourth century Christian hermit and also fifteenth century Renaissance scholar.

Jerome's study in this image looks a little like my own, except that whereas his lectern is tilted at a forty-five degree angle so that he can read his book, what I have open in front of me and tilted at a similar angle is a Macintosh iBook G4 laptop. And unlike him, I can see my text in the dark, since the computer screen glows at night like a television set with its own internal bioluminescence.

A lot has changed since Jerome's (and Van Eyck's) day, which is, of course, the primary reason why I have written this book. It is a document meant to chronicle the stresses of a major cultural shifting in sensibilities, one with, I believe, catastrophic consequences for all our traditional printed media.

While I am certainly no technophile, it is also important for me to point out that I am not exactly a technophobe, either, as the following text might lead one to believe. Like Jerome, I spend most of my time in my study, reading, but unlike him, a lot of what I read is electronic. The Internet has become an essential tool to my existence as a writer and has created a co-dependency that I am loathe to admit. It seems nowadays that I am always on it, checking email, watching videos on YouTube, looking something up on Wikipedia, or searching for books on Amazon. These sites have completely hi-jacked my life, but it wasn't always this way. I can still remember starting out as a writer fifteen or so years ago and never using the Internet because I didn't then know what it was, or even care. Now it composes my environment as a total surround. And I'm a little bit concerned about this, because I often wonder what would become of me if something should ever happen to the Internet? If Paul Virilio's global accident that he has been predicting for years should ever become a reality, and some unforeseen catastrophe unplugs the Internet, then where will we be? A civilization thrust back into the depths of a new (and very) Dark Age, apparently.

And speaking of the dark side of things, one of the main reasons I have written this book is to investigate the often overlooked — indeed, usually ignored — *shadow* side of all these new gadgets. Just as in the case of Nietzsche's perception of the grim horrors that underlay the Apollonian beauties of the gleaming marble of the Greek temples and the smoothly polished contours of Classical statues, so likewise, there is a whole hidden dimension to the existence of this new world, a dimension of chaos and cultural destabilization — of bloodletting, in other words — that needs, I believe, to be illuminated. I find these gadgets to be novel and fascinating, but I also think we need to be aware of the *costs* involved in bringing this new digital cosmos into being.

In ancient myth, this was the role of the sacrificial victim, the Christ or the Moses, the one who was *left behind* or *murdered* specifically so that a particular world could come into being and flourish on the remains of that death. While the New World thrives, the old one that was sacrificed to make the new one possible is kept alive through the performance of the ritual that reenacts the sacrifice. At a Jewish wedding, the wine glass is stepped on in order to remember the destruction of the Temple by the Romans in 70 A.D. In the Christian sacrament, you eat the body and drink the blood of the Christ because it is *God's* blood that is keeping you alive and your world functioning.

Traditionally speaking, the purpose of myth and ritual is to keep alive, to *never forget,* the sacrifice of the one whose death made possible the world *inside of which* you now live. Heidegger may have insisted that being-*in* did not mean existing "inside of" a spatial container, but this is precisely the sense in which it should be understood here.

So, likewise, the wonderful new digital cosmos in which we are all swimming about nowadays depends for its existence upon the sacrifice of a Cosmic Being, which, like Tiamat, has had to be killed and cut up in order to create the very substance, indeed, the very *epidermis* of the new world inside of which we now dwell. Indeed, the bubble, the sphere — to borrow from Peter Sloterdijk — the very *container* inside of which we *Ek-sist* has been constructed out of the fragments of the death of the body of the Word (which, remember, was made flesh, and so can, after all, be killed) which, once upon a time, we actually took inside of our very bodies as a form of (Catholic) nourishment.

The purpose of this book, accordingly, is to remind us of the murder of an entire way of life that has existed for centuries, a way of life made possible by the architecture of European capitalism, an entire mediatic ecosystem that is now disappearing, and must disappear, if the new media universe is to thrive.

This book, I would hasten to add, is not a collection of mere objections to the new media environment — although there are, admittedly, some of those — but rather an attempt to follow the contours of the *structure* of the process whereby one world disintegrates while another takes its place.

It is a study of media Death and Resurrection in action.

Introduction to a
Catastrophic Bifurcation

When Worlds Close Down

Every culture opens a window onto a particular world horizon that is accessed via one or another form of media. Normally, the process of articulation and unfolding of a cosmos is two-fold, that of annunciation and transmission: annunciation, that is, of a vision to one sort of prophet, while another one, receiving the vision, then creates the necessary medium for transmitting it on a mass scale. Thus, Abraham, living in the Mesopotamian city of Ur, hears the voice of an obscure and hitherto unknown god that tells him to leave the land of his birth and migrate to another land, Canaan, which this god will make known to him. Generations later, after enduring the collective traumas of Egyptian servitude, the vision descends to Moses, who invents the medium of the alphabet and brings it down from the top of the mountain as the new means for communicating the Hebraic vision of a *non-visual* deity who makes his will known via a *non-pictographic* script.

Later, reiterating the structural dynamics of the same process, an illiterate carpenter will venture into the desert in quest of a new vision bestowed upon him by a descending dove — the ancient signifier of the love goddess Aphrodite — in which the dove's *revised* meaning will now stand for a religion of *an*-erotic brotherly love. A generation or two more and a man named Saul, hit by a vision on his way to Damascus, will change the signifier of his name to Paul and then invent the new literary medium of the Christian epistle as

5

a means for conveying this desert vision to the other members of the worldly City of God.

The vision, then, comes first — whether that vision is of an acoustic or imagistic nature — while the medium for transmitting it is then invented subsequently. Note that the morphology of the process of world-formation implies that a literate mentality is absolutely unnecessary for receiving world-shaping Visions that become foundational for entire civilizations. Literacy only becomes necessary, along the lines of the Shannon-Weaver model of communication, for *sending* that Vision along the constraints of one or another cultural channel to a receiving audience.

When, however, worlds *close down* and visions *become extinct,* so too, their corresponding media disappear. Thus, Egyptian hieroglyphs vanish at the end of the fourth century when the vision that had animated Egyptian civilization for three thousand years had crumbled and fallen into desuetude. The cuneiform tablet, likewise, had by then already disappeared (end of the first century) along with the Mesopotamian way of life that Abraham was already paying farewell to in about 1800 B.C.

Likewise, when the literate world configured in the fifteenth century by the advent of the printing press — a world structured by individuality, nationalism and abstract, three-dimensional space — begins to disappear somewhere in the middle of the twentieth century in a haze of violent, earth-shaking battles and academic disputes in which their corresponding metanarratives are taken apart, dismantled and deconstructed — then it is only a matter of time before the media which made that world possible, which had fed and sustained it for centuries with printed books, magazines, newspapers and bookstores, also begin to vanish.

Which brings us to the edges of history, where we, today, currently find ourselves gazing off into the abyss of a new media extinction event in which absolutely *all* the media which have built and shaped a literate Gutenbergian cosmos for five centuries are, within the space of about a decade, *ceasing* to exist.

Extinction Event

What made this ecosystem possible in the first place was a society equipped with printed reading matter and the corresponding mercantile economy of booksellers, shopowners and vendors which came into being in order to purvey those texts in the form of identical copies of mass-reproduced objects to a European public whose vision had been honed to a keen edge by the recent invention of lenses. Spinoza, lest we forget, made his living as a lens grinder, and the achievements of natural philosophers like Roger Bacon, Galileo and Descartes were made possible, to a very large degree, by their fascination with the properties of optical devices. This was a culture, in other words, that was thoroughly fascinated by the dynamics of *vision,* and everything that it produced, from printed books to depth-perspectival oil paintings, were manifestations of this fascination.

The new digital world that is coming to replace this optical horizon of Western civilization, on the contrary, is one based upon the revelation of the integrated circuit: a world of hidden, *non-visible* electromagnetic fields of force. This invisible cosmos of photons and electrons traveling at the speed of light — think of the old iconic RKO tower beaming its zigzags to all quarters of the compass — now cocoons the entire planet in a sort of invisible macrosphere composed of ghosts, phantoms and etheric information searching for antennae like Shannon's proverbial receiver waiting to catch and rearrange the data into an observable, yet phantasmic, reality of pulsing signals given form as recognizable images.

This is a new cosmos altogether, one that is moving too fast for the media of old Europe, with its linear first-one-thing-then-another logic to keep up with. And since it can't keep up, that world, together with all its media of communication, is dissolving into the slag heap of melted visions and worn out cosmologies along with all of history's other discarded world horizons.

The sum total of these vanishing media, however, is currently amounting to something of an extinction event analogous to all those other great geo-ecological extinctions which scientists and environmentalists have mapped out for us. But whereas those events — there were five of them, the most recent being the one that killed off all the dinosaurs approximately 65 million years ago — took place offstage, as it were, in a distant temporal horizon that is inaccessible to our contemporary mode of experience, the current media extinction event is happening right in front of our eyes.

One morning, for instance, I woke up to do a Google search only to find out that record stores had disappeared while I wasn't looking. Indeed, I read that Tower Records had closed the doors of its last store in December of 2006, just a few years after Apple's release of its iPod in 2001 and its iTunes Music Store in 2003. Tower Records, *gone?* But how could this be?

And that's not all: bookstores may soon follow, for they have been closing their doors steadily since the advent of Amazon.com in 1995, and now, with the release of the third generation Kindle in August of 2010, the book itself as a physical entity may soon go the way of CDs, records and tape cassettes. Borders Books, moreover, has called it a day, and Barnes and Noble is doing nowhere near the kind of business that it once used to. DVDs, too, may not last much longer, as Netflix's streaming of movies on their website begins to catch on, and the movie studios themselves introduce Video on Demand services which will make movies available over the Internet within a mere 45 days of their theatrical release.

Newspapers, furthermore, which came into being during the early part of the seventeenth century, and magazines, which originated about a century after that, are folding up at an alarming rate. Newspapers that have either filed for bankruptcy or will be transferring to exclusively online versions include *The Philadelphia Daily News, The Minneapolis Star Tribune, The Miami Herald, The Detroit News, The Boston Globe, The San Francisco Chronicle, The Chicago Sun Times, The New York Daily News, The Fort Worth Star Telegram* and *The Cleveland Plain Dealer.*

The Tribune Company, furthermore, which owns both *The Los Angeles Times* and *The Chicago Tribune* filed for bankruptcy in December of 2008. Not long ago, *The Christian Science Monitor* shifted from a daily to a weekly paper, while *The Washington Post*— the very paper that uncovered the Watergate hotel break-ins back in 1972 — announced in 2009 that three of its regional bureaus in New York, Chicago and Los Angeles would close.

The list of magazines that have folded up in the past decade is cause for similar alarm: *Mirabella, Mademoiselle, Lingua franca, The Partisan Review, Book Magazine, Circus Magazine, Premiere Magazine, Life, House and Garden, PC Magazine, Playgirl, Vibe, McCall's, Teen Magazine, Country Home, Gourmet Magazine,* and many other, more obscure titles.

The actual physical world space of capitalism, too, seems to be breaking apart and destructuring, for retail stores are collapsing all around us like singularities into the dead space of economic penury: in June of 2008, FedEx announced that they were removing "Kinko's" from their store signs, having already purchased the company in 2004; in February of 2010, meanwhile, Hollywood Video filed for bankruptcy and has now vanished along with Kinko's. KB Toys, Linens 'n Things, the Sharper Image and Steve & Barry's have all folded up for good. Blockbuster intends to close some 20 percent of its stores, while Starbucks has plans to shut down 600 or so of its stores, and Circuit City has closed its doors (its rival, Best Buy, meanwhile, is reporting loss of market share for the first time ever as of 2010). Sears, too, is in dire straits, with a ten percent loss of its revenue since 2005, when it made a desperate merge with Kmart. Sales at J.C. Penney's have declined by six percent, and other stores like Macy's, the Gap, Zales Jewelers, Foot Locker, Dillard's and Whole Foods are all cutting back and closing stores. Shopping malls themselves, furthermore, are in a state of decrepitude, and are becoming an increasing economic, as well as visual, blight all across the American landscape.

Not since the end of the fourth century A.D., when the Christian Emperor Theodosius outlawed paganism, has there been any comparable Media Extinction Event. In 384, Theodosius banned the ancient practice of haruspicy (the examination, that is, of the entrails of animals for omens, which had been practiced since the early days of the Sumerians); pagan feast days were declared work days in 389; a few years later, in 391, the Serapeum, a temple annex of the great library of Alexandria, was sacked and burned under his orders, resulting in the loss of countless manuscripts; in the same year, moreover, Theodosius issued a new decree outlawing blood sacrifice and insisting upon the closure of all pagan temples; also in 391, the eternal fire in the Temple of Vesta in the Roman Forum was extinguished and the Vestal Virgins disbanded; the last Olympic Games took place in 393. The fourth century was, furthermore, the final century in which Egyptian hieroglyphics were written.

Subsequent centuries have featured assaults on books and learning (as for example, when the Arabs finished off the Alexandrian library in the seventh century), book burnings and barbarian invasions, but nothing on the scale of what happened in the fourth century, in which pagan media of all kinds were forcibly extinguished. What is happening today is, of course, not taking place at the point of the sword, but as part of the internal exigencies of capitalism. Nevertheless, the scale of the two events is just about commensurate.

The Internet vs. the Printing Press

If an extinction event is characterized by a vast reduction of species biodiversity in favor of fewer of them, then I think it is possible to theorize that ever since about the year 1995, when the National Science Foundation released control of the Internet to the private sector, we have been living through an analogous phenomenon on the plane of media and culture. A single colossal entity, the Internet, together with a handful of electronic gadgets which swarm around it like a cloud of flies, is emerging from the devastated mediascape as a powerful force of centralized communications. Almost every digital gadget in existence is compatible with the Internet in some way, including the personal computer itself, without which, we should remind ourselves, the Internet would not even have been possible.

I think it is important, though, *not* to see this, as is commonplace in most contemporary discussions of the social effects of the Internet, as analogous to what happened with the rise of the printing press in the middle of the fifteenth century. There are some important reasons for this.

The printing press, for one thing, emerged out of world circumstances which were entirely favorable to it, for its nature as an ocular medium was already consistent with the optically based aptitudes of the society that gave birth to it. It simply brought this specular gaze, which was already being honed by painters and Scholastic philosophers, to a fine focus.

The Internet, on the other hand, is not an ocular medium, but a digital one, and as such, it is inherently *incompatible* with the Gutenbergian nature of the print-based society into which it crashed like a bolt from the blue. Its advent is sudden and discontinuous, whereas that of the printing press had been more gradual and evolutionary.

Elizabeth Eisenstein, in her magisterial two-volume study, *The Printing Press as an Agent of Change*,[1] made the argument, back in the 1970s, that the effects of typography were not so much evolutionary as *revolutionary* and that its effects were rather more sudden than her media studies peers had then assumed. But it should be pointed out that the word "sudden" is a relative thing: her idea of the "suddenness" of the printing press involved it exerting its effects over the course of about a century and a half. The damage wrought by the Internet to our media landscape, on the other hand, has taken place in about the same space of time as the proscriptions of Theodosius in the fourth century, namely, over the course of a mere *fifteen years*. This is neither evolutionary nor revolutionary, but *catastrophic*.

Indeed, the disturbing and transformative effects of the printing press are undeniable, as Eisenstein describes them: from approximately 1450—1600, the advent of typography favored a shift away from scriptoria and professional ("lay") stenographers to printers, which created new jobs for typesetters and compositors while putting scribes completely out of work. It also forced the Renaissance bookdealer, who had previously made his living selling illuminated manuscripts as works of art, to close the doors of his shop for good. Illuminators themselves found work for a time applying the same old techniques to the new medium, for the first printed books, "incunabula" as they are called, were virtually indistinguishable for a time from illuminated manuscripts.

The printing press also created intellectual property laws and the concept of "fame" as we know it, for it eroded the anonymity of oral sayings by fixing one's name in place on the title page, thus permanently associating the individual with a particular text that had sprung from his own brain like Athena from the head of Zeus. The unleashing of hordes of new texts, meanwhile, created the conditions for the possibility of the encyclopedically learned scholar, like Erasmus or Montaigne, thus transforming the mythic figure of Saint Jerome into a quotidian reality. The individual was no longer part of a vast social machine but rather cut loose from the Medieval collectivity by the linear framing processes of printing, as though saints were now being removed from niches where they had been buried in the walls of Gothic cathedrals and taking on their own lives as articulate men capable of explaining the symbolic subtleties of the Gothic edifice to a vast new reading public.

Thus, the overall impression that is conveyed by the details of this media revolution is one of linear continuity with the optically embedded structures in the mentality of the pre-printing press Western episteme. The sense of order and organization that is associated with typography — indexes, Arabic numerals, title pages and citations — is consistent with the already extant tendency toward linearity and ocularly inspired thinking that is evident in the Medieval scholastic mentality. Thus, if any culture was going to produce mechanized printing, it would surely have come forth out of the implicitly ordered and organized mentality of the Scholastic universe that had already dedicated itself to carefully detailing, arranging and tracking Classical texts preserved from the ruins of antiquity.

With the Internet, on the other hand, what is most strikingly evident is its *discontinuity* with the surrounding culture out of which it emerged, a culture that had built itself around printed media for five centuries prior to its advent. The Internet actually reverses and disrupts all of these structures: on the ironically named website Project Gutenberg, for instance, texts are simply dumped in and stripped of all their sensuous elements, fonts, typefaces, and indeed all haptic sense of texture have been removed from the books, and consequently, one is presented with a collection of unreadably bland documents that no one would ever want to spend much time bothering about. Blogs, meanwhile, are sloppy, informal and disorganized, and are rarely, if ever, proofread for grammatical and spelling errors with which they are normally saturated. Even on professionally designed websites, moreover, images are routinely misaligned, out of place or just plain incorrect. On Amazon.com, for instance, it is not uncommon to encounter book covers matched with the wrong captions, and so forth.

Many of these Internet sites, furthermore — as Andrew Keen points out in *The Cult of the Amateur*— are in reality low budget operations with little in the way of ad revenue to finance them and so cannot afford to pay good journalists and writers to create worthwhile articles and essays. As a result, there is a vast decrease not only in the quantity of *kinds* of available media, but also in the *quality* of the information that is offered as a monolithic substitute. We are being forced, in other words, to trade off a diversity of media sources — magazines, newspapers, etc.— for only *one* kind of media: digital. The disappearance of diversity, especially of media, is never a good thing, for in this case, it amounts to a massive cultural impoverishment. As a result of the elimination of choices, we are increasingly forced to rely more and more on the Internet in order to get access to our media, our news and our information, articles, essays, reviews, etc., which is only *one* means of purveying such media, and arguably, not even the best.

So the Internet is a force of disruption and discontinuity in the evolution of the Western mediascape and is in no way analogous to the revolution in printing inaugurated by typography in the fifteenth century. It is rather the incarnation of a *new* kind of mentality altogether, one in which technology, learning and information occur at the speed of light via digitization. It is a mentality that is at its best when its concern is with images, pattern recognition and icons; at its worst when it attempts to take over and mimic the functions of the Gutenbergian landscape that it is in process of dismantling.

Thus, the printing press *builds up,* favoring structurally organized hierarchies of knowledge, whereas the Internet *tears down,* favoring nomadologies of one sort or another (along with their attendant antipathy to knowledge apparatuses: historically, nomads are illiterate). To borrow from the language of the French philosophers Deleuze and Guattari, then, we can say that the Internet is a *nomadological technology* while the printing press is a technology of *state apparatuses.*

The Internet and Radio

There *is* another medium, however, that serves as a much better analogy to the Internet, and that is radio.

In the last quarter of the nineteenth century, the telegraph had given birth to two further media: the telephone, in which the disembodied human voice was transmitted across vast distances through wires; and the wireless telegraph, in which the atmosphere was stained with Morse code signals which saturated it in all directions simultaneously. The wireless, in turn, gave rise, about the year 1920, to radio, in which the heavens crackled with human voices and music coded into the ether like a technologized version of the ancient elemental spirits which were once thought to flit about amongst clouds, fields and trees intermittently.

Radio, you might say, added an *ear* to the ocular world of Gutenberg that had been missing since the days of the fifteenth century when oral traditions began to drop out and give way to printed works. The Medieval *jongleur* and the court storyteller — basically involved in staging Medieval radioplays — were obsolesced by the Renaissance man of the printed book whose *written* stories, plays and novels began to favor the eye at the expense of the ear. Radio brought back the Medieval storyteller and transplanted him into the middle of the suburbs, where the denizens of the average living room became his new audience.

But radio was a very different kind of medium from anything that had gone before it because it was the first medium to offer its content "free" to the public. The initial problem that it raised, correspondingly — and it was a problem that would later be raised again by the Internet — was how the new medium would pay for itself.

The inceptual imagination of radio was that it would be a sort of ennobling medium that would bring the arts and culture to the living rooms of suburbia (just as Starbucks later brought espresso from the cafes of Vienna to the sidewalks of Main Street). There was great reluctance, consequently, to freight the new medium with advertising, since in those days the living room was thought to be a place where the crass vulgarities of the marketplace did not belong. President Hoover's comment that it was "'inconceivable that we should allow so great a possibility for service, for news, for entertainment, for education, and for vital commercial purposes, to be drowned in advertising chatter'"[2] now seems almost comical in its naivete.

Various solutions were suggested: a private tax, perhaps, or else wealthy endowments from some Andrew Carnegie type of philanthropist?

Eventually, the aura of advertising that began to glow around the names of various programs, like the *Everready Hour* or performers like the Vicks Vaporub Quartette, began to provide the answer.[3] Within just a few years, the previous resistance to advertising had vanished, and the medium was so completely hi-jacked by advertisers that they actually began to dictate the content of shows, writing them and selling them as package deals to the networks. Eventually, radio became the one medium to draw its *entire* source of revenue from advertisers, and this solved, once and for all, the problem of how to pay for the new medium.

Another issue that radio raised was that of intellectual property rights, just as the Internet has done in our own day. The answer to the question, should royalties be paid for the right to use and broadcast music over the air? may be obvious to us, but back in the 1920s, it wasn't obvious at all. In 1922, the American Society of Composers, Authors and Publishers (ASCAP) demanded royalties for music played on the air, reminding one of the various suits filed by the Authors Guild and a convocation of publishers against Google in 2005 for the right to scan books electronically. Back in the 1920s, however, broadcasters pointed out that copyright holders were being greedy, since it was thought that by playing their music on the air, they were already getting free advertising. But, of course, we know very well how the copyright issue turned out.

Now the link between media and economic landscapes is not usually thought much about, but radio, too, had devastating effects on the economy of the 1920s just as the Internet has had in our own time, for as Paul Starr has pointed out, "radio in the 1920s, like the Internet three-quarters of a century later, plunged record (as well as sheet music) sales into a deep downturn," for rather than pay for the records, people preferred to listen to the music broadcast over the air for free.[4] The record companies managed to solve this particular problem by putting out the recordings of such hitherto overlooked music as jazz, which wasn't then being played on the radio — since it was considered "disreputable" — and thus served to create the jazz explosion of the 1920s.

There *are* of course important differences between the two media that should not be overlooked: the fact, for instance, that whereas the Internet is not owned by anyone, radio fell very quickly into the private ownership of just a few large networks. The damage inflicted by radio on other media, furthermore, has come nowhere near that which has been wrought by the Internet, for though radio was as different from printed media as the Internet is — coming down, as it were, from heaven to earth — it was not a medium that sought to *replace* and *imitate* those other media like some ersatz invasion of the body snatchers, but rather supplemented them with the invention of new literary genres like the radio play.

Radio, though, not only caused a downturn in the sales of records, it also siphoned off advertising revenue from newspapers and magazines — just as the Internet has done today — and may therefore have contributed to shifting the economy into that turbulent flow which we call the Great Depression. Perhaps not coincidentally, the advent of the Internet, too, was followed about a decade later by another Great Depression (although it has not yet been called this) and so it may be that we need to be more attentive to the politically and economically destabilizing effects of these new media on the respective societies into which they were born.

Destabilizations

The great media essayist Neil Postman, in his writings, used to point out that the one thing we almost always forget to ask in our excitement over the possibilities unveiled by new technologies is what way of life will be *un*done by this or that new gadget. This is a question which I think needs to be asked today more than ever. For every new technology invented, new vectors of turbulence are introduced into a society, and those vectors can sometimes result in explosive bifurcations which can be surprisingly destructive of existing socio-political configurations.

The role of television in the destabilization of the Soviet Union, for instance, which Gorbachev had, for the first time in Russian history, allowed to broadcast Politburo meetings live in the late 1980s, has yet to be studied, but the effects of Twitter during the 2009, presidential elections in Iran, very obviously catalyzed the transformation of the crowd into a plasma that nearly overwhelmed Ahmedinajad's regime. Then there is Xerox's invention of the copy machine, which came into widespread use in the late 1960s, and which enabled Daniel Ellsberg to photocopy the Pentagon Papers and hand them over to the *New York Times,* which published them in 1971, revealing a whole series of lies and cover-ups on the part of the U.S. government which set in motion a chain of events that would lead to the conclusion of the war a few years later.

It was Harold Innis, the cofounder of the American media studies tradition, who first remarked in his *Empire and Communications* that the rise of radio as a new medium in the 1920s may have contributed to destabilizing the economy and thus indirectly bringing on the Great Depression.[5] In his other great media studies book, *The Bias of Communication,* Innis even suggests, rather cryptically, that the invention of the telegraph in the 1840s may have played a role in the outbreak of the Civil War: "As in England the telegraph destroyed the monopoly of political centres and contributed, in destroying political power, to the outbreak of the Civil War."[6] There does, then, appear to exist an interesting pattern of economic depressions and wars occurring in the wake of volcanic periods of technological upheaval: the depression of 1837 — 43, for example, followed immediately upon a major public works project of building railroads, canals and urban roads.

The problem is that while healthy economies are able to integrate the turbulences caused by new technologies, economies that have already been weakened for one reason or another — by, say, old age or dwindling resources — may not be able to withstand the impacts of new innovations, especially if there are a lot of them occurring within a short space of time, as was the case in the 1920s. As a result, the proliferation of new gadgets creates structural instabilities in the economy which gradually accumulate and then, if conditions are right, brings about a catastrophic bifurcation in which the economic system collapses. As the system then restructures itself, it must take the new technologies into account, favoring certain of them, while excluding others. Thus, the evolution of economies and technologies are involved in an intimate feedback loop of structural coupling in which changes made in one sphere (i.e. technology) create changes in the other sphere (the economy) which then feed back into the original sphere and change it to suit the needs of the new situation.

As the philosopher Bernard Stiegler puts it in his book *Technics and Time:*

> The transformations of the technical system regularly bring in their wake upheavals of the social system, which can completely destabilize it when "the new technical system leads to the substitution of a dominant activity for an out-dated activity of a totally different nature...." The relation between the technical

and social systems is thus treated as a problem of consumption, in which the economic system is the third component: the development of consumerism, accompanying constant innovation, aims at a greater flexibility in consumer attitudes, which adapt and must adapt ever more quickly, at a pace obviously not without effect on the specifically cultural sphere. The twentieth century thereby appears properly and massively uprooting — and this will always provide the theme, in terms of alienation and decline, of the great discourses on technics.[7]

It therefore seems not implausible to me to suggest that we are caught in a period of turbulence similar to the one which took place in the 1920s — and before that, the 1830s — in which the new medium of radio — together with all sorts of new domestic gadgets such as the electric oven, the dishwasher, the refrigerator, etc. — exerted so many stresses on an already weakened economy that it brought about the total collapse of that economy.

The current crisis, admittedly, is a many body problem which involves multiple layers of interfolding causes — subprime loans and credit default swaps are only the surface layer, in my opinion — but surely the massive proliferation of gadgets during the years from 1995 to 2008 — i.e. the Internet, digital cameras, video games, handheld devices, etc. — has played a major role in the present collapse, since it has forced us into a survival mode in which we have to adapt very rapidly in a *very* short space of time to tremendous economic, political and technological changes. As P.W. Singer remarks:

> ... we experienced more technologic change in the 1990s than in the entire ninety years beforehand. To think about it another way, technology in 2000 was roughly one thousand times more advanced, more complex, and more integral to our day-to-day lives than the technology of 1900 was to our great-grandparents. More important, where they had decades and then years to digest each new invention, ours come in ever bigger bundles, in ever smaller periods of time.[8]

Just to take one example: as I was in the midst of revising this book, I came across an article in *The Atlantic Monthly*'s online journal in which the writer described how he thinks the iPod will become obsolete soon as the result of new cloud computing music websites like Grooveshark, rdio.com, or emusic.com. The writer points out how he no longer has any need for the iPod, since he uses his smartphone to download all the songs he wants, after paying his website a mere $36.00 annual fee for unlimited song downloads. What does he need an iPod for, or even the iTunes Music Store, in light of such a development?[9]

This is a pace of change that is absolutely breathtaking and it is nearly impossible to keep up with its demands. Indeed, by the time this book is published, much of it will have been rendered obsolete by new gadgets that have come along in the meantime.

The effects of such a rate of change upon the human psyche as well as the organization of society is nothing short of catastrophic, which is precisely why we periodically require catastrophes and breakdowns in order to give ourselves time to readjust and catch up with it. To quote Marshall McLuhan: "Most people take a long while to adjust to quite simple changes. And when invited to readjust their entire lives every few years to very vast changes, people tend to fall apart."[10]

Thus, the world that we have come to know — especially the one those of us who have reached middle age grew up in — is now collapsing all around us. We have entered a cultural and social *pralaya,* from which, I have no doubt, the world that emerges will bear only faint resemblance to the one inside of which we were encased up until the late 1990s. As different, say, as the 1950s were from the 1930s, two decades straddling either side of the catastrophes of the Great Depression and the Second World War, respectively.

The present book, then, is a report from the battlefield, as it were, meant to chronicle what it is like to live through such a shift, and how our perceptions and actions are being forced to change so drastically in order to adapt to the world that the new media are currently *un*making all around us.

First, a Brief Note on the Self-Luminous Nature of the New Technologies

Paul Virilio once insisted that in order to understand technology properly, one must first understand religion. Here is a case in point:

In Indian philosophy, a distinction is made between two different types of matter known as *sthula* and *sukshma*. Whereas the former is said to refer to physical matter, the latter denotes subtle, or visionary matter. Physical matter refers specifically to the mode of experiencing objects in the waking state, where each object is separate from every other object and all are illuminated from without. They are not self-luminous, as are the objects of subtle matter (*sukshma*), which are more proper to the visionary realms of dream and myth.[1] The forms of our dreams are not illuminated by the sun, or by anything else for that matter, for they are *self*-luminous, pulsing with their own weird internal bioluminescence like those glow-in-the-dark fish in Paul Klee's paintings. The physical body, moreover, is *sthula sarira,* while the subtle body is *sukshma sarira.* (The subtle body is what transmigrates from one lifetime to the next in the theoretical framework of Hindu metaphysics.)

But does this distinction not parallel the one Marshall McLuhan made between "light *through*" as opposed to "light *on*"? "Scribal culture and Gothic architecture," McLuhan writes, "were both concerned with light *through*, not light *on*."[2] Hence, the quality shared by the *illuminated* manuscript and the Gothic cathedral with its bejeweled interior of stained glass

19

is that of diaphaneity, or transparency. The light from another world shines *through* all cultural phenomena of the Medieval era. But after Gutenberg, as McLuhan continues, "the new visual intensity will require light *on* everything. And its idea of space and time will change to regard them as containers to be *filled* with objects or activities."[3]

Thus, McLuhan's Medieval cosmos of the world as revelation, as light *through* phenomena in the form of signs and symbols present everywhere, is essentially equivalent to the Hindu notion of *sukshma,* or subtle matter, in which visionary objects give forth their own internal radiance. The Gutenberg world, by contrast, was a world that was *awakening* to the light of day, a gradual emerging from the Medieval dreamworld of radiant signs and wonders, to a world dominated by *sthula* forms, in which the laws of waking consciousness, together with three dimensional space as articulated simultaneously in depth perspective in painting and in Newtonian physics, came to predominate. The evolution of painting from 1500 to 1900 is one of a gradually increasing realism, in which a cold, sober vision of a real world extended in real space filled with real things triumphed over a world populated by monsters, angels, demons and devils. Western cultural history, as reflected in both the sciences and the arts, is a tale of the gradual victory of *sthula* over *sukshma.*

But ever since about the year 1995, when the Digital Revolution began to take off, technologies of light, *luminous* technologies, that is to say, have begun to triumph over technologies of matter, technologies, that is, which move physical objects about through space. We are living now in a world that has increasingly come to be dominated by *sukshma* technologies, of ubiquitous self-luminous video screens of all shapes and sizes, in some cases — as in Shanghai, China — the size of buildings. *Sthula* technologies — of roads and bridges, highways and automobiles, buildings and power stations (what economic historians have traditionally called "fixed capital") — are of course still around and will be for a long time to come, but the accent has shifted now to the technologies of self-radiance (a new form, in other words, of "circulating capital.") This becomes evident to anyone walking down the streets at night of a megalopolis such as Tokyo or Shanghai, New York or San Francisco, cities which glow at night with all the incandescence of molten lava pouring across dark hills.

This book chronicles the new living conditions which this shift is burning into the world all around us. Technology is in the process, arguably begun by the Japanese after World War II, of what Arnold Toynbee called an "etherealization," in which it is becoming ever more refined, subtle and luminous. It sends human thoughts racing around the world at the speed of light, leaving *sthula* technologies, which are primarily designed for moving physical bodies about through space, lumbering to catch up.

It is a world, in short, that each day comes to resemble more and more a dream.

Thus, we are witnessing the transubstantiation of Western waking consciousness into a virtual dream world, the digital literalization of the Hindu cosmic vision of the world-as-dream, which we now possess the proper technology to create as a daily living "reality."

It is very possibly the strangest world the planet has ever seen.

Or ever will.

PART I

IN WHICH THE INTERNET RECREATES THE WORLD-AS-CAVERN

1.

José Saramago's 2000 novel *The Cave* tells the story of one Cipriano Algor, a modern ceramics artist who sells his pottery to a store in the local shopping mall, a gigantic mother-of-all malls type of complex. One day, the authorities at the mall tell him they no longer need his pottery, for people now prefer to buy industrialized plastic products instead. Worried about how he shall continue making a living, his son-in-law, who happens to work as a security guard at the mall, is given a promotion which allows him and his wife to go and live inside the mall. Algor, apparently having no other choice, decides to go with them. Once there, he hears about an archeological finding that has been discovered beneath the mall and decides to go investigate on his own. At the site, he finds that the excavators have unearthed a cave: going inside, with a single flashlight to guide him, he stumbles upon the bodies of five dead people sitting bolt upright. Behind them is a stone bench and beyond it, the charred remains of a fire. The excavators, in other words, have discovered Plato's cave. And no sooner have they discovered it, than they begin selling tickets to it as a kind of theme park attraction. Algor decides that if his values are to remain intact, he must leave the shopping mall, known as the Centre, itself a modern incarnation of Plato's cave.

Saramago's complex, multifaceted novel works on several levels, one of which is to show that, in our contemporary consumer paradise, we have retrieved and recreated Plato's cave as a gigantic dome of entranced shoppers dazzled by the profusion of electronic shadows cast upon its walls. Indeed, Saramago's novel perfectly captures the sense that our contemporary, hidden cosmology is indeed the reconstitution of a vast cavern inside of which we have all become like Plato's prisoners mistaking so much shadow for substance.

I think it is possible to be even more specific, though, and say that it is the Internet itself which is transforming the world into a huge echoing cavern in which all the conditioning modalities proper to orientation in space have been removed. In the caves of Paleolithic man — which, as Saramago's novel implies, lie at the ultimate root of our Western mentality — the animals were painted onto the walls with casual disregard for direction: they float — disconnected from all contexts — like astronauts in outer space, for whom the very idea of such orienting vectors like horizon lines or compasses is meaningless. In a cave, point of view is simply irrelevant, for there is no horizon and there is no longer any such thing as upside down.

Inside this world-as-cavern, the Internet is recasting each of us as a being made out of light, a being which is simultaneously co-present everywhere. Online, we are all present everywhere on the planet at once. We exist in a state of pure simultaneity, like light particles, for which neither time nor space exists. We are disembodied, figures floating without grounds. All the limitations associated with embodiment in a material world are gone, for the Internet not only eliminates hierarchies, it also abolishes the very idea of physical location in a specific place. Hence, while online, one is denuded of historical and cultural context, from all the conditioning logics of worlds, to use the philosopher Alain Badiou's phrase. We are thin slices of geometry, figures without grounds drifting free of history. Thus, the end of history, as it turns out, was actually about the triumph of electronic technology, which renders all linear processes simultaneous and obsolesces anything that transpires or unfolds in time, such as cultures in historical modes. All linear structures disappear; all sequential logic vanishes into the all-at-onceness of pure acoustic simultaneity.

Thus, pilgrimages and journeys are now obsolete. There is no longer anywhere to go, since you are already there. In a world of pure simultaneity, in which everyone is located nowhere and yet co-present everywhere, there is no longer room for anything so antiquated as goals, journeys and pilgrimages. All center-periphery models are simply liquidated.

2.

The Internet is an inherently decentralizing — and destabilizing — technology. No one owns it, no single government or corporation controls it, and this makes it absolutely unique as a technological medium. When applied to any sort of government or corporation that bases itself upon a center-periphery model of power — Microsoft, let's say, or some authoritarian regime such as that of Thailand — it acts like a solvent upon such structures and works to dissolve them, unless intrusion counter-measures are erected against it. In North Korea, the Internet is illegal for precisely this reason, and in countries like China, Burma and Malaysia, its use is carefully monitored and controlled. It is a kind of technology which travels across national boundaries injecting information exactly as viruses land upon cell walls and disrupt them with their own genetic codes, hijacking the cell's machinery by forcing it to replicate copies of the virus. The Internet is a viral technology.

It is interesting, therefore, that in precisely the decade and a half since its introduction, walls and fences have been going up along the borders of nation states everywhere, as though to counteract the threat posed by such pathogenic technologies. It was Andre Leroi-Gourhan, in his *Man and Matter,* who said that whereas technologies tend to be universal, it is cultures which are ethnically specific and tend to counter such universally adopted technologies by insisting all the more fiercely upon their local differences.[1] Hence, we find walls being built, or being planned to be built, along the borders between Israel and the West Bank, Saudia Arabia and Oman, along India's border with Bangladesh, along the borders of Thailand and Malaysia, Brunei and Limbang, Beijing and North Korea, Uzbekistan and Tajikistan, etc. Societies resort to such defensive measures whenever an invasive presence is sensed, and there is nothing more (subliminally) invasive than the all-encompassing electronic technology of the Internet. Indeed, no greater threat to centralized power structures exists than the Internet, which asymmetrically amplifies the power of the individual user out of all proportion to his social status as a statistical element of a crowd "plasma," which tends to average him out of significance. The Internet actually *reverses* the averaging effects of crowd phenomena, extracting the individual out of such social plasmas and placing him on the map as a force to be reckoned with, as in the case of the May, 2007 cyberattack on an entire country by one individual, when Russian hacker Konstantin Goloskokov shut down the government sites, businesses and banks of Estonia virtually single-handedly.[2] Likewise, such Internet organizations as WikiLeaks, Amazon or Google represent a new type of corporate structure, for they are founded and run usually by only one or two people, since the power of the Internet is such as to amplify them with all the force of resonant feedback as institutions unto themselves in the global social arena.

Thus, in an age in which nation states are dissolving and reconfiguring into more amoeba-like structures composed of heterogeneous ethnicities vying against one another, we are seeing the rise of new collective social structures — such as Arjun Appadurai's 'diasporic public spheres' which use the Internet to configure themselves as transnational entities around the globe (such as Al Qaeda, for instance, or the hacker group Anonymous) — and also the rise of rogue individuals whose power is extended by global electronics into significant social modules unto themselves. Google *is* Sergei Brin and Larry Page, just as Wikipedia *is* Jimmy Wales and Amazon.com *is* Jeff Bezos.

3.

The first message sent by Samuel Morse's telegraph in 1844, "What hath God wrought," finds its analogue in the first message sent over the Internet in 1969, when it was created by the Department of Defense and known as ARPANET, which was "L-O." This was supposed to be "LOG" for "LOG ON" but since the system crashed when the letter "G" was typed, the first message was determined by the machine itself to be "L-O" or "Hello." Reinvented by Tim Berners-Lee's creation of the World Wide Web in 1989, complete with color graphics, sound, hyperlinks and URLs, ARPANET was decommissioned by the U.S. government in 1990. Run by the National Science Foundation until 1995, at which point it was turned over to the private sector, where it is currently owned by nobody, we can regard the Internet as the most dangerous tool in the world.

It has destabilized the U.S. economy twice, first with the bursting of the dot-com bubble in April of 2000, and then later on, more severely, with the crash of the stock market in 2008, which I am convinced was actually a catastrophic bifurcation in which a cascade of accumulating causes — small vortices of economic disruption such as the closing of record stores, the folding of newspapers and travel agencies, the closing of video stores, etc.— sufficiently weakened the economy to allow it to be all but taken down by the collapse of the housing bubble.

A complex dynamical model is necessary to understand this latter crash, since such models normally take into account the accumulation of multiple causes which act with asymmetric force to suddenly bring down an entire system, whereas most attempts by economists and historians to make sense of the 2008 crash has been in terms of linear, mechanistic causal models: we hear that it was caused by the failure to regulate credit default swaps, for instance (this is the explanation given by PBS's *Frontline*), or the sudden failure of the population to repay their subprime loans (the explanation given by Niall Ferguson in his PBS documentary, *The Ascent of Money* which, interestingly, doesn't even mention credit default swaps). But almost nobody mentions the Internet as a causal factor since, in order to see it as such, one must step back and view a larger picture in which a number of economic and social flows overlap with one another: the Internet's decade long destabilization of the U.S. economy with mini-collapses and failures crossing with Stock Market flows, derivatives speculation and real estate loans to create a single gigantic picture of economic systems failure. The inherent nature of the Internet as a technology, remember, is to destroy all center-periphery relationships, including one in which the world economic center is localized to Wall Street in New York, while the rest of the world is peripheral to it. The impact of the current crisis, however, is to scatter and disburse the world economic center to a number of locations simultaneously: London, Beijing, Tokyo, Mumbai, etc.

We are not living in a world, as some would like to maintain, in which technological innovations and economic ebbs and flows exist like parallel lines that never meet. The two are in reality tightly interconnected in a subtle and intricate web of multiple causes and effects.

So in the chapters which follow, I examine five crucial Internet sites and the socio-cultural effects which they are bringing about: YouTube is destructuring copyright laws; Facebook is rewiring human social relations; Wikipedia is redefining the word "encyclopedia" and actually exemplifies a knowledge crisis; WikiLeaks is assaulting governments and corporations worldwide by exposing their secrets; Amazon.com is destructuring and dismantling the entire book industry. Each one of these sites does not just "exist," then, as a useful tool; they are actually melting down and reconfiguring the basic socio-cultural structures of our society. The lineaments of the new world that is presently coming into being as a result are all but unimaginable, but I think we can be certain of at least one thing: it won't look anything like the world we lived in prior to 1995.

1

Amazon.com, the Kindle and the Collapse of the Book Industry

Word vs. Byte

The ancient power of the orally spoken Word was such that, once uttered, it had the magical effect of bringing *things,* tangible things, into being. In the Egyptian theogony of Memphis, the creator god Ptah brought all the gods, and indeed the entire world, into being simply by pronouncing their names. On the first page of the Old Testament, likewise, God *says,* "Let there be light," and light emerges. "By the word of the Lord the heavens were made," goes Psalm 33, "and all their host by the breath of his mouth.... For he spoke, and it came to be; he commanded, and it stood forth."

The power of the spoken Word in these ancient traditions was such that by merely pronouncing it correctly, it could actually alter the very physical composition of the world, bringing forth singularities and Events as sacred ruptures in the flow of profane banality. When Mohammad, for instance, was meditating in his cave and the angel Gabriel descended to him and spoke *a single* word, "Recite," Mohammad brought the Koran and along with it, an entire civilization, into being. Or when, in the Christian tradition, Gabriel descends once again, this time to Mary, and tells her that she has been chosen to become the mother of God, the myth is actually a vision of conception *through the ear,* just as in the Hindu tradition when, in the *Shiva Purana,* the god Shiva sees Vishnu in the guise of a beautiful woman named Mohini and masturbates, the seven sages preserve his semen on a leaf and then pour it into the ear of Anjani, the daughter of Gautama, who then gives birth to Shiva in the avatar of the monkey hero Hanuman: it is the same idea, only literalized.[1]

Thus, the creation of the world, the birth of a religion (Islam), the advent of a God incarnate on the physical plane as a monkey: each of these Events is a non-repeatable, non-reproducible singularity, a one time only occurrence that is pregnant with numinosity precisely because it can never be repeated or mass-produced by anything as profane as the capitalist megamachine.

Computer technology, however, actually reverses all this. The power of the byte confers upon humanity the ability not to bring forth new physical worlds, but rather to dismantle them. With the power of the byte, things do not originate, they *dis*-originate, or better, dis-integrate. When Jeff Bezos, for instance, founded Amazon.com in 1995, the power of the byte enabled him to dismantle the actual physical existence of the bookstore. Within a mere five years of Amazon's inception, independent bookstores everywhere had begun closing their doors. In the San Francisco Bay Area alone we have the closing of Gaia Bookstore on Shattuck Avenue in 1999; Cody's Bookstore on Telegraph Avenue in Berkeley in 2006; A Clean Well-Lighted Place For Books in San Francisco itself; then in 2007, the Cody's store in San Francisco — which had been in business since 1956 — closed; in 2009, in Berkeley once again, Black Oak Books, and then in San Francisco, Stacey's — which had been in business for 85 years — and also Abandoned Planet in the Mission — in business for 16 years — all closed down. In 2010, Modern Times Bookstore in the Mission, which has been open for 39 years, was reporting that it didn't have enough money to pay its bills. In Menlo Park, California, Kepler's Bookstore closed its doors on August 31, 2005, but then, with community support, somehow managed to reopen a few months later. In Seattle, Elliot Bay Bookstore narrowly escaped closure by relocating in 2009 to a better neighborhood, while Spine and Crown Books can no longer afford to pay its rent. In Los Angeles, meanwhile, The Bodhi Tree is scheduled for closure sometime this year. And this is just on the West Coast. The number of closures broaden as you go across the nation.

The big chain stores are sinking, too. Borders Books has now become a capitalist memory and Barnes and Noble is in trouble: its stock, once valued at $45 a share is down to $13 a share, and every quarter, its earnings reports are smaller and smaller. It is not likely to survive, either.

The age of the bookstore, it would appear — which began in northern Europe in twelfth century Paris as a service by-product of the birth of the university — is coming to an end. Indeed, I suspect that within a mere five to seven years, the bookstore will have joined the record store as nothing more than a capitalist memory.

Not a Bookstore

The important thing, then, to grasp about Amazon.com, is that it is *not* a bookstore. We always try to understand a new medium through the form language of an earlier, vanished medium: thus, the automobile was first thought of as a "horseless carriage" when in fact, it was nothing of the kind, but rather a radically new technology for moving people about through space; the railroad, likewise, was called "the iron horse"; and film, when it first began, was referred to as a "photo-play," and so on. As Jeff Bezos himself has commented: "... when we first started Amazon.com, we had very conscious discussions where we talked about the fact that we were not a bookstore, but we were a book service. I do think that is a better way to think about it. Thinking of yourself as a store is too limiting. Services can be anything."[2]

Amazon, it is important to remark, does not own a bookstore of any kind, nor has it ever run one. Yet it obsolesces the bookstore precisely because it speeds up the functions of a traditional brick and mortar store by applying electricity to the whole operation. As a result, it has swallowed up the traditional bookstore in its entirety, along with Books in Print, in order to create a virtual simulacrum in which every book in print is theoretically available at the touch of a button. If the content of a new medium, as McLuhan always said, is an older medium, then in the case of Amazon, the bookstore becomes the *content* of the new electronic medium of Amazon.com, along with Books in Print, the video store, the record store, the toy store, the video game store, etc. It is not a bookstore, but a retail *service* designed as a totalizing retail medium. The old Parisian arcades that Walter Benjamin wrote about in his *Arcades Project,* which is the ancestor of the shopping mall, has been swallowed up entire by Amazon:

it is a virtual arcade, not a bookstore. If you could plug in an entire arcade, and send electricity racing through its various stalls and shops, its iron and glass roofs, its masonry walls, the result would be Amazon.com, the world's first virtual arcade.

And the *effect* of plugging in such an arcade?

The effect is to dematerialize not only the stores themselves, collapsing them and recreating them as two-dimensional icons in cyberspace in which the capitalist *functions* take place independently of any material substrate, but also the merchandise *inside* the stores, as well. Amazon does not just wish to virtualize the bookstore, but to actually remove the knowledge *content* from the printed page and offer it for sale as an entity unto itself. This, then, is the ultimate result of the Kindle, which simply takes the axioms set up by Amazon and follows them through to their logical conclusions. The whole operation, from start to finish, is a dematerializing one. The capitalist process, when accelerated to light speed, simply removes the transactive functions from the material conditions in which they are embedded, just the way credit cards remove transactions from their material substrate in actual money.

Thus, Amazon should not be blamed for what it is, since it is simply making *explicit* what had been merely *implicit* in capitalism all along: namely, the desire to remove the flow of capital itself from the real world of material goods, and to separate it off into an abstract realm all its own, a virtual flowing river — an Amazon — of pure decoded flows.

The fact that it also happens to be sweeping books along up into this river of virtual flows is merely a by-product of the undertaking.

A Transcendentalist Operation

This overall dematerializing tendency, not only of the Internet generally speaking, but more specifically, of Amazon.com itself, is perhaps rooted in the rather transcendentalist orientation of its godfather, Jeff Bezos, a man who grew up reading primarily science fiction and fantasy novels like *Dune,* Robert Heinlein, *Lord of the Rings,* etc. Indeed, as Bezos matured, his biographers tell us that he dreamed of one day going into outer space, or of building a space station, which many believe, in fact, to be the ultimate end goal of all his labors.

> He made no secret that he wanted to build a commercial space
> station [Robert Spector remarks] because, he believed, the future

of the human race was not on Earth; the planet might be struck
by a foreign object from outer space.... In a 1982 *Miami Herald*
feature story on all the high school valedictorians in South Dade
County, Jeff was described as hoping to one day build space
hotels, amusement parks, yachts, and colonies for 2 or 3 million
people orbiting the planet.[3]

Thus, Bezos is something of a transcendentalist who views the Earth —
and along with the earth archetype, then, everything that it would com-
prise, such as physical matter, the senses, ecology, plants, trees, *paper*— as
something to be *escaped from* at all costs. This was, of course, precisely the
myth of Plato's cave: the seeker of knowledge leaves the cave behind —
i.e. the realm of the senses — in order to gaze upon the sun of intelligible
(non-sensual) Truth, the Truth of Being in opposition to the illusions of
Becoming, that lay beyond it. The problem with the river of Becoming is
that it never *is,* according to Plato, and can therefore never be relied upon
as a stable base for knowledge; only the mind's penetration of the Forms
comprising the imperishable realm of Being, which is stable and unchang-
ing, enables it to create a foundation of knowledge worth taking the trouble
to learn.

This idea, then, later became the basis of both Gnosticism and Neo-
Platonism, for the goal of the former was the attainment of *gnosis,* or the
knowledge of the Eternal God that lay beyond Yahweh and his planetary
archons who had constructed the world as a prison for the soul enslaved
to the senses and tricked into believing that the physical world was real.
In the case of Neo-Platonism as defined by Plotinus, the goal was union
with the One — which Plotinus claimed that he had achieved on precisely
three separate occasions — and to disengage one's mind from the senses in
order to learn of the realm of Nous, the static and incorruptible reality of
divine knowledge which lay beyond the *anima mundi*— also incorruptible,
but in motion — which the demiurge used as a blueprint to hammer out
the created world.

What all of these thought systems have in common — and this
includes mainstream Christianity — is a shared antipathy to the physical,
created, earthly world, Heraclitus's flowing river of the senses that you
could never step into twice.

A great deal of modern science fiction, furthermore — as I have written
about elsewhere[4]— especially of the Cold War variety from Heinlein to
Asimov, retains this Gnostic-Platonic antipathy to the earth in favor of a

plan for making use of technological gadgets to enable an actual physical performance of the Platonic myth of leaving the earth behind in favor of the incorruptible realm of the heavens.

Jeff Bezos, as a kid growing up in the culturally deprived suburbs of Houston, Texas, inherited from his reading of these authors this ancient Neo-Platonic substratum that is hidden (or, better: *submerged*) in the works of Asimov, Clarke and Heinlein like a code. Hence, his adoption of a virtual technology like the Internet, which enabled him to create Amazon.com as a tool for dematerializing the entire book industry from printed page to constructed wall is a direct result of his science fiction-based education.

Thus, the entire book industry is being collapsed by one man, using (albeit naively) the hidden tool of the ancient mythology of Gnosticism to disrupt and dismantle centuries of visually-biased print-based transmission of learning.

So if you think mythology is only for the Edith Hamiltons and the Bulfinches of the world and that it can have little effect upon physical reality, then I would advise you to think again. A transcendentalist mythology is currently being used as an epistemological tool by one man with a suburban education to deconstruct and dis-originate the *entire* book industry.

E-Readers

Which brings us to the Kindle.

The first Kindle, designed by Bezos himself, was released in November of 2007. The second generation model came out in February of 2009, while in August of 2010, the third generation model was released.

The latest Kindle, which, as of this writing, is the third generation model, is only ⅓ of an inch thick and weighs 8.7 ounces. It has a six-inch screen that is not backlit, so it isn't hard on the eyes, and can be read in bright sunlight, even at the beach, although it cannot be read in the dark without exterior illumination. It can hold over 3,500 books and documents and has WiFi access, no matter where you are, to the Amazon Kindle store, from which any of the 630,000 books therein contained can be downloaded onto your device in less than a minute, for a fee of about ten bucks.

It is this latter point which is the most interesting, for it reduces the costs of books and makes them available to the reader outside the bounds of the bookstore at any time of the day or night and no matter where he or she happens to be located. With the Kindle, you don't go to the books, the books come to you. And if you happen to be traveling, you no longer have to carry all those heavy books onto the plane with you: indeed, if the whim strikes you while on a 14 hour flight, you can download Gibbon's unabridged *Decline and Fall of the Roman Empire* and start reading. Students especially, who have since the twelfth century when the university came into being, been burdened with lugging heavy volumes around, are quite relieved to no longer have to do so.

In short, there has never been a greater threat to the existence of the book industry in the five centuries since Gutenbergian technology has been printing books. And who needs bookstores when you can download any book you want at any time of the day or night? Their disappearance now seems guaranteed.

Of course, the Kindle has its limitations: so far, it only comes with a black and white screen and this makes it difficult to appreciate those big Barnes and Noble coffee table books on the pyramids of ancient Egypt or the history of Impressionism that we like to get as Christmas presents. But for that purpose, Steve Jobs has kindly supplied us with another gadget, namely, the iPad, which comes in full, lucid Technicolor and also has all kinds of features such as that when you touch the screen, the image gets bigger, or else shrinks, depending on your preferences.

Between the iPad and the Kindle, then, it does not appear that the printed book stands much of a chance, despite the protestations of media theoreticians like Ted Striphas, author of *The Late Age of Print,* whom I quote here verbatim: "People ask me if the printed book is going to go away. The simple answer to that is no. Absolutely not."[5] Striphas insists that the book will merely become one medium striving for attention amongst all the others. Maybe. But the history of book media actually tells a different tale.

The clay tablet existed right alongside the papyrus scroll for several thousand years; indeed, their peaceful coexistence seems to have been guaranteed by the fact that they were the media preferred by two completely different civilizations, the Mesopotamians, who invented the clay tablet due to the resource scarcity on the alluvial plane between the two rivers, and the ancient Egyptians, who had the world's monopoly on papyrus in the Delta of Lower Egypt. Indeed, both media seem to have disappeared precisely as the result of a new form of the book as medium, namely the parchment codex, which came into being sometime in the first century

A.D. amongst the ancient Romans, the very century in which the clay tablet disappeared forever.

However, the parchment codex, though invented by the Romans, existed right alongside the papyrus scroll for about three or four centuries before the scroll disappeared entirely in the seventh century A.D. The reason for its disappearance seems to have been cultural, for the scroll had remained the medium of choice for pagan writers all along, while the codex had been the preference of the Christians, and when in the early sixth century A.D., the Byzantine emperor Justinian ordered the final closing of the schools in Athens, this seems to have also marked the end of the use of the papyrus scroll as well. So the form of the book that we have inherited down to the present day, the rectangular codex with a spine and interior leaves, has remained the unchanged form of the book as a medium since the seventh century A.D., that is, for over a thousand years.

The advent of the printing press in the fifteenth century did not change the *form* of the book, for the codex remained its basic matter, only the manner and means by way of which the codex was produced, namely through mechanized printing, which had the tendency to eliminate illustrations, for by the middle of the sixteenth century, the illuminated manuscript was gone. *Entirely.* The stark, black and white, line by line linearity of the printed page had triumphed and illustrations were no longer in color. It took only a century, but the new medium of the book as a mechanically printed text *did* in fact wipe out the illuminated manuscript as a medium. Handwriting continued, of course, but not as a means of making publicly marketable books. So Ted Striphas may have to back up a few steps when he asserts that the printed book will *never* disappear.

All prior forms of the book, in fact, *have* disappeared: the clay tablet is gone, the papyrus scroll is gone, even the Southeast Asian palm leaf manuscript and the Chinese bamboo book are made no longer. The illuminated manuscript, too, has vanished, except maybe as the private hobby of a few antiquarian bookmakers who feel nostalgic for the good old days pre–Gutenberg. They are *all* gone: the printed book is now the last man standing.

So I don't think we have any justification whatsoever for saying that the printed book will not face its extinction at the hands of the e-reader. It *will* disappear. You can count on it. The only thing up for debate now is *when.* A century from now? Decades? Years?

Retrievals and Disappearances

In a way, though, of course, the old media do not *entirely* vanish, for they live on in the form of the various retrievals by new media that McLuhan spent the entirety of his career pointing out for us. The automobile, for example, retrieves the knight in shining armor; the radio retrieves the power of the orally spoken utterance; capitalism retrieves the modality of the hunter / gatherer, and so on.

Looking at the iPad and the Kindle, insofar as their *structures* are concerned, I would say that they are both based upon a retrieval — rather ironically so — of the very first form of the book as the Mesopotamian clay tablet. (Indeed, the iPad is now referred to as a "tablet computer.") Their *contents,* however, are different: while both of them presuppose the book as content, it is not the same *idea* of book that each retrieves. The Kindle, for example, with its black and white screen retrieves the book as Gutenbergian product circa 1600, which was almost entirely void of (color) images. The Kindle is, in short, a Gutenbergian manuscript that has been plugged in and turned on.

The iPad, however, retrieves the book as illuminated manuscript. It is, in fact, simply an illuminated manuscript that has had electric current sent pulsing through it. Indeed, when one glances at the screen of an iPad, the first thing that strikes one is how similar it looks to a piece of stained glass. The illuminated manuscript emerged at about the same time as stained glass — in the seventh century A.D.— and attained its apotheosis as a medium at about the same time, i.e. the twelfth and thirteenth centuries. Both are illustrations of the Medieval phenomenon of light *through* rather than the Gutenbergian idea of the printed text as something that is not self-luminous and requires exterior light *on* in order to see properly. (Remember that the Kindle requires an exterior lamp to read it properly at night.)

I have not the slightest doubt that these new e-readers will replace the printed book as a medium. The printed book replaced the scribal manuscript because it simply offered too many advantages that the manuscript could not match: it was cheaper, could be made much, much faster, tended to be more accurate, and could be mass produced. The technology of the manuscript simply could not keep up, so it disappeared within a century. Some of the Florentine bibliophiles of the fifteenth century, by the way, did resist the printed book, regarding them as inferior objects that they did not wish to disgrace their libraries with. The bookseller Vespasiano da Bisticci, specializing in manuscripts, spurned the new printed books, but this proved to be his undoing, for he was "forced out of business in 1478" as a result of the demand for printed books.[6]

Elizabeth Eisenstein, in her book *The Printing Press as Agent of Change*, cites an amusing anecdote to the effect that as soon as Gutenberg and Schoeffer had finished printing their Bible, John Fust, their financier, set off with an armload of them to Paris to sell to students but that, when he got there, he was confronted by a guild of manuscript dealers who called the police on him, insisting that only someone in league with the devil could have access to so many books at once.[7] One can easily reimagine this situation transposed to the present day, in which Jeff Bezos, arriving with the Kindle, causes a similar nervous anxiety amongst contemporary bookstores selling physical printed books. Given the similarity of the two situations, I don't think it requires too much of a leap of imagination to guess where the future is headed.

The advantages which the e-reader confers over the printed book are just about as numerous as the advantages which the printed book had over the manuscript: the e-readers are easier to transport; they can store thousands of books on them at a time; they make books cheaper; they can send any book that is in print — and which is carried and made available by Amazon — directly to your lap, wherever you happen to be in the world; and they don't use paper, which cuts down on global deforestation, surely an issue that will become more and more pressing as global warming heats up in the decades to come (unless we return to the practice of making paper from rags, which was how it was fabricated clear up until the middle of the nineteenth century whereupon it shifted to being made from wood pulp).

Needless to say, the e-reader destroys the very concept of the used book, with its resale market value, since there is no physical object for the owner to resell. This means, of course, that they represent the twilight of the bookstore as a totality, for they are based on a technology that is inherently antagonistic to the bookstore, since they tend to *centralize* books into occupying *one* piece of matter, whereas the printing press *decentralizes* and disperses books out into the world from a center to a periphery. It was precisely this dispersion principle that the bookstore came into being in order to market to a reading public.

The e-reader eliminates both book and bookstore alike, and may even wipe out publishers, too. Who needs a publisher when you can just market your own book directly on the Internet to the public for a small fee to download it onto your gadget, while you, the author, pocket most of the money, which reverses the normal situation in publishing?

Thus, the future of the entire publishing industry looks very grim, indeed. In fact, a whole world is collapsing, a world that was configured around the advent of the printing press in the fifteenth century and has remained relatively stable for five centuries, a world based on the mechanical printing of books, their dispersion to bookstores, schools and public libraries and thus, to an entire industry devoted to propagating literacy based upon the technological medium of mechanized print.

The e-reader, together with online retailers like Amazon.com and Alibris, are dismantling, destroying and crushing the Gutenberg galaxy with a sense of utter, absolute finality that is hard to brook. The process may take a few years, but make no mistake about it: it *is* happening.

As a kid growing up in the suburbs of the Southwest, bookstores were my favorite place to go. They were a light from another world, a world signifying culture, ideas and the mind, that was inspiring and uplifting by contrast with the dismal banality of life as a teenager in culturally deprived Phoenix. Even a bookstore in a shopping mall, like B. Dalton or Waldenbooks — remember those? — was an oasis in the desert of crudity and vulgarity represented by the megalopolis of gas stations, parking lots and strip malls that surrounded me on all sides.

Now, with their disappearance, kids like my son will grow up in a world without bookstores or record stores as havens to remind them that there is more to life than the grim animal struggle for survival of living in a soulless megalopolis. Our cities, with their disappearing neighborhoods, and their proliferating airports, convenience stores and gas stations, will be that much more impoverished; they will become hellish places, cultural wastelands frequented by brutality and violence with no spark from a higher world to remind us that there is something beyond all this that redeems it, and makes the hell of survival under such conditions capable of redemption.

Instead, my son will have to go to museums and libraries — if they survive, that is, as public funds are siphoned off from them and redirected toward fighting wars in foreign lands that have the purpose of making us "safer" — as a substitute for spending a quiet afternoon surrounded by the artifacts of the highest values which the human mind has to offer. Hopefully, at least museums will survive this cultural holocaust that we are living through at the transition to the third millennium after Christ.

Hopefully.

2

YouTube and the
Twilight of Copyright

Glass-Cased Installation

Let's imagine that we put YouTube inside of a glass-cased installation of the type used by Damien Hirst for one of his animal exhibits, such as his famous *Formaldehyde Shark*, forever imprisoned behind aqueous blue glass with mouth wide open in a rictus of imminent death.[1] Suspended this way, we could walk around it in three dimensions, carefully examining it as an anatomical specimen with a very exact morphology, flayed and splayed before us with pins and needles holding back layers of cartilage that enable us to peer inside it to the very depths of its anatomy.

Considered morphologically, what would we find?

An Evanescent Horizon

Imagine this: a vast horizontal plane stretching to the horizon — a *gray* horizon, perhaps — upon which is displayed an infinity of squares, like the façade of a skyscraper. Imagine further that each of these squares is pulsing with a dim, flickering light, the kind of light that paints the interiors of living rooms at night with blue, spectral luminescence. Within each of these squares there resides a different image, indeed an entirely different *set* of images, images that are in motion.

If you can conjure this vision in your mind, then you have perceived the metaphysical structure of YouTube, the implicate structure that exists beyond the limited and evanescent window of spacetime that is explicate on your computer screen.

Partial Objects

A cross-section of YouTube thus reveals that it is planar in structure and, like comic books or American cities, cellular in composition. These picture cells can be plugged into and turned on by the image-hungry receptors of the human psyche that is always seeking for partial objects to salvage the half-submerged contours of its hidden neuro-anatomy.

There is a scene in Steven Spielberg's movie *A.I.* that perfectly illustrates this: at one point early on in the film, the boy robot, wandering in the woods at night, witnesses a futuristic garbage truck dumping its refuse of broken body parts from discarded robots of all shapes and sizes. A band of "living" robots then descends upon this midden heap, scavenging it for parts: one who is missing an arm retrieves an arm from the pile and fastens it onto his mangled stump. Another whose jaw is hanging loose tears the old piece away and replaces it with a better one. And so on.

YouTube, likewise, functions in a similar way as a vast electronic image heap through which the contemporary individual sifts out those particular images that he will find to be most compatible with the neuroreceptors of his own psyche.

Electronic Decay Rate

Electronic society is already showing early signs of decrepitude. This is evident everywhere we look, especially in the profusion and superabundance of its images, which have become its accursed share: worn out advertising images; old television commercials, piling up like the electronic equivalent of stacks of rotting tires; swamps of decaying movie images, haunted with celluloid ghosts; postcard snapshots of Grand Canyons and Las Vegases; Brooke Shields and her bluejeans; Farah Fawcett and her hair; Humphrey Bogart and his hat; *Star Wars*, James Bond, Indiana Jones; shopping malls with their video ads for The Gap and Macy's; McDonald's, Taco Bell, Coca-cola. Images; images everywhere, proliferating without aim or purpose. A veritable rag and bone shop of images.

What to do with this surplus, which now haunts us like the surplus wealth of the Kwakiutl Indians who had to build potlatch bonfires to consume it all?

Each medium is invented for a purpose, and the specific purpose of YouTube is to drain off this iconic efflux of our overloaded sensorium. It is an electronic potlatch designed to consume the accursed share of our own neurologically-saturated iconophilia.

Founders

YouTube was founded in February 2005 by Jawed Karim, Chad Hurley and Steve Chen, partially in response to the December, 2004 Indian Ocean tsunami which claimed the lives of over 300,000 people. There were no camera crews around to film the catastrophe, and so it was the first large-scale disaster to be chronicled primarily by cell-phone camcorders. "Karim perceived that viewers who attempted to watch these virally spread videos ran into all sorts of technical difficulties, and he figured that a site that made uploading and watching any video effortless would fill an unmet need."[2]

In February of 2004, Flickr had been launched as a site for the public to upload photos from their digital cameras with descriptive tags on them. Thus, just as photography had preceded the motion picture, so Flickr was succeeded by YouTube, a sort of "Flickr for videos."

Cultural Memory

Every civilization requires a way of storing its memory. In pre-literate societies, cultural memory is stored as oral recitation of patterned verses keyed by mnemonic formulae. In literate societies like ancient Mesopotamia, there were libraries at places like Nippur and Ebla where the baked clay tablets were stored on shelves for quick retrieval. Alexandria and Pergamum had their great libraries of scrolls, just as we have our own huge libraries containing aisle upon aisle of printed books and folios.

The history of human media, however, can be divided into *two* great divisions: there is the realm of inscriptions that extends from the caves of Paleolithic France and Spain and reaches all the way to the printed books of the twentieth century; and then, beginning in the early part of the twentieth century with the advent of electric media such as the cinema and radio and going all the way down to the present proliferation of video screens everywhere.

Why these two divisions?

Because there is nothing in the first phase that cannot be captured in the pages of a printed book: from cuneiform tablets to illuminated manuscripts, the printing press was *the* great repository of the Word of literate civilization in its entirety. *Nothing* escaped it: from every petroglyph inscribed on a stone surface to every palm-leaf Buddhist text or Chinese bamboo book, *everything* that the human species has ever recorded in one medium or another has appeared somewhere in the pages of a printed book.

But this is not the case with electric media, which is the *one* medium that resists confinement by the pages of the book. How do you create the book equivalent of one of Bill Viola's haunting video installations? Or a movie? Or a rock and roll song?

All electronic media have been engulfed by YouTube, which has captured and encompassed them with the same kind of thoroughness which the printing press once exhibited in swallowing up all previous forms of written communication. Once upon a time the "memory" of electronic society was television, but now television, too, has disappeared inside of YouTube, along with movies, music, old commercials, talk shows and everything else.

YouTube is thus a gigantic electronic midden heap stuffed full of outworn, overused images, dead icons, old ads and other mediatic effluvia.

And this is why big corporations are so misguided in their efforts to protect media like film and music from being coopted and stored in the electronic museum of YouTube. They simply don't understand what the medium is trying to do, for they are still thinking in the now outmoded Gutenbergian terms of "intellectual property" laws, an archaism left over from the days of the printed book.

Free Movies

Indeed, increasingly more and more often, movies can be found and watched on YouTube in their entirety, for free. I no longer even bother to rent movies at Blockbuster, since every third or fourth title I enter into the YouTube search database comes up. Of course, the movies are segmented into ten or fifteen minute blocks, but this is not much of an obstacle. Movies I have seen lately in their entirety include: *The Ring, The Double Life of Veronique, A.I., Minority Report, The Terminal, The Grudge,*

In the Mouth of Madness, Altered States, Dogville, Dancer in the Dark, The Exorcist, The Invasion, No Country for Old Men, Encounters at the End of the World, etc. Not a bad showing. And more movies are uploaded everyday, although occasionally they are blocked or pulled by YouTube or the film's copyright owner.

I think this is an act of futility, though, since it is basically equivalent to a stroke of "bad conscience." If you're going to host a site that features video content that can be shared by everyone, you're either going to have to follow through on the implications of what you've set up, or you might as well just close up shop. If the people who own copies of these movies want to share them with others, then it should be allowed. What's the harm?

Well, of course, there *is* harm. That's the way it is every time a new medium comes along in this society. As Neil Postman was fond of pointing out, in our excitement about the possibilities of new gadgets, we almost always forget to ask, what way of life will this new thing *undo*?

I don't, for instance, foresee entities like Blockbuster surviving this new democratization of video file sharing, much less the rise of Video on Demand technologies which the movie studios are in process of implementing, and in which first run studio movies will be available over the Internet or cable within 45 days after the movie's theatrical release. Netflix has turned its primary revenue over to streaming movies live, and as a result, it is becoming a major player in the media landscape. Indeed, this may do to the DVD what the iTunes Music Store did to the CD: render it effectively obsolete. So, not only is the film industry going to have to rethink how it goes about distributing its DVDs — or whether DVDs will even continue to be produced at all — but the music industry, too, is in big trouble.

For instance: when I wrote my book *Dead Celebrities, Living Icons,* I was still thinking in terms of the old media when it came time to do my research. For my chapter on the Beatles, I actually went out and *bought—* can you imagine it?—*all* of the Beatles' records in order to listen through them one by one so that I could write the chapter. What I should have done was to look them all up on YouTube, where each album can be found today and listened to in its entirety, for free. This would have saved me, a poor scholar indeed, a lot of money.

As a result of this easy availability, the film and recording industries — indeed, the *entire* media apparatus — are in the midst of what the mystics call a "Dark Night of the Soul," for the world which brought them into being is now crumbling and they are simply going to have to endure the agonies of a death and rebirth.

The Gutenberg Episteme

Copyright laws came into being as one of the emergent properties of the Gutenberg revolution. Indeed, they were created as a by-product of the printing press and the literate world of booksellers and publishers which that particular medium made possible.

According to Elizabeth Eisenstein, the first intellectual property laws began to emerge near the end of the fifteenth century, just a few decades after the printing press was up and running. In 1469, a Venetian printer obtained the right to print and sell a given book for a given interval of time. In fact, the state of Venice was the first to provide legal protection for inventors in 1474. "Printing," she writes, "forced legal definition of what belonged in the public domain. A literary 'Common' became subject to 'enclosure movements' and possessive individualism began to characterize the attitude of writers to their work. The terms 'plagiarism' and 'copyright' did not exist for the minstrel. It was only after printing that they began to hold significance for the author."[3]

The first official copyright law, however, was the British Copyright Act of 1709, also known as the Statute of Anne, which came into force on April 1, 1710. Its full title was: "An Act for the Encouragement of Learning, by vesting the Copies of Printed Books in the Authors or purchasers of such Copies, during the Times therein mentioned." It granted publishers a legal protection of 14 years (21 years for those books already in print), which could be renewed by the author, if he was still living, at the end of that term.

In America, Congress passed a copyright law in 1790 which granted the author similar terms. By 1831, it "extended the initial term of copyright to twenty-eight years and broadened the scope to cover musical compositions; by 1870, it had expanded copyright to include translations and dramatizations."[4]

But these developments, in turn, were embedded in the larger episteme of the Gutenbergian world that had begun to configure itself as a morphologically distinct structure of the European mind starting around 1500. The printing press was invented in 1439 or so, but by 1500, the

Medieval world was coming to an end. A number of structures came into being simultaneously at just about this time throughout the European arts and sciences, making this an epoch to be demarcated from the Medieval one preceding it.

Painters, for one thing, routinely began signing their canvases at this time, a rare occurrence in the Middle Ages, in which the artist was regarded more as the functionary of a larger social machine than as an individual genius. Artists like Leonardo da Vinci, Hieronymous Bosch or Albrecht Dürer began to take on more and more idiosyncratic traits, traits which separated each of them off into stylistic worlds unto themselves. Leonardo's universe is a microcosm that cannot be fully understood without learning the semiotics of his worldview, whereas prior to that time, the semiotics of the Christian worldview were more or less the same for everybody. Bosch may have been a member of a strange and heretical sect known as the Adamites, and this means that his paintings are unintelligible without some knowledge of their ideas. And Michelangelo's cosmos presupposes a study of Neoplatonism in order for his works to make any kind of sense to the viewer, as Erwin Panofsky demonstrated in his *Studies in Iconology*.[5]

In the Medieval episteme, by contrast, there was no such thing as "originality." The stories recounted in the popular romances of the time, such as the Grail legends or epics like *The Song of Roland*, were rarely original tales, but had rather been recycled from traditional oral storytellers (called *jongleurs*) who had passed them on. The ideal of the author who committed these texts to writing was not to innovate, but rather to take an old and well known tale and remake it anew. Thus, Gottfried von Strassburg betters all previous versions of the Tristan legend with his own unrivalled romance, while Wolfram von Eschenbach creates the greatest version of the Perceval quest ever written. Even as late as 1600, most of Shakespeare's plays are based on recycled legends out of the works of the ancients. There is very little in Shakespeare that is new in the sense of originality of content.

But it is precisely during Shakespeare's time that the European novel was being (re)invented by the Spaniards (*Tirant lo blanc, Don Quixote, Lazarillo de Tormes*). Don Quixote is one of the first heroes of Western literature not to be based upon a previously extant character. Cervantes simply made him up, a novelty at the time.

In the same century, Descartes was busying himself in philosophy discovering the ego, for in his writings, the basic ontology of an absolute subject-object dichotomy was created, an ontology that would continue all the way down to Heidegger, who was the first to begin to deconstruct it. The equivalent to this occurred in painting from about 1500 on with the rise of the individual portrait study beginning with the Van Eycks in the north and in the south with Giovanni Bellini's *Doge Loredano*. This idea of the individual as a totally unique being, ontologically speaking, parallels the invention of new, three dimensional characters in the novel.

Nationalism, though largely a creation of the eighteenth century, begins to emerge at about this time, as well, for the nation state is brought to a focus as *the* great political structure of Western European civilization. All its subsequent wars, down to World War II, are based on the presupposition of nations as imagined communities (to borrow Benedict Anderson's term) with coherent and distinct identities that are geographically and linguistically bounded.

With the rise of the printing press, furthermore, the spread of the vernacular languages were favored at the cost of the dominance of Latin as the universal language of learning. Descartes is still writing in Latin in the middle of the seventeenth century, but by the eighteenth, *all* of Voltaire's works are written in French (as Anderson points out).[6] With the creation, furthermore, of things like indexes, tables of contents and numbered pages, the author as an entity unto himself began to assume more and more importance, for it now became possible with proper citation to keep track of him and his intellectual property.

Hence, the advent of copyright in the eighteenth century was but one structural feature of the larger episteme of the revolution brought about in European civilization by the advent of the printing press.

Diasporic Public Spheres

That episteme, of course, now lies in ruins all about us.

Take, for instance, the nation state. Currently, walls and fences are going up everywhere across the globe as literalizations of nation state borders, as though to shore up the fact that geographical boundaries drawn upon maps and agreed upon by nations are no longer effective as "ideas" but rather must become physicalized in order to be convincing. The fence upon the U.S.–Mexico border is perhaps the most conspicuous example, as well as the one separating Israel from the West Bank, but there are also cement block walls going up around the slums of Rio de Janeiro; a security fence separating Thailand from Malaysia; Brunei is walling out Limbang; an electrified fence built by India along its border with Pakistan (while Pakistan has proposed building a fence along its border with Afghanistan), and another one along India's border with Bangladesh; one separating Beijing from North Korea, Uzbekistan from Tajikistan, Botswana from Zimbabwe, United Arab Emirates from Oman, Kuwait from Iraq, and Saudi Arabia from Yemen to its south and Iraq to its north. One may even go up some day along the U.S.–Canadian border.[7]

Clearly, the nation state no longer works as an "idea," especially since these walls are built mainly for the purpose of keeping other ethnicities "out." (One builds walls as a last resort, in order to keep out the "flow" of liquidity — i.e., humans, floods, etc.— that has been all too frequently pouring in.) The geographical lines drawn on maps and agreed upon by the UN have little consequence in today's world where it is becoming more and more apparent that postnational structures and organizations are succeeding nationalisms. As the philosopher Slavoj Žižek writes:

> This is why, in the new global order, we no longer have wars in the old sense of a regulated conflict between sovereign states in which certain rules apply (humane treatment of prisoners, prohibition of certain weapons, etc.) What remains are "ethnic-religious conflicts" which violate the rules of universal human rights; they do not count as wars proper, and call for the "humanitarian" intervention of the Western powers — even more so in the case of direct attacks on the U.S. or other representatives of the new global order, where, again, we do not have wars proper, but merely "unlawful combatants" criminally resisting the forces of universal order.[8]

During the Yugoslavian break up of the 1990s, what mattered was not so much where you were *at* geographically as who you were descended *from* sanguinally: whether you were a Serb, a Croat or a Bosnian Muslim, not whether — or where — you lived in the vanished nation state of Yugoslavia. Nowadays in Iraq, the term "Iraqi" is completely meaningless, since what is important is whether you are a Sunni, a Shi'ite or a Kurd; in Afghanistan, whether you are Pashtun, Tajik, Uzbek or Hazara; in Rwanda, whether you are Hutu or Tutsi; in Canada, whether you are Québécois or Anglophone; in Darfur, whether you are black or Arab; in Sri Lanka, whether you are Tamil or Sinhalese; in China, whether you are Uighur or Han, and so on.

Benedict Anderson, in his *Imagined Communities*, pointed out how the nation state was largely a creation of the age of print capitalism, in which the ability of those who could not stand in each other's proximity face to face could yet nevertheless conceive of themselves as a single, "imagined community" via literary media such as the novel and the newspaper, in which Malaysians, say, or Indonesians could see themselves unified as a single group. But now the disintegration and breakdown of the nation state has occurred in tandem with the explosion of the new electronic media to bring forth other kinds of postnational communities, usefully termed by Arjun Appadurai "diasporic public spheres," in which people of certain groups or ethnicities, scattered across the globe, can partake of the same community in diaspora, as it were, via electronic technologies such as the Internet. Writes Appadurai:

> These diasporic spheres are frequently tied up with students and other intellectuals engaging in long-distance nationalism (as with activists from the People's Republic of China). The establishment of black majority rule in South Africa opens up new kinds of discourse of racial democracy in Africa as well as in the United States and the Caribbean. The Islamic world is the most familiar example of a whole range of debates and projects that have little to do with national boundaries. Religions that were in the past resolutely national now pursue global missions and diasporic clienteles with vigor: the global Hinduism of the past decade is the single best example of this process. Activist movements involved with the environment, women's issues, and human rights generally have created a sphere of transnational discourse, frequently resting on the moral authority of refugees, exiles, and other displaced persons. Major transnational separatist movements like the Sikhs, the Kurds, and the Sri Lankan Tamils conduct their self-imagining in sites throughout the world, where they have enough members to allow for the emergence of multiple nodes in a larger diasporic public sphere.[9]

Should we be the least bit surprised, then, that the idea of copyright, which came into being along with the advent of the nation state, the printing press and individuality is now, along with the disintegration of the nation state into these various postnationalisms, entering into the period of its twilight?

The Hitler Parodies

The YouTube Hitler parodies are a case in point.

In 2006, a Spanish user posted a short clip from the movie *Der Unter-*

gang (*Downfall*) showing Hitler going into a rant in front of his closest advisors as he realizes that the Germans cannot avoid losing the war. The user inserted his own subtitles to modify the semiotics of the scene, in which Hitler now goes into a rant over the lack of new features in Microsoft's Flight Simulator X. Soon, clips were posted showing him ranting about everything from how cell phone keys are too small for men's hands to send text messages, to the boredom and ennui of moving to South Dakota.

Constantin Films, the company which owns the rights to *Downfall*, began asking YouTube in 2010 to take down the videos. YouTube complied, as it almost always does with such requests, but this only caused more parodies of the scene to be uploaded, some of them featuring Hitler reacting to the video being taken down. Currently, there are plenty of these clips on YouTube, and I have to admit, they are quite funny.

What's even funnier, though, is that the movie *Downfall* itself can be watched on YouTube currently for free. As of this writing, the entire film comes up if you type in "Downfall Part 1." (It is, incidentally, one of the best movies ever made about Hitler; Bruno Ganz's performance is astonishing. If you haven't seen it, you need to.)

What interests me about this episode, though, is not so much the freedom of speech issues that it raises — those are obvious — but rather the Hydra-like nature of YouTube as a medium that it illustrates. When, in Greek myth, Hercules cut off one of the hydra's seven heads, two more sprang up in its place. We may term, then, the repressing of electronic content on the Internet that pops up elsewhere the Hydra Effect. When, for example, Facebook recently shut down Kim Jong-il's Facebook page, it simply sprang up under another name: the Hydra Effect in action. The same thing occurred when, in December of 2010, servers denied WikiLeaks access, and clones of the site simply sprang up elsewhere as fans of WikiLeaks reproduced it.

If industrialization was all about mass production, then electronic technology is based upon feedback and resonance: the instantaneous proliferation of series is part of its very nature as a medium. When something is fed into it via the Internet, the recording industry, the film industry or what have you, the result is *instantaneous* mass proliferation of the image (or song, etc.). Suddenly, the psyche is bombarded with image clones that not only overwhelm it but may also overload it with cognitive "noise," the type of noise that erodes personalities and tilts them toward doing dangerous things like shooting their favorite celebrities or killing everyone at school. If the besieged individual doesn't know how to turn it off, he can very quickly find himself in a kind of madness. Indeed, the attainment of fame via electronic technology involves precisely this process of image avatar proliferation which can and often does drown the psyche of the hapless performer in an ocean of mental feedback.

YouTube as a medium is a kind of machine for absorbing and draining off this electronic resonance effect. It traps image clones, as it were, and holds them in its keep like a huge virtual castle. In this respect, it is doing society a very great favor, since the image proliferation is thereby kept under control. If you want to participate in it, you can go to the site and spend hours, as I have, wading through videos.

Copyright, on the other hand — like today's lizards and birds left over from the Age of the Dinosaurs — is a vestigial survivor from an earlier epoch in which such image proliferation was simply unheard of. Books are mass produced *objects*, certainly — they were, in fact, the first mass produced good to circulate through the capitalist system — but as physical objects, there are real limitations upon how many of them can be produced.

Electronic *images*, on the other hand, are not objects in the same way as mass produced goods can be said to be objects. They exist as part of the ancient realm of phantoms, ghosts and shades, and so the laws and logic governing them are much closer to the morpho-dynamics of ancient myth than they are to three-dimensional mass produced capitalist objects. They do indeed proliferate like mythological beings: the hydra, say, or those skeletons that Cadmus fought when he sowed the dragon's teeth into the earth.

Electronic images do not just reproduce, they *swarm*. Their proliferation is instant and magical and moves with the logic of dreams. They proliferate so fast that the old left to right, first one thing then another logic of the Gutenbergian world of intellectual property laws and copyright are left scrambling after them, disoriented and confused.

Copyright laws — at least as we have come to know them — belong to an age of creaking windmills, tri-masted sailing ships, chugging factories and Newtonian motions of planetary bodies trundling along through Euclidean space. They were not made to exist in the Einsteinian universe of speed-of-light electrodynamics of bodies which move so fast that the eye cannot keep track of them.

As they exist today, copyright laws need to be scrapped and rethought. They need to change, metamorphose and transform into a new kind of creature altogether: one that can accommodate the needs of twenty-first century Internet users. Their governing metaphor must shift from that of a rigid skeleton that breaks when you bend its bones too far, to a more gelatinous, amoeba-like organism that is fluid and can move and shift in ways that befit the phantom-like nature of electric culture.

The owners of YouTube originally sold their company to Google in October of 2006 precisely because they realized that they did not have the capital to combat lawsuits filed against them by big corporations. They knew they had created a technological infrastructure that was exciting and ingenious in its power to turn control over electronic media back to the consumer, just as Michel de Certeau in his book *The Practice of Everyday Life* describes the power of the user to reterritorialize production through tailoring consumption to suit his own needs.

The corporations are just going to have to face it: people like watching movies and listening to music on YouTube, sharing these creations with others, remaking them, reworking them, cutting and pasting them. Indeed, the cut up novels of William Burroughs (*The Soft Machine* [1961], *The Ticket That Exploded* [1962] and *Nova Express* [1964]) had already foreshadowed by several decades the coming of this cut and paste culture.

Legislation, in our society, is not made to control and contain the arts, rather it is the other way around: the laws exist to reflect the creative status of the artistic practices currently in vogue. The printing press came first; *then* the new copyright laws that governed its usage. It is the laws, then, which must change to conform to the new media, not the new media to the old laws.

Welcome to the Remix Society.

3

On Facebook We're All
Being Flattened Together

Faciality

"The face is not a universal," write Deleuze and Guattari in *A Thousand Plateaus,* and indeed, it is not, for in different sign regimes the face takes on different values and must be constructed accordingly.[1] The "face" that is presupposed by Facebook is what Deleuze and Guattari refer to as the "face of Christ," or in other words, the average White Man.

In Byzantine art, for instance, a vast majority of the images are composed of white people gazing directly at the viewer with intense, dark eyes. The icon of "Christ Pantocrator," of which the oldest example comes to us from Saint Catherine's Monastery in Mount Sinai, dating from around the sixth century A.D., is archetypally demonstrative. In it, Christ is depicted as a young white man with long brown hair who gazes at the viewer with eyes that cannot be avoided. It is a searing gaze that penetrates right into you, brooking no evasions. The same goes for the mosaic of Justinian with his staring retinue of white men at San Vitale in Ravenna.

This art of the *en face* visage was practically non-existent prior to the Byzantines, for amongst the ancient Greeks, faciality is something else altogether, and rarely meets or greets the viewer's eye. In ancient Greek sculpture, the face always *avoids* the viewer: Praxiteles' Hermes is looking down at the infant on his arm; Myron's disc-thrower is looking back behind him as he readies for the throw; Polyclitus' spear bearer gazes somewhere off into the distance, fixated on we know not what. This is not an art that foreshadows the photos of people on Facebook, which *is* already prefigured, however, by the Byzantine Christs.[2]

The Mask Is Inimical to Facebook

In a primitive — or, as we say nowadays, "aboriginal" — society, the face as such does not even exist. It has vanished into the mask of a deity or else disappeared beneath a cartography of scarification and paint. It assumes the configurations of a god or an animal and connotes not individuality or subjectification but the presence of a being from another world.

In Mesoamerican civilization, which was far, indeed, from being a "primitive" society, this tradition of the face engulfed by a mask was carried to the point of being an obsession, for in this society, the individual was nothing without a mask or a headdress of some sort. Hence, the ubiquity of the motif, found constantly reiterated in their sculpture and in the regalia of soldiers like the Aztec eagle warriors, of the human head peering out from the mouth of a divinity or beast which has swallowed it up. The human face as we in the West have come to know it scarcely existed, for in Mesoamerica, if you did not embody the presence of a deity, you were simply not an effective presence.

Facebook could not, therefore, function in a signifying regime of masks. A collection of "friends" wearing masks would defeat the whole point of the site, which is designed — ostensibly, at least — for people to connect with one another, an impossibility if a deity is in the way. Nobody wants as their "friends" on Facebook a bunch of deities and astral spirits.

So, the particular kind of faciality presupposed by Facebook is a specifically modernist one in which the human individual has been carefully differentiated out from the realm of transpersonal forces and is thought to be a self-sufficient individual or subject whose thoughts are his own. In a signifying regime of masks, on the other hand, the assumption is not that one is a self capable of articulating and originating his own thoughts but rather that he is an *assemblage,* a tissue of consciousnesses which are speaking through him. One has no idea who or what sort of an entity one might be relating to under such circumstances. Is this "friend" identifiable as David Smith — as it were — or am I to regard his utterances as more properly belonging to the rain god Tlateutli?

The assumption of Facebook is that we are relating *not* to a collective assemblage, but to a specific and unique individual whose faciality is embodied by, and sufficient to, the visage that he presents in his photo.

Our technologies are always embodiments of cultural assumptions. We often use them assuming that they are the only possible and logical way of manifesting technological aims and functions, but this is rarely the case. They are always produced, as Heidegger would put it, out of a particular and very specific understanding of Being, that is, of being *intelligible* as a technological artifact. Facebook is the technological product of a culture that does not identify Being with *a* god or *the* gods, but rather understands it as having been shaped by the human intellect alone and apart from the cosmos.

And why is this important for a mere social networking site on the Internet, the alert reader may well ask? And the answer is that the ontological status of the individual on Facebook has *everything* to do with what it means to be *on* and communicating *with* others on Facebook because the particular kind of faciality presupposed by Facebook is, I believe, actually at odds with how the technology itself makes it possible for these individuals to communicate with each other.

You Have a Friend Request

Allow me to explain.

Facebook is based on the concept of "friending" people. Either someone sends you an invitation to be their friend or vice versa and you then click on the "accept" or "ignore" button depending on your opinion of what you know about this person.

Now, what is the nature of these "friends"? In most cases, they are actually people about whom we know very little, next to nothing, usually. All we see of them is a photograph of their face (typically, anyway) and a handful of facts about them, such as that they like to collect comic books or go to see romantic comedies or read trashy mystery novels, etc. Maybe they have a "friend" or two shared in common with you.

But that's about it. Unless you already happen to know the person well — and this, in my experience, is rare on Facebook — you actually end up knowing very little about these "friends." In other words, these are people who have been simplified to the status of electronic trading cards, just as in the case of baseball trading cards, in which there is a photograph of the "star" on one side of the card while on the reverse, you find a handful of statistics about his batting average, say, or how many homeruns he has hit. On Facebook, then, people do not actually relate to other people, they relate to icons, in almost the same sense in which our celebrities are icons.

Celebrities are digitized human avatars who have descended into the electronic media, where they have been cloned, replicated and accelerated around the globe at dizzying speeds through oceans of human faces. A celebrity is actually not a real life three dimensional human being at all, but a two-dimensional construct of a human being who has been flattened out — as all objects are at the speed of light — crushed, and over-simplified to a cliché or stereotype of his or her own making. These flattened icons bear very little relationship to the complexities and idiosyncrasies of the real three dimensional person who generated them. The public thinks it "knows" very well who the person is, but in fact, it is in love with a fantasy figure that has no real independent existence outside of electronic circuitry. "Real" flesh and blood people usually have very little in common with their two-dimensionally generated icons, as fans, to their disappointment, often find out.

It's the same way with Facebook: real people with complex personalities have been flattened out, crushed and simplified to a stereotype: it is impossible to have any sort of real relationship with such a stereotype, for people always amount to far more than what their profile describes. I, John Ebert, for instance, may be described on Facebook as a writer of books who loves to listen to rock and roll music and is currently single, but this hardly captures me as a personality. For example, based on this profile, the viewing public has no idea whether I am introverted or extraverted; whether I have a good sense of humor or am dull; whether I am assertive around others or passive and accepting, and so on. In short, I am not my Profile. And neither are you.

So the point I am making here is that Facebook, by its very nature as a medium, excludes the possibility of depth and complexity from all human relationships. And of course, the idea of a "friend" is someone who knows you in depth, not someone who has collected you as an electronic trading card.

So these "friends" are not really "friends" at all, but electronic trading cards, human individuals who have been transformed into commodities. You can go shopping for as many "friends" on Facebook as you want, but the chances of actually having a stimulating conversation with any one of them are about nil.

That's the other thing about Facebook as a medium: it's designed for the user to interact with others in the form of just a couple of sentences which are no sooner posted than they are whisked away into the flow of messages that are posted by others. And the more "friends" you have, the faster this stream moves, so the less likely it is that anyone is even going to see what you've posted, assuming that you *can* post anything in two or three lines that is even worthwhile to say. (Twitter is even tougher in this respect, due to its 140 character limit per tweet.)

So, like television, Facebook is an inherently anti-intellectual medium. You cannot discourse with others about complex philosophical ideas on it because this isn't what the medium was designed to do, anymore than television was. You can't even hold meaningful, intimate conversations with "friends" about deep personal issues, since the medium won't tolerate it. Indeed, the site was designed by Harvard students as an electronic equivalent of their bar and dance club "chatter," and if you've ever tried to have a conversation with someone in a dance club, then you know what I'm talking about: the results are similarly frustrating.

So given these limitations, one begins to wonder whether Facebook is of any use for anything *at all?*

But the popularity of the site indicates that it *does* serve a purpose, a purpose that people want, or possibly even need.

The Disappearance of Neighborhoods

When we look at the superficial nature of the chatter on Facebook ("Just got back from the Bermudas!" "Where's the party this weekend?" "Elvis Costello sucks!") it is evident that it represents a type of communication that linguists have termed "phatic." That is to say that the chatter is not designed to convey facts and actual useful information, but simply to create a "sociable" atmosphere. Now, people would not have needed a site that is based almost exclusively on creating a sociable atmosphere unless the conditions for such environments had disappeared elsewhere from the society. And indeed, when we look around at our cities, it is quite evident, I am afraid, that they have.

Phatic environments of communication are most common in neighborhoods in which people are out walking around, as Michel de Certeau, in his book *The Practice of Everyday Life* points out. "Walking," he says, "...alternately follows a path and has followers, creates a mobile organicity in the environment, a sequence of phatic *topoi*."[3] Indeed, the kinds of chatter on Facebook are similar to the kinds of communication that goes on in neighborhoods when people are walking up the street to get a cup of coffee from their local café, read the newspaper, or who are just out for a stroll in the warm evening air. People living in such neighborhoods bump into each other, say "hello!" to their neighbors, or talk superficially about the weather, just as they do on Facebook.

The kinds of environments, however, in which people *don't* do this are becoming more and more common, especially in cities where, as Jane Jacobs never tired of pointing out, the automobile has been allowed to completely take over and force the city officials to redesign their cities around them, instead of people. Automobiles destroy neighborhoods and communities because they have an inherently decentralizing effect upon cities. They act with an almost elastic force upon them, elongating and stretching their geometries to absurdly vast proportions.

I happen to know something about this because I was born and raised in Phoenix, Arizona, a city where the automobile has dictated absolutely *every* civic feature on the map. When the nearest coffee shop is so far away from your living space that you need to climb into your automobile to access it, as you do in Phoenix, the pedestrian is actually eliminated from the city streets. *There are no pedestrians in Phoenix.* At any given moment, one actually has to look around very hard to try and spot one.

Phoenix, of course, is not alone in this, for it is actually happening — or has already long since happened — to most cities in America, with a few notable exceptions such as New York or San Francisco. *People have disappeared from the landscapes of our cities.* If this doesn't alarm you, then it should.

When communities and neighborhoods disintegrate, people retreat, withdrawing alone into the cool interiors of their air-conditioned houses. Or else they go to shopping malls, where they can be alone together. (But of course, now our shopping malls are disappearing, too.)

So, with the vanishing of neighborhoods in which phatic communications normally take place as part of the daily routine of living, we should not be at all surprised when such fugitive environments reappear on Internet sites like Facebook. What we destroy with one kind of technology, we often reinvent with other technologies.

Facebook is an electronic neighborhood where virtual *flaneurs* can go strolling, saying "hello" to "friends," or else they just try to convince themselves that other people *do* exist out there who are as lonely as they are.

But the problem is that Facebook is a poor substitute for real human contact. It is a virtualization and replacement for the kinds of tangibility that human relations need in order to thrive and flourish. In coffee shops, after all, you can have long, interesting conversations with real friends. A great deal of European literature was worked out this way, in coffee shops such as the Café de la Regence or Café Procope (one of the very first) or Les Deux Magots in Paris, places frequented by the likes of Rousseau, Voltaire, Joyce, Picasso, Sartre, Henry Miller, etc. As I have already pointed out, Facebook does not allow for the possibility of long conversations of *any* kind.

But its very existence is a testament to the fact that communities and neighborhoods are disappearing everywhere from our maps.

The World Isn't Flat, You Are

As I have said, the particular kind of "faciality" presupposed by Facebook is one in which human individuals are thought to be three dimensional entities who have decoupled from the transpersonal realm of spirits, gods, ancestors and other assorted deities. This is what is connoted by the signifier of the photograph of a person's face, which is a way of saying "I am me" and not some other entity that is part of some larger dimension of existence. Indeed, the West, since at least the Middle Ages, has been built up out of this idea of the differentiated individual human who is a self-sufficient subjectivity unto himself. This has been the case in philosophy since Descartes: "I think, therefore I am" is really another way of saying "*I* exist, *I* am an entity with my *own* thoughts. Gods and spirits and ancestors do not speak through me, for me or on my behalf."

(And in fact, as the Austrian philosopher Franz Borkenau has pointed out, this tradition is as old as the invention of the I-Form of speech, which first appears in runic inscriptions in the Norse languages of old Denmark circa 400 A.D. It is at this point that the pronoun "I" is separated out from the verb: "I, Hlegestr from Holt made this Horn," found on a golden horn, may be the earliest appearance of the pronoun "I."[4])

But as we have seen, the nature of Facebook as a medium overrides all this, for it transforms such individual subjectivities into two dimensional trading cards. The individual is absorbed back into the same Electrotopic fantasy land occupied by celebrities and therefore ironically becomes a sort of hollow mask of himself.

On Facebook, we are all tautologies, for on it, we become our own masks.

But of course, all of this is part of a larger endeavor of our civilization to flatten out depths into surfaces, to crush complexity, ambiguity and multi-dimensionality into simplicity and advertising logo simple-mindedness.

Television flattens political issues into sound bites; the automobile flattens cities into wastelands; celebrities are a flattening of the human personality into an icon; Hollywood movies flatten complex stories into formulas and clichés; books are becoming ever more and more shallow (and even flattening into non-existence via the e-reader); zero casualty wars (i.e., drones); caffeine-free coffee, Coke and Pepsi; non-alcoholic beer. All is flattened, simplified, detoxified and destroyed.

On Facebook, human relationships are the latest casualty of this process. But at least we're not alone.

We're all being flattened together.

4

Wikipedia; or, The Catastrophe of Knowledge

Not *an Encyclopedia*

Whatever else it is, Wikipedia is no encyclopedia, as its tagline "the Free Encyclopedia" would have us believe. It is no more an encyclopedia than a movie is another kind of book. Rather, it is a very different kind of text from anything even remotely resembling a printed book, or indeed, a book of *any* kind; it is so different as to constitute something of an epistemological crisis regarding the very notion of the concept of "knowledge."

The word "encyclopedia" comes from the Greek words *enkyklios paideia,* meaning "general instruction," or, more literally, "training in a circle," the "circle" (*kyklos*) referring to the "curriculum" of the arts and sciences. But Wikipedia, of course ("course" as in "running in a circle," like a chariot race), has no "curriculum" because it is not organized according to any sort of a plan or "paideia" of instruction at all. It is, instead, an accident of knowledge, composed out of the wreckage of shattered words and disconnected information, wrenched free of context and splashed across the information superhighway as an obstacle that is impossible to avoid.

Thus, I think the disaster of Wikipedia justifies our taking some time and glancing back over the history of the book in order to gain an aerial view, as it were, over the scene of this knowledge derailment.

A Miniature History of the Book

1.

The first books were simply small, round clay tablets that could be held in the palm of the hand (like primitive iPhones) and upon which Sumerian scribes (known as *dubsars*) drew pictographs with pointed reed styluses about 3400 B.C. in the city of Uruk, where writing was first invented. The earliest writing came into being strictly for practical reasons, in order to keep track of the transactions of ur-capitalism; literary works were not first written down for about another eight centuries, sometime around 2600 B.C., and found at sites such as Abu Salabikh and Shuruppak.

The pictographic signs themselves, though written vertically in columns and read from right to left, were originally arranged in no particular order, leaving it up to the reader to supply things like syntax and grammar. Only in the Early Dynastic III period at Shuruppak (c. 2600 B.C.) were grammatical elements first written down. The tradition of writing words and grammatical elements according to their *spoken* order first began in the period of Eannatum of Lagash about a century later.[1]

Mesopotamia was the first, and also the *only* civilization ever to use clay as a medium for writing, since the alluvial plain was poor in just about every resource but clay. All media have their limitations and the drawback with clay is that pictures are difficult to draw on it. The initial solution to this problem was to rotate the pictographs 90 degrees, for at first, the direction of the scribe's hand had moved over the clay from right to left in vertical columns. The disadvantage of this method was that the hand could smudge what had already been written, so to rotate the figures 90 degrees also meant that the vertical columns became horizontal. In this second phase (c. 3000 B.C.), the tablets became larger and the signs more abstract, with fewer curves.

In the Early Dynastic I period (c. 2900–2700 B.C.), curvilinear forms were dropped altogether. The earlier stylus was replaced by a reed with a triangular wedge at the tip which could be pressed into the clay in order to create words with an almost Morse code-like rapidity and thus, cuneiform proper was born (from Latin *cuneus* meaning "wedge-shaped"). The direction of writing shifted now, as well, and was read from left to right.

The Epic of Gilgamesh may very well be the earliest complete book. It was written down on a series of twelve (originally, eleven) clay tablets by the Babylonians of around 1750 B.C. in the language of cuneiform Akkadian. The tablets were baked in kilns so that they would be "permanent." This was the kind of text that could not be easily altered once it had been baked (by contrast with Wikipedia, say, where "knowledge" appears and disappears without warning).

According to a Sumerian myth, it was actually Gilgamesh's grandfather, Enmerkar, who was supposed to have been the inventor of writing in Sumer. The story concerns a rivalry between the cities of Uruk and Aratta (a city in Iran), in which Enmerkar prays to his goddess Inanna to make Aratta supply his city with precious metals. He sends a messenger across the mountains to deliver riddles to the king of Aratta, and after two such trips back and forth, the runner returns to Uruk, exhausted. Enmerkar's next message is too long for the runner to remember — orality, in other words, has become an overheated medium — and so Enmerkar is forced to invent writing as a substitute to supplement the runner's memory:

> This speech was long and difficult to understand;
> The messenger's mouth was too heavy and he could not repeat it.
> Because the messenger's mouth was too heavy and he could not repeat it,
> The king of Kulaba formed some clay and put words on it as if on a tablet.
> Before that time the inscribing of words on clay (tablets) did not exist;
> But now, in the sun of that day, it was indeed so (established) —
> The king of Kulaba had inscribed words as if on a tablet, it was indeed so (established)!

However, when the messenger carries this new medium to the King of Aratta, there is a problem:

> The king of Aratta set a clay lamp
> Before the messenger.
> (In its light) the king of Aratta looked at the clay (tablet).
> The spoken words were but nails, and his brow darkened.
> The king of Aratta kept staring into the clay lump.[2]

The king is of course illiterate — as was everybody in the world at that point, except Enmerkar — and so he cannot read the message. But the invention of writing gives Uruk an asymmetric advantage over Aratta, which is then required to submit to Uruk, its acknowledged cultural superior. The message is clear: he who has writing is superior to those who do not, and those who do not must submit to the yoke of those who do. (Notice that the back and forth treks of the messenger between the two cities imitates the way in which the eyes scan a text, moving back and forth across the surface of the clay tablet.)[3]

The clay tablet was not only the earliest form of the book to come into existence, but also the "first form of the book to have become extinct," as Frederick Kilgour remarks, for by the second century A.D., it had vanished from the earth.[4] Its decline had been heralded when, in the middle of the second millennium B.C., the appearance of West Semitic alphabet-like syllabaries came into being, which were a much more efficient instrument of writing. Clay tablets were an extremely durable medium, however, for they had remained in existence for over 3500 years, alongside more perishable media such as the papyrus scroll. Indeed, Egyptians as late as the time of Akhenaten, in the middle of the fourteenth century B.C., were still writing on clay tablets, for the Amarna texts were written down at the city of Akhetaten in cuneiform Akkadian, implying that the medium still had its advantages.

2.

By the time of the First Dynasty of Egypt, c. 2900 B.C., the Egyptians were already using and making the form of the book as a papyrus scroll. Papyrus was made out of dried strips of a plant known as *Cyperus papyrus*— which the Egyptians had a monopoly upon, since it was only found in the Nile delta — which were laid together, slightly overlapping, with a second layer added on top of the first at right angles. Moistened and hammered with a mallet, the two layers adhered together to make a single sheet of writing material. 20 sheets were then assembled to make a roll.[5] The earliest surviving papyrus scrolls date from the reign of King Den at Saqqara (the fourth king of the First Dynasty), and although they had not been written on, there is little doubt as to their purpose, especially since the hieroglyphic sign of a roll and that of a scribe's utensils already existed at that point. Papyrus rolls, when new, were white and then gradually yellowed with age, like paper.

Writing in Egypt, though, had already originated c. 3200 B.C. in connection with the tomb of the Scorpion King, where over 150 bone and ivory plaques have been found inscribed with the earliest recorded hieroglyphs.[6] Hieroglyphs can be written from right to left or left to right and also in vertical columns, depending on the scribe's intention. The scribe in Egypt (known as a *sesh*—after Seshat, the goddess of writing) was very highly esteemed, by contrast with his role in Mesopotamia.

> He who knew how to write [remarks Mohamed Hussein] could enter the "cursus honorum," attain the highest state appointments and thus participate in government. The ramification of the administration, which from the early days of the Old Kingdom expanded, absorbing more and more people, created an extremely self-assured class who, because of their education and knowledge, regarded themselves as being above the masses of illiterates. They prided themselves in having access to higher education, to classical writings and to the doctrines of life and of knowledge and security as well as in not having to do any physical work. Intractable pupils were told in well-chosen words about the advantages of the scribe's profession: "As far as the scribe is concerned, whatever post he may occupy in the state, he will never be in need."[7]

The scribe's writing kit — by the end of the Fifth Dynasty, anyway — consisted of a long wooden palette in the shape of a rectangle, with an opening in the middle in which could be kept his reed pens. At one end of it were two ink wells for red and black ink (the god Osiris, incidentally, was associated with the black, fertile soils along the riverbanks of the Nile, whereas his enemy Seth was associated with the color red, the color of the deserts of Upper Egypt). The scribe wetted and cut the reed, dipped it into the ink, and then wrote his hieroglyphs upon a sheet of papyrus, using the red ink as rubrications for section headings, dates, titles of spells or the beginnings of paragraphs.

If it is true that the nature of the medium determines the content of what is expressed by means of it, then we can see how the medium of the clay tablet was unfavorable to the development of a pictographic script, since such images were difficult to draw legibly in moist clay. The medium therefore favored a more abstract script which eventually surfaced as cuneiform, whereas papyrus was a medium that favored pictographs, since they were easily drawn or inked upon the page. Egyptian writing, therefore, always retained its pictographic origins and was closely aligned, as we have seen, with funerary art from the very beginning.

The earliest sacred books in Egypt were the *Pyramid Texts*, carved upon the walls of the pyramid of Unas (c. 2375–2345 B.C.) at the end of the Fifth Dynasty. Egyptian tombs were essentially books in stone, as the German scholar Jan Assmann elaborates:

> ... the most important common denominator of tomb and
> book is authorship — a denominator without parallel in other
> cultures. Where else does the owner of a tomb figure as the
> "author" of his burial place and the life recorded within...? This
> "literary" element is unique to the monumental Egyptian tomb.
> For the Egyptian, the tomb was the most important thing in the
> world, the "work" for which he lived and in which he invested
> both his financial resources and his intellectual powers; his
> tomb recorded in a visible and preeminently durable form his
> acts and designs, his exits and entrances, his value and signifi-
> cance, his virtue and his standing. The noble Egyptian planned
> his tomb during his lifetime and left a record of that activity in
> his biographical inscription.[8]

Indeed, the Egyptians actually invented the genre of the autobiography as the direct result of the inscribing of this personal life history — by the nobles, however, not the pharaohs — upon the stone walls of their tomb-texts. These autobiographies originated in the Old Kingdom from about the time of the early Fourth Dynasty, and over the course of the unfolding of subsequent dynasties, they became ever longer and more boastful as the power of the nobles rose to a climax during the Sixth Dynasty.

The Egyptians, however, never produced an epic of the stature of *Gilgamesh*— although they were masters of the short story — but their Books of the Dead are the closest analogue, constituting essentially an epic journey to the Underworld told over the course of many generations, paralleling Gilgamesh's journey to the island underworld of Dilmun, where he encounters Utnapishtim, the caretaker of the dead.

Egyptian hieroglyphs became extinct near the end of the fourth century A.D., during which time the emperor Theodosius outlawed paganism, and proscribed the cults of Isis. The papyrus scroll, however, continued as a literary medium down to the seventh century A.D., during which time it, too, became extinct (although it continued to be used for utilitarian documents until the eleventh century). It was probably not a coincidence that it was during the sixth century when the Byzantine emperor Justinian ordered the final closing of the schools of Athens, from whence Greek intellectuals then fled into Persia, where they were welcomed.

3.

Among the Greeks, meanwhile, the papyrus scroll continued to be used as the preferred form of the book, although parchment — which had been in use since 1600 B.C.—came into prominence as a new material for scrolls around the time of Herodotus. Parchment is made from dried animal skins (calf, sheep or goat) and by the sixth century A.D., it had become the preferred material for writing upon. In the second century B.C., however, there was an intense rivalry between the libraries of Alexandria and Pergamum, a rivalry so fierce that it caused King Ptolemy V Epiphanes (c. 205–185 B.C.) to stop shipment of papyrus to Eumenes II, the king of Pergamum, so that books could no longer be manufactured there. Pergamum responded by stepping up the manufacture of parchment as an official substitute for papyrus (thus: Latin for "parchment" is *pergamenum*).[9]

The Greeks, meanwhile, had inherited the alphabet from the Phoenicians (or else the Canaanites, whose script is known as "Ugaritic") and added (a total of seven) vowels to it, although it is equally possible that the alphabet *could* have been invented by Hebrews in the Sinai peninsula (known as the "proto–Sinaitic" script).[10] The ghosts of earlier pictographs can still be discerned in the alphabetic letters. The letter "A" for instance is an upside down bull's head (*aleph*); the letter "B" is a stylized drawing of a house (*beth*); the letter "G" is a camel's hump (*gimmel*) rotated to a vertical position, the letter "D" a doorway (*daleth*) and so on. Now, instead of several hundred or more signs, the individual had only to master roughly 25 in order to learn to write, greatly simplifying the process.

The earliest Greek inscriptions—if we overlook Mycenaean Linear B—date from around the middle of the eighth century B.C., contemporary with Homer. As in the case of ancient Egypt, they actually come from a funerary context, for the earliest written inscription that we posses comes from a Dipylon vase dating to about 750 B.C. which would have been used to adorn a Greek burial mound in the Kerameikos cemetery at Athens.

The direction of early Greek writing originally read from right to left, before shifting to *boustrophedon* ("ox-turning") in which every other line is read in the opposite direction, thus imitating the path of a bull plowing a field. By the end of the fifth century B.C., Greek writing stabilized in the left to right direction that has been standard in the West ever since.

Writing on papyrus had begun to come into fashion in Greece in Ionia in Asia Minor, not on the mainland, somewhere around 500 B.C. It didn't become fashionable in Athens until a century or so later, thus preparing the ground for Euripides.

The first public library in Greece opened in 330 B.C., while Euripides is said to have been the first man to own his own private library. Indeed, the book trade in Greece originated as a direct result of the popularity of Attic tragedy, for by the time of Euripides, plays were widely read after their performances.

4.

Thus, in the West, the book has gone through three distinct transformations: the clay tablet, the papyrus scroll and the codex. Each phase has been of extremely stable duration: from the Egyptians of the First Dynasty (c. 2900 B.C.) to about the seventh century A.D., the book was a scroll for nearly 3600 years, as was the clay tablet, which existed right alongside it from 3500 B.C. to about 100 A.D. Then, with the codex, which was invented around 100 A.D., the book has retained a stable form to the present day (approximately 2000 years), for our current books are of course also codices, mechanized codices, to be exact.

The phase of the codex has itself undergone three sub-phases: first, the codex as a standard Christian book form; then, with the illuminated manuscript, coming in around 500 A.D., it undergoes transformation into a luminous medium which survives until about the year 1500, whereupon, with the printing press, the codex is mechanized and mass produced.

Now, as I have said, the codex itself was born somewhere around the first century A.D. in ancient Rome. It evolved from the use of hinged wooden writing tablets with wax surfaces that could be inscribed like the clay tablets of the Mesopotamians; these wax surfaces could also be completely erased when heated, just as sun dried clay tablets could be wetted and then erased. However, these tablets could hold at most only about twenty or so pages of text.[11]

At this point, the very geometry of the book undergoes transformation, unrolling from the topology of a spiral to that of a flattened planar surface. The codex is "made by putting single sheets, cut to the same size, on top of each other, stitching them together in the middle and then folding them."[12] For a long time, a codex consisted of a single quire of rectangular sheets of parchment, vellum or papyrus with a spine, although the tendency of papyrus to tear away from the stitching with age favored the use of parchment for codices.

Thus, the curvilinear book gives way to the rectilinear, right-angled book, the preferred form of writing for the Christians. All the Nag Hammadi texts, containing most of the Gnostic writings, for instance, were written in the form of codices. In fact, as Kilgour points out, during the first three centuries A.D., 92 percent of the Bibles produced were codices and only 8 percent were papyrus rolls.[13] The pagans, though, tended to continue writing on scrolls.

For a few centuries, the scroll and the codex overlapped, but the tipping point came near the end of the third century A.D., when the number of codices began to exceed the number of scrolls. By the seventh century A.D., the codex had completely wiped out the scroll as a medium.[14]

One wonders why it didn't happen sooner, for the codex had several advantages over the scroll. It had a spine, for instance, upon which the incipit of the text could be written, which made codices easier to find and store in a library. Also, they could be written on both recto and verso, unlike scrolls, which could only be written upon one side. And they were also easier to carry and transport than scrolls.

Why, then, did it take so many centuries (roughly six) for the codex to put the scroll out of business? As Kilgour remarks: "certainly a reluctance to accept change was a major obstacle."[15]

5.

Papyrus fell out of use in Europe by 716 A.D., whereupon parchment came to replace it during the Carolingian dynasty.[16] The epoch of parchment, in turn, would begin to wind down by the 13th century, while paper, in the meantime, had already been introduced into Spain by the Arabs near the end of the eleventh century. The Arabs had acquired the art of making paper from the Persians, while the Persians had acquired it from the Chinese who had invented it in 105 A.D.

Parchment tended to be linked with a monopoly of knowledge developed by ecclesiastical organization, whereas a monopoly of knowledge developed by political organization was favored by paper, which also tended to give voice to the vernacular languages at the expense of Latin. As Harold Innis writes:

> Parchment was slowly displaced by paper in the universities, churches, and monasteries. The Greeks began to use paper in manuscripts in the twelfth century and Italians in the thirteenth century, but it was sparingly used, in spite of the very high cost of parchment notably in the thirteenth century, until the fifteenth century. Monasteries continued to support the slow and costly production of parchment manuscripts. Writing on

parchment required strength and effort. "Their fingers hold the pen but the whole body toils." Working six hours a day the scribe produced from two to four pages and required from ten months to a year and a quarter to copy a Bible. The size of the scriptures absorbed the energies of monasteries. Libraries were slowly built up and uniform rules in the care of books were generally adopted in the thirteenth century. Demands for space led to the standing of books upright on the shelves in the fourteenth and fifteenth centuries and to the rush of library construction in the fifteenth century.[17]

The illuminated manuscript, meanwhile, was largely an invention of the seventh century. It is simply a more beautifully illustrated codex. Its charismatic early examples are books like the Codex Aureus, the Lindisfarne Gospels, or the Book of Kells, which date from between 700–800 A.D. These texts were written on vellum with iron gall ink, *the* staple ink used in Europe until the nineteenth century. These were big, heavy books, incidentally, weighing over 20 pounds each.

Words at this time were normally run together without separation clear down to about 675 A.D., when, with the Book of Durrow, Irish monks invented the practice of clearly separating the words from each other on the page in order to make them more visible and easier to read aloud. Kilgour also points out that modern punctuation — such as parentheses, quotation marks, commas, etc. — was largely an innovation of the twelfth and thirteenth centuries, along with subject indexes, tables of contents and the practice of silent reading, all of which *preceded* the printing press.

It was around the year 1439 when the ancient culture of writing with ink by hand was crossed with the civilization of the Machine — specifically, the wine press — to produce mechanized printing, which was, of course, invented in Mainz, Germany by Johannes Gutenberg, who was the first to perfect the use of blocks of movable metal type. Walter Ong gives us an excellent description of the printing process in his book *The Presence of the Word:*

> What was crucial for this ultimate locking of sound in space was the invention of movable alphabetic type cast from matrices which had been made with punches. When this development was matured it entailed a large number of steps in fixed sequence. One started by cutting punches in a hard metal (iron or steel), one for each letter of the alphabet, with the letter raised on the end of the punch as a letter is on a typewriter key. These punches were struck into pieces of softer metal to form

matrices (that is, if we translate this Latin word, "wombs"). Still softer metal, molten, an alloy of lead, was then brought into contact with the matrices to cast types, which were made in large quantities for each letter. A font (that is, a pouring) of these types was stored in a case, a large tray with box-like compartments, one for each letter. The typesetter took his copy to the case and set type on a composing stick (a small tray-like holder), later transferring it to a galley (a larger tray), proving it and correcting the proof sheets and subsequently the type in the galley. The type was moved onto the composing stone with other type from other galleys and locked in a form or chase. This chase was transferred to a press into which it itself was further locked. After makeready, the type was inked, the inking apparatus (originally daubers, later rollers) moved aside, paper brought into contact with the locked-up type, the platen of the press squeezed down on the paper, the platen then removed, and the printed sheet taken off the type. Some twelve to sixteen steps, dependent on how one figures the units, intervene here between the written word (already one remove from the spoken) and the printed sheet.[18]

Thus, printing enabled the mass production of books, for presses could produce up to 3,600 pages per workday, as opposed to the mere few pages produced by Medieval scribes in the scriptoria. The earliest manuscripts, up until about the sixteenth century, were known as incunabili (Latin for "swaddling clothes"), which indicated the infancy of the new medium.

One of the main advantages of the printing press was the drastic decrease in the cost of books. Christopher de Hamel synopsizes these dramatic price differences for us:

> The chronicler Hartmann Schedel happens to record the prices which Sweynheym and Pannartz were asking for printed books in 1470: St. Augustine (1468 edition) has dropped now to 5 ducats; Cicero *De Oratore,* 1469, is only 19 *grossi* (there were 24 *grossi* to a ducat); Cicero, *De Officiis,* 1469, is one ducat; Caesar, *Commentarii,* 1469, are 2 1/2 ducats; Pliny's massive *Historia Naturalis,* 1470, containing 378 leaves, is the most expensive at 8 ducats. Compare the prices at which Vespasiano offered manuscripts of the same texts for sale in Naples in *c.* 1457: Cicero, *De Oratore,* at 9 ducats; Cicero, *De Officiis,* at 5 ducats; Caesar, *Commentarii,* at 18 ducats; and in 1463 the secretary of the king of Naples was prepared to pay Vespasiano up to 60 ducats for a manuscript of Pliny's *Historia Naturalis....* The printers could produce books more accurately and more cheaply for about one fifth to one tenth of the price of a manuscript.[19]

This new economy also began to favor the popularity of the vernacular languages, for by the end of the sixteenth century, French was in and Latin was out.

Here is Harold Innis, once again:

> That the sacred character of the scriptures in the Middle Ages was expressed in sculpture and architecture had disastrous implications following the expansion of printing with its emphasis on the scriptures. Greek scriptures following the translations of Erasmus and a concern with the possibility of translation into the vernaculars destroyed the monopoly of the church as expressed in Latin. In the Reformation print was used to overwhelm sculpture and architecture as interpreters of the scriptures. Translations into the vernaculars gave them a sacred character and gave a powerful drive to nationalism.[20]

Thus, the decentralizing effects of the printing press, which aided and abetted the rise of Protestantism by circulating vernacular copies of the Bible and other ecclesiastical texts, brought to an end the age of the domination of the State by the Church, and of the Word by the Image.

6.

Now, step back from our panorama and observe the sequence: the history of the book follows a trajectory along the chain of being from clay (earth), to papyrus (plant), to parchment (animal), to paper (wood). (In Southeast Asia, books were written on palm leaves in India or on strips of bamboo or pieces of silk in China.) It is, in other words, all very tangible, concrete and elemental. Having the ontological status of concrete "things," these media were designed to outlast the lifetime of the individual who composed them and in some cases, as with clay and parchment, to last for a *very* long time. Knowledge thus has the status in these ancient societies of something permanent (more or less), a Big Other that is already in existence when the individual is born and will continue to exist after he is gone. There is nothing *ad hoc* about it.

A body of wisdom is there to be consulted; it is something which has a shaping influence on the individual's life. Knowledge worth knowing, in other words, is not easily acquired, but it *is* worth the trouble of storing up in writing, where it will take on an existence that is independent of the merely transitory phenomenon of biological life.

There is also a sacred dimension to writing, traditionally speaking, since each one of these civilizations had patron deities of writing who were thought to have invented it for the purpose of giving the scribe access to the sacred realm. Writing in Mesopotamia was thought to have been invented by the grain goddess Nisaba (later displaced by the Babylonian god Nabu); in Egypt, by the astronomical goddess Seshat (later displaced by Thoth); in India by the goddess of eloquence Saraswati, who was later displaced in this role by Ganesha, who was said to have written down the *Mahabharata* while taking dictation from Vyasa; in Greece, by Hermes, who was assimilated to Thoth during the Alexandrian age; and in Christianity, the angel Gabriel occupied this role (although St. Jerome, the patron saint of archivists and librarians and the first to translate the Bible into Latin, seems to have displaced him. Hence, the custom of placing a pair of lions in front of libraries, which continues to the present day, is a recognition of Jerome's patronage, for whom the lion was a sort of *vahana*).[21]

Thus grounded in a transcendent dimension, writing has an ontological status in these civilizations that it no longer has for us, for the god guarantees that what is written and stored up as Truth is ontologically grounded in an invisible reality that is not only divine, but valid for all eternity.

Of course, things nowadays are no longer this way: Saussure and the deconstructionists have assured us that the relationship of the signifier to the signified is totally arbitrary, that there is no necessary dependence whatsoever between a word and the concept or reality to which it refers. Any word can be substituted for any concept. The very idea of a sacred language is ridiculed. Sacred *for whom?* For every elite that has privileged access to a transcendent knowledge base, some group of people is being oppressed or marginalized: the price for the access of the *Brahmin*, via Sanskrit, to the ultimate reality, is that the *shudra* will have molten lead poured into his ears if he happens to overhear a sacred recitation.[22] Nowadays, especially since the French po-mo revolution, we have sided with the *shudra* and have therefore exploded and deconstructed the pretense to authority of all traditional knowledge systems whatsoever.

So the relationship of the signifier to the signified *must be* arbitrary, otherwise you will become the victim of a knowledge-power movement by the elite group which has privileged access to the transcendent dimension represented by an authoritative knowledge base.

Back to Wikipedia

But now all this finds its technological equivalent with the triumph of the video screen, where the word no longer exists in any sort of concrete way to tangible things at all. Incarnated in the silicon chips of integrated circuits, it is as ghostly and intangible as the angels were once considered to be.

The image of a text on a computer screen is just that: an *image* of a text. It is no longer a text proper. It exists in a state of virtuality and potentiality, without ever having attained the ontological status of completion that is necessary for a text to convey anything even remotely as reassuring as the idea of knowledge.

With Wikipedia, furthermore, knowledge is never "complete." It never even attains the status of knowledge, for the information that appears on Wikipedia may disappear within minutes. A knowledge base which appears and disappears without warning *cannot* be regarded in any way, shape or form as an encyclopedia *of any kind*. If what I just read a few minutes ago may have disappeared since I read it, and thus no longer has the status of being "true," then what I have read cannot be regarded as knowledge at all, but rather something more akin to the status of rumor, which is information that may or may not be true and may even change its status in the very process of its utterance.

One of the most amusing things about Wikipedia is how often its "editors" place at the headings of various articles the warning that "this article needs proper citation." Sometimes the threat follows that unless the status of "proper citation" is achieved, the information that has been anonymously posted may be "deleted."

Let's face it: the very *concept* of Wikipedia completely undermines any such print based notions of proper citation. Citation by whom? The articles are not signed; all information is posted anonymously. What would be the point of citation? To confer some sort of authoritative status on what has been posted? Yet how can there be any official status if the information posted on Wikipedia is by definition posted by faceless, nameless "non-experts," come one, come all? Proper citation doesn't change the fact that the information has not necessarily been posted by an expert.

Knowledge Crisis

Wikipedia, then, bears scant resemblance to any traditional idea of the book or encyclopedia as we have come to know it. The history of the book prior to the twentieth century, as we have seen, has been a history of concrete objects in which and upon which, stable references have been inscribed to an *objective* world that is not going to disappear any time soon. To borrow from Zygmunt Bauman, that is, what was true at sunset today is not in danger of ceasing to be true at sunrise tomorrow, as is the case with us moderns.[23]

In such a bizarre case as ours, with knowledge and facts appearing and disappearing by the moment, it is nearly impossible for the beleaguered individual to plan ahead for more than a few days at a time. Plans that are made based on one set of data that has become obsolete within a matter of hours are not really plans at all and cannot function as such. The human individual, in such a society, is caught in a temporal horizon of the present moment that he cannot get free of, since there is no longer past or future within which to structure his actions effectively. Loyalties must change, as Bauman has said, by the moment. What skills the individual was valued for yesterday are today as obsolete as eight track tapes and vinyl records. The individual is forced to become a *bricoleur* ready to adapt at a moment's notice to the exigencies imposed upon him by the new "memo." And if he cannot keep up, then he falls by the wayside of "progress."

Wikipedia reflects the status of knowledge in a society in which knowledge has become merely provisional. Indeed, in such a society, there almost seems to be nothing worth knowing at all, since everything learned is destined to become obsolete in a few minutes anyway.

If this isn't a knowledge crisis, then I don't know what one is.

Borges, Prophet of Wikipedia

With the advent of Wikipedia and the phantom nature of its "knowledge" in which lines of text, whole paragraphs, or indeed even entire articles may abruptly disappear, we no longer have a tangible text at all, but a phantom one that has the ontological status of one of those virtual objects out of a Borges short story than any kind of traditional idea of a text.

The artist, as Marshall McLuhan was fond of saying, is the Distant Early Warning system of a society, and Borges, in his fiction, was indeed the first to perceive the coming of electronic texts, for their fantastical nature is already clearly sketched out there. Think of the cosmic library in "The Library of Babel" that keeps growing and growing until it is so large that it essentially *is* the universe. Bizarre forms of knowledge are stored within this library; books that do not make any sense, or in which only one or two lines seem to be intelligible, or that go on and on interminably about some minor point. Or those phantom encyclopedias in "Tlon, Uqbar, Orbis Tertium," which describe a nonexistent world in which plagiarism does not exist and in which all authors are essentially the same author and consequently nobody signs his name to anything. Or the novel in "The Garden of Forking Paths" in which *all* possible outcomes of the plot are simultaneously written because they are all equally compossible. No event can be said, with any certainty, to have taken place, since it is just as possible to say that in a parallel universe that event did *not* take place.

Indeed, these virtual objects, with their illogicality, paradoxical reasoning and fantasmatic natures are clear foreshadowings of the coming of an electronic "artifact" such as Wikipedia, which bears every evidence of being their physical realization. *Nothing* is more Borgesian than the *a*-logicality of Wikipedia with all its insistence on a publicly alterable database of articles that "may be deleted" at any moment. Why offer the site to the public, then, in the first place? Just *who* is it anyway that lies behind this phantom database of non-truths and inexpert citations?

Once again, the ontological nature of electronic technology is far more akin to the logic of myth and dream than to traditionally inscribed media.

Wikipedia is a sort of encyclopedia of *Als Ob,* in which all possibilities are equally true. It corresponds to the phase space of a Leibnizian reality of monadological compossibilities, a virtual world that runs parallel to the real world but only rarely manages to actually intersect it. It is a Garden of Forking Knowledge Paths in which Napoleon may have existed, for instance, or he may not have, depending on that day's editorial whims.

Who Needs It?

The key thing about knowledge traditionally speaking has always been context: who said it? Who published it? What university financed it? What institution paid for it? Who is saying what is being said, and what is motivating this person to utter it? All of these things must be weighed in order to properly evaluate what you are being confronted with as "knowledge."

But with Wikipedia, all of these contexts have disappeared. Knowledge has taken on a free-floating status in which News from Nowhere uttered by nobody in particular is drifting about in the ether for whoever wants it.

Such a knowledge system, furthermore, exists in a temporal horizon that is locked into a pure present. There is no future, there is no past, only what somebody just wrote on the site a few minutes ago. Unplug the system and the knowledge disappears. If an economic or an electrical catastrophe should ever happen to shut down the Internet, all the "knowledge" on it would disappear, utterly. In this case, there would be nothing remaining for the future, no records in which future historians — assuming there are any — can look back and say, "Oh, at this point, they believed that." Only a knowledge lacuna in the void of history.

Our electronic media reflect more and more as time goes by the amnesic, aphasic nature of the contemporary Western episteme. We are currently suffering from a kind of intellectual equivalent of Alzheimer's and our new technologies, from iPhones to MiniMacs reflect this, with all of their user interfaces, virtual graphics and electronic alterability.

Only in a culture as intellectually senile as ours could a site like Wikipedia ever flourish.

5

WikiLeaks and the
Death of Culture

Intelligible Sphere

WikiLeaks was founded in December of 2006 by Julian Assange together with a group of Chinese dissidents, journalists, mathematicians and technologists from countries as diverse as Taiwan, Europe, Australia and South Africa. Assange himself is a former computer hacker from Australia who claims to have founded the site for the express purpose of "exposing injustice." "Our primary targets," he told a *New Yorker* essayist, "are those highly oppressive regimes in China, Russia and Central Eurasia, but we also expect to be of assistance to those in the West who wish to reveal illegal or immoral behavior in their own governments and corporations." He has argued that a "social movement" to expose secrets could "bring down many administrations that rely on concealing reality — including the U.S. administration."[1]

WikiLeaks appears to represent the advent of a new epoch for journalism. Assange says his approach differs from traditional journalism in that it models itself after scientific papers, in which citations indicate that the reader can check the source material for himself in order to verify the accuracy of the article in question. In traditional journalism, readers usually cannot check the journalist's sources and so just have to rely on their reporting, which is often biased or even wrong. On WikiLeaks, one finds entire source documents, mostly unedited, with few annotations. They are primary sources obtained anonymously and display an intriguing range of topics, from the hacked emails of Sarah Palin to the official torture instruction manual from Guantanomo Bay.

WikiLeaks is thus a classic example of the kinds of asymmetric power that the Internet is capable of bestowing upon a single individual: through electronic amplification, he can become powerful enough to take on big, arrogant institutions such as governments, banks and other corporations which pride themselves on being able to intimidate the little guy. The Internet is, as I have said — and as is well-known — an inherently decentralizing technology, one that acts as a solvent upon hierarchies of all kinds, which draw their power from older, now obsolete center — periphery models.

Thus, Nicholas of Cusa's fifteenth century aphorism that "God is an intelligible sphere whose center is everywhere and circumference nowhere" sounds like a prophecy forecasting the coming of the Internet, which destroys all center — periphery power structures and disburses margins everywhere. It is indeed, hostile to hierarchies of any, and every sort, be they religious or political. WikiLeaks simply takes this characteristic of the Internet and magnifies it disproportionately.

Armor of Light

When the individual is online, he is no longer just himself, for the resonant effect of the Internet is such as to scale him up to mythic proportions in which he is garbed in an armor of electronic light, like the figure of the Anthropos in the Manichean creation myth who suits himself up in armor made out of light particles so that he can descend into the material world and do battle with its army of demons. Single-handedly, the Anthropos drops down into the physical world and fights an army of devils who have gathered in order to launch an assault upon the kingdom of light, but he fails in his task, for the demons tear off his armor of light particles and devour it. The myth goes on to recount how the cosmos is eventually constructed out of the fragments of their scattered bodies, and so the narrative is a description of the Manichean idea that the world is made out of particles of light which have fallen and become entrapped in the world of matter. The task of cosmic evolution, accordingly, is to redeem those fallen particles of light, eventually restoring all of them to the heavens, whence they originated.

This scenario isn't actually all that far off from what Assange is doing in his Internet battles against the world's governments and corporations, for without the Internet, it is unlikely that we would ever even have heard of him. By means of suiting himself up, though, in its protective coating of light, he is able to take on governments single-handedly via the process of information warfare and as a result, such governments are currently wringing their hands over him as they would over a rogue nation state like North Korea. Indeed, the U.S. government wishes to have him declared a terrorist and extradited so that he can be tried on grounds of "treason," although as he points out, he isn't even a U.S. citizen. However, the hyperbole of the language is a measure of the degree of threat which he, a mere individual, poses to an entire government. Indeed, fighting him doesn't seem to be all that much different from going up against a rogue state like Iran or Libya.

So the Internet is changing the rules of all the old strategic wargames, for it has created new enemies of mythic power and amplitude. Instead of redeeming captured light particles, Assange's task has been to redeem chunks of secret information which have been captured and locked up into the keeps of the world's information dungeons. Once set free, these secrets can roam about cyberspace inflicting damage like viral pathogens assaulting the organs of a single gigantic immune system.

Assange, then, is an Internet pathogen and the world's governments are currently scrambling about trying to develop antibodies with which to combat his assaults.

Thus, the world's first cyberwar is really an immunological battle whose outcome will determine the future conduits for the circulation of the world's information networks.

The Cultural Function of Secrets

WikiLeaks' release in November 2010 of over 200 diplomatic cables filled with information embarrassing to world governments is actually the Fourth Act of its year-long war against the U.S. government: the first three acts had taken place earlier in that year, beginning with the release on April 5, 2010, of a video which WikiLeaks entitled "Collateral Murder," and which they posted on its website and on YouTube. The video was a seventeen-minute edited version of a longer, unedited thirty-nine-minute video — also posted — of a U.S. Army helicopter attack carried out on Iraqi civilians on July 12, 2007, in the district of New Baghdad. The video showed remarkably clear footage (taken from the gunsight camera of one of the attacking Apache helicopters) of an aerial attack on a group of pedestrians milling about the streets of the city, two of whom were actually Reuters reporters, both killed during the attack. The video displays the unhesitating glee with which the U.S. military proceeds to massacre these civilians, including two children in a passing van who happened to be on their way to school with their father (they both survived, though their father did not).

The following month, in May of 2010, the U.S. military arrested a twenty-two-year-old soldier, Private Bradley Manning, for allegedly leaking the video as well as a landslide of other documents which WikiLeaks would spend the rest of the year releasing. Manning had gotten himself arrested when he bragged to a computer hacker named Adrian Lamo about turning the documents and video files over to WikiLeaks. Lamo then turned him over to military authorities.

WikiLeaks then proceeded to move on to its second assault on the U.S. government when, in July of 2010, it published a collection of more than 90,000 classified documents giving very specific accounts, day by day, of the entire Afghan war, covering the period from January 2004 to December of 2009. Initially, 15,000 of the documents were withheld, so that they could be redacted for the names of individuals and informants whose lives might be endangered by making such knowledge public. But not all the names were redacted; and in fact, a military spokesman pointed out that "the Taliban had said it would study the WikiLeaks documents to punish collaborators with the Americans."[2] Three newspapers, *The New York Times, Der Spiegel* and *The Guardian,* were given copies of the documents on condition that they not be published prior to WikiLeaks' release of them. (It has been said that the site has released more classified documents in the past few years than the rest of the world's media combined, and this is a sobering fact: it has made more than 1.2 million documents available since 2006.)

The *Times* reported that these documents revealed the war to be considerably bleaker than the official accounts given of it by the military. Pakistan, for instance, was shown to have consistently aided the Taliban who were known to have used the same kinds of heat-seeking missiles which had enabled the mujahedeen to defeat the Soviets in the 1980s, a fact not hitherto disclosed by the military; the presence of secret commando units like Task Force 373 was made known, a classified group of military special ops forces which were sent out on assassination missions to kill insurgent commanders; Predator drones were seen to occasionally go rogue, and the military would have to send out F16 fighter jets to hunt them down and destroy them; the Afghani people's dissatisfaction with the U.S. imposed government under Hamid Karzai revealed that they generally felt they were *worse off* than they had been under the Taliban; and so on.

This leak was then followed by another when, on October 22, 2010, WikiLeaks released an even larger batch of classified military documents known as The Iraq War Logs, which amounted to nearly 400,000 documents chronicling the war from January 1, 2004, to December 31, 2009, as told by soldiers in the United States Army. This time, the names of civilians were carefully redacted from all the documents.

Then, on November 28 of the same year, WikiLeaks released over 200 diplomatic cables that contained a great deal of embarrassing information to world governments, such as the U.S.'s secret war against Al Qaeda in Yemen, in which it was revealed that the Yemeni government was willing to pretend that it was they who were launching the shells and not the U.S. ("We'll continue saying the bombs are ours, not yours,'" the cable reads); or the Saudi government's private antipathy to Ahmadinejad, in which King Abdullah insists that the U.S. unleash bombing runs against Iran at the earliest possible convenience; Vladimir Putin's chummy relationship with Italian right wing leader Berlusconi; China's hacking into the Google database to control the flow of information in that country; or the Chinese government's private cooling of relations with North Korea, in which one official is quoted as having stated that "North Korea is behaving like a 'spoiled child'" and so on. What's more, Assange claims to have in his possession over 250,000 such cables, which he plans on releasing a little bit at a time over a series of months.

The U.S. government in turn has tried to declare Assange a terrorist—"Congressman Pete King has called for WikiLeaks' designation as a terrorist organization," remarks *Time* magazine[3]—while British authorities, meanwhile, have jailed him on suspicious charges involving a sexual scandal the timing of which leads one to suspect political motivations behind it. It seems likely that he will be extradited by the United States—if Swedish authorities, from whence the charges stem—decide to allow it, and tried for illegally releasing classified information to the public.

Clearly, the U.S. government is terrified that so much of its dirty laundry is being hung out to dry in such glaring profusion. Governments depend for their power, to a large degree, upon the keeping of secrets out of the hands of a public which they inherently mistrust. If it reveals anything, the WikiLeaks scandal shows that the U.S. government is no different in this respect from any other of the world's authoritarian regimes. Knowledge is not just power: it is a weapon, like plutonium, a weapon which must be kept out of the hands of those who might inadvertently cause it to explode.

Now, let me just say that while I am all for the individual making use of Internet technology to scale himself up to the size of a mythical Anthropos fit to take on world governments single-handedly, I do think it is necessary for us to pause and step back for a moment in order to look at some of the larger socio-cultural implications raised by the democratization of such secrets.

Is it possible, for instance, that the keeping of certain secrets might actually play a crucial role in the smooth flowing of cultural metabolism, and that making them public might actually be tantamount to an act of cultural sabotage and demolition?

As Nietzsche would say, in Assange, it is *resenttiment,* not creativity, that has here become active.

Disrupting Culture

Assange has theorized that "when a regime's lines of internal communication are disrupted, the information flow among conspirators must dwindle, and that, as the flow approaches zero, the conspiracy dissolves. Leaks were an instrument of information warfare."[4] This statement neatly summarizes his organization's primary endeavor, which is to say that it is a fundamentally *disruptive* one.

The French philosopher Regis Debray makes a useful distinction in his book *Transmitting Culture,* between what he calls "communication" and "transmission": communication involves a sender and a receiver linked by some kind of medium embedded in a temporal horizon of seconds, minutes or hours; transmission, on the other hand, has to do with the handing down of culture from one generation to the next, which requires decades, if not centuries or millennia. In the one case, we have a horizontal coupling between the living regarding the ephemeral (and historically short-sighted) concerns of the moment, while in the other, the coupling is between the living and the dead, and the concerns not of the moment, but rather of generations. Here is how he puts the matter:

> Communication prompts an instantaneous response between
> parties, by synchronizing and connecting them like a thread: a
> communicative network runs its course between contemporaries
> (sender and receiver present to one another simultaneously at
> either end of the line). Transmission takes its course *through*
> time (diachronically), developing and changing as it goes. A
> thread *plus* a drama, it links the living to the dead, most often
> when the senders are physically absent. Whether configuring the
> present to a luminous past or to a salvific future, mythical or
> not, a transmission arranges the effective force of the actual
> with reference to the virtual.... Communication excels by cut-
> ting short; transmission by prolonging, even if it must condense
> its ample forms of expression into the emblematic currencies of
> the motto, the logo, the apologue, the parable, and so on. Reli-
> gion, art, ideology: these variegated categories of transmission
> all aim to thwart the ephemeral by the ploy of drawing out,
> particularly in the Western context, with its grand undertakings
> of constructions built to last.[5]

WikiLeaks, I think it is safe to say, falls under the category here of communication: its concerns are inherently *a*-historical and its task blithely indifferent to the cultural continuities which build and shape civilizations. It is not the least bit interested in preserving cultural lines of continuity and transmission but, like the Arabs under T.E. Lawrence during World War I whose task it was to destabilize the Ottoman Empire by blowing up its railroad tracks, with disrupting such lines of communication. Indeed, it is structured in such a way as to actually *freeze* and *arrest* the process of cultural transmission, for as Debray points out, family secrets, state secrets, professional secrets, secrets of all kinds, are an inherent part of the process of cultural transmission. But it is precisely such secrets that WikiLeaks is designed to expose, at any and all cost.

Thus, with its primary aim of short-circuiting the transmission of secrets, WikiLeaks is, in essence, *inimical* to the flow of culture, a great deal of which depends for its functioning upon the maintaining of secrets. Take, for example, the case of initiates into the mystery cults of the ancient world who were required to proceed, as in Mithraism — a religion popular amongst Roman soldiers — along a grade from one revelation to the next. The profaning of such mysteries by making them public would actually ruin the impact of the revelation and deprive such initiates of what is known universally in world religions as a 'second birth' into forms of secret knowledge designed to alter and transform consciousness. In an age in which *all* secrets must be known, such initiatic experiences would be an impossibility.

Now, of course, it can be argued that we are actually talking about two separate categories of secrets here: those having to do with religious mysteries, on the one hand, with which the likes of Assange have nothing to do; and political secrets, on the other, which are a matter of public interest and must therefore be published. But WikiLeaks is actually only one small slice of the kinds of antipathy to culture exemplified by the Internet as a whole; it is a sort of localized example of a much larger tendency, namely, that in the age of the Internet, *nothing* is sacred any longer: *all* shadow zones must be flooded with light, recklessly and impatiently. The fact, for instance, that in the release of the Afghan War Diaries, Assange did not take the time to sit down and redact the names of all the civilians whose lives might be jeopardized by such information, and that *all* the documents were dumped onto the public at once, followed within only a couple of months by the Iraq War Log and the release of the diplomatic cables barely two months after that; all these facts are evidence of the kinds of haste and impatience for results that characterizes the amateur. The Internet is a machine for actually *speeding up* the process of culture, but in doing so, the resulting product is invariably of inferior quality. There is a reason why good wine takes so long to make.

Secrets, though, are actually inherent to the smooth functioning of *any* and *every* organization. Even Assange's organization depends for its functioning upon the keeping of certain secrets, which he doesn't deny: it is extremely protective, for instance, of its sources, which it must be, since the site publishes anonymous submissions and leaks of otherwise unobtainable documents. Keeping the identities of its sources "secret" is essential to the very existence of WikiLeaks. If it couldn't keep them secret, it would very quickly disappear from the Internet.

So, it is actually the case, I would argue, that *every* organization — whether political or religious — depends upon the keeping of certain secrets in order to function at all. Indeed, "secrets" are the secret to the metabolism of culture, without which it would simply not *be*. Making *all* secrets public, therefore, is effectively tantamount to an act of cultural demolition characteristic of the amateur who does not have the patience to spend the time that is necessary to produce artifacts of worthwhile and lasting value.

Years of skillful diplomatic maneuvering, of carefully cultivated alliances and relationships, are simply undone in a matter of *minutes,* and all by an individual who is merely out to make a name for himself. The culturally destructive effects of all these new digital media are, in the case of WikiLeaks, brought to a focus and become evident in concentrated form, for the antipathy of WikiLeaks toward cultural transmission and construction is symptomatic of the attitude of the digital revolution toward culture — toward traditional media, that is — taken as a whole. Assange's attitude, when it comes down to it, is more or less the same as that of Bill Gates, Jeff Bezos or Jimmy Wales: *all* of these men share a similar mentality in that they could simply care less about the fate of traditional media. All that matters to them is advancing the cult of Digital Progress, no matter what the cost.

The Death of the Event

Let's take a look at the problem of the Internet's hostility to culture from a slightly different angle: the point of view of those kinds of religious singularities that are foundational acts in the process of bringing forth worlds.

Consider, for instance, the ancient religious idea of the pilgrimage: in order to go and find the sacred object or geographical place, you had to physically move your body from one point in space to another, where the object was to be found. This is why religious cities, such as Jerusalem, once occupied the bull's eye centers of old Medieval maps. The ancient sacred city is the holy place, the center from which all power radiates. To get to the city is to get to the source of the Power.

Such sacred localities are spatio-temporal singularities. The whole point of going to find them is that they cannot otherwise be replicated, like original works of art. The core pillar of Islam is built around the Haj, the sacred pilgrimage to Mecca that is required of each true Muslim. This is one reason why the Arabs don't allow electric media near the Ka'ba, on the suspicion perhaps that to reproduce it electronically would render the whole point of the pilgrimage obsolete. Pilgrimages, furthermore, *take time:* but then, why take the time nowadays when you can just surf the Internet for digital photos of sites and watch video files posted by tourists on YouTube?

The Internet, we need hardly remind ourselves, dismantles and collapses all the old center-periphery models that once structured and built entire civilizations. Such technology decouples events and sacred places from their spatio-temporal coordinates and brings *them* to *us*. Nowadays, we no longer have to go to them; they come where we're at. Thus, the Internet renders the age of Events as singularities obsolete. There is no longer any event that can take place upon the surface of the earth that is capable of becoming a singularity and hence of forming the foundation of a Truth Event, in the sense defined by the philosopher Alain Badiou in his *Being and Event,* since no event that occurs is required any longer to stay confined to its GPS coordinates.[6]

Thus, the military's attempt to confine a massacre that takes place in a battle in an Iraqi suburb, let's say — Haditha, for instance — to top secret status is essentially an effort to nail down the parameters of the event to a specific latitude/longitude, and to confine it to one point in time. Once the electronic replication of the event, however, is made public via the Internet, the event has been decoupled from its spatio-temporal coordinates and made instantly accessible, at the speed of light, to every computer in the world. It is therefore no longer unique, or even "top secret." In fact, it is no longer even an event at all, but an electronically stored memory of an event, a digital echo, as it were.

The founding of new religions — which occurs slowly, through processes of cultural "transmission" extending over generations — thus becomes an impossibility in an age dominated by Internet technology, since all religions depend upon the occurrence of Truth Events as their founding singularities: the holy city of Karbala is sacred to the Shi'ites precisely because it was the one and only point in spacetime where Husayn ibn Ali was beheaded. Thus, to physically put one's body there is to go to the center of an Event with a religious aura. The world's current religions, in which such Events have already long since taken place, and have had sacred geographies and ancient iconographies constructed around them, are generally immune to electronic replication, since centuries of human psychological investment have been put into them and such investment cannot easily be stripped away by a technology that is only a few decades old. However, the Internet does render it difficult for the possibility of any new Truth Events to take place since the moment they occur, they can be instantly replicated and shot through the matrix around the world and thus stripped of their aura.

There is simply no time, under the conditions of electronic society, for such an Event to take place, for in an Age dominated by "real time" the deferred space of extended time that is necessary for the mind to process the *implications* of such events is no longer there. All mental responses and public commentaries on events nowadays must be *immediate,* since the temporal cascade of events coming at us from all directions at the speed of light means that another event will be coming just minutes after this one, and another one after that, so the mind must process them very quickly. It cannot be allowed to linger too long on the implications of any single one of them. This, then, is not an age in which culture that doesn't take place at the speed of light can function.

Thus, the Internet transforms Debray's diachronic plane of cultural transmission across the generations to the horizontal and *a*-temporal plane of mere communication between senders and receivers motivated by the simple — and simplistic — curiosity of the tourist. The Internet, like almost all forms of electronic technology, is an inherently shallow one, for such technologies move too fast to allow room for the kinds of reflective and thoughtful ponderings that the human mind requires in order to produce worthwhile observations. It took Immanuel Kant an entire lifetime to think through all the implications of his masterpiece *The Critique of Pure Reason,* which he did not write and publish until he was in his 60s. It is, then, little wonder that in today's media landscape, which is dominated by lightspeed technologies which are inimical in both aim and function to the reflective capacities of the deeper mind, that the publishing of such profound and life-altering books has virtually ceased altogether.

The Event Which Never Happened

Take the uprising at Tiananmen Square as an example of a political Event of the kind which, for the Chinese, never officially happened. The event was broadcast live on CNN in 1989, and it has been thoroughly recycled through Western cyberspace ever since. The image of the man standing in front of the line of tanks has taken on the status of an icon for us, since we interpret him as the signifier of a brave individual standing up against totalitarianism. For us, it has merely become an image that is fit to be printed upon T-shirts.

But in China it has retained the status of an Event, albeit a hidden one, precisely because the Chinese government has effaced all traces of its existence. When one performs a Google Image search in China on the words "Tiananmen Square," the only images which come up are pictures of happy tourists. All references to the Truth Event have been expunged, thus protecting its status as a hidden secret Event charged with significance for Beijing — the Event Which Never Happened but which, paradoxically, led to Deng Xiaoping's importation of capitalism into China in the early 1990s. In a show on PBS's *Frontline* entitled "Tank Man," three contemporary students at Beijing University, when confronted with a picture of the Tank Man, have no idea what it refers to.[7] It is, to them, a meaningless image, but to the Chinese intelligentsia, it signifies the birth of Chinese authoritarian capitalism and is therefore an image that is kept carefully out of the hands of the people so as not to remind them of the blood spilled during the massacre for which they were bribed with Western capitalism.

Most Truth Events, in fact — which function as founding acts for religions in the ancient world — were actually based upon murders. The crucifixion of Christ, for instance, is the founding event of Christianity; in The Book of Genesis, it is Cain's murder of Abel (or, more properly, the *thwarting* of such an event in Yahweh's intervention of Abraham's sacrifice of Isaac); in Zoroastrianism, it is the murder of the Primal Ox and the Primal Man which brings the cosmos into being. Indeed, ancient creation myths are filled with accounts of the murder of a primordial being by way of which the world of time, of sex and temporality, of man's life as a sexed and mortal being, were brought into existence. Such Events generally became the central secrets of ancient religious rituals and liturgies.

But the Internet is a machine for transforming all things private into public domain, and it therefore destroys all secrets; as such, it is the enemy of all traditional societies everywhere, for such societies are based upon keeping special knowledge and access to certain sacred objects out of the hands of an impure and profane public. In an age dominated by Internet technology, the Mystery cults of the ancient world, as I need hardly repeat, would have been an impossibility, for their aura and functioning specifically depended upon the taking of an oath by their initiates not to reveal the content of their mysteries. And the ancients could keep a secret, for in all the Classical writings that have come down to us from those whom we know to have been initiated into the Eleusinian Mysteries — Aristotle, Plato, Cicero, et al.—*not one word* of their content was ever uttered. As a result, we have only the vaguest idea of what went on in them. Such a thing would be an impossibility under the conditions of electronic circuitry, which insist on making all secrets known *immediately.*

Julian Asange thus finds himself today in the role of the Tom Cruise character in Stanley Kubrick's last film *Eyes Wide Shut* in which the initiate who witnesses the mysteries of the sex cult is enjoined not to breathe a word of its existence to outsiders on pain of death. Public knowledge of the cult's existence would cause it to disappear altogether, so it is essential that the protagonist not disclose it to anyone. The world's governments and corporations are now in the role occupied by the sex cult in Kubrick's film, for WikiLeaks has made them very anxious indeed about the public divulgence of what Slavoj Žižek has called their "hidden obscene underside."

WikiLeaks has devoted itself to exposing secrets everywhere with reckless abandon and brash, arrogant insouciance, but in doing so, the Internet has merely become a means and extension for the hand of the cultural amateur to meddle in things for which he has little patience, or tolerance for taking the time and trouble to understand. What can years of the cultivation of diplomatic subtleties in relationships involving the balance of political power mean to an ex-hacker, who harbors in his knowledge of manipulating circuitry the ability to bring years of the accumulation of such relationships crashing down at the speed of a byte? The frightening thing about the Internet is how drastically it amplifies the power of *anyone* who uses it: now, even the Philistine, by means of it, becomes a force to be reckoned with.

As a result of the Internet, Events — be they political or religious — have now lost their status, and their corresponding strength, as singularities. And since culture depends for its existence upon the founding of such singularities, as I have demonstrated in this essay, it is scarcely necessary to point out that the Age of the Internet is an age that is absolutely incompatible with the flourishing of human Culture. It is the kind of technology that a society produces when it is *on the way out.*

Information War

On the other hand, we also need to point out that WikiLeaks itself has been the cause of a cultural singularity, for with the advent of "Cablegate," it has inaugurated the world's first Information (Cyber)War. This, indeed, is a singularity unto itself.

When WikiLeaks posted the first batch of diplomatic cables on November 28, 2010, it became the object of a cyberattack, in which a number of organizations attempted to deny it Internet service: Amazon, for instance, pulled the plug on the servers which it had been allowing Assange to use for its site (Assange's response to this action was, in effect, to point out that if Amazon doesn't believe in freedom of speech, then it shouldn't be in the business of selling books; he does have a point here); the Swiss bank PostFinance announced that it had frozen Assange's assets, while PayPal denied it service and both MasterCard and Visa refused to process any further financial contributions to WikiLeaks.

In retaliation, a group of globally dispersed hackers known as Anonymous — an example of one of Arjun Appadurai's diasporic public spheres — launched what it called "Operation Payback," and began an assault on all those it deemed to be enemies of WikiLeaks: they flooded the websites of PostFinance, MasterCard, Visa, Amazon and others with page requests that had the result of temporarily shutting down these sites. Assange, however, has denied any association with this organization, claiming that he is not a hacker, but a journalist. (However, Assange *is* formerly a hacker, and as this essay should have made clear, he bears all the characteristic hallmarks of the hacker mentality: resentment against those who are capable of taking the time and trouble to produce culture; a desire simply to destroy and bring down anything and everything which stands, be it government or corporation, heedless of consequences; and the taking of sadistic pleasure in simply thwarting and subverting the efforts of those who are capable of creative, and not simply destructive, acts.)

WikiLeaks, meanwhile, has managed to survive by drifting around the Internet from server to server. A Swiss-Icelandic company known as Datacell has taken over PayPal's role of processing financial contributions to the site. Supporters of Assange, in addition, have "mirrored" the site by posting hundreds of exact clones of it, thereby making censorship very difficult. According to the *New York Times,* there are now at least 208 WikiLeaks mirror sites up and running. "'Cut us down,' said a message on the WikiLeaks Twitter feed ... 'and the stronger we become.'"[8] This is a classic illustration of what I have called "the Hydra Effect" of electronic replication.

In ancient mythology, the magical power of the spoken Word to exert effects upon the physical world was considerable, even dangerous. Oedipus slew the Sphinx simply by solving the riddle which it had posed to him, causing the monster to commit suicide by throwing herself over the edge of a cliff. Yahweh brought the entire world into being — as did the Egyptian god Ptah — by merely pronouncing certain syllables, while the efficacy of

Hindu mantras is such that one can induce transformations of consciousness by pronouncing all the vowels together in the form of the sacred syllable "AUM." The Hebrew golem, likewise, is animated by pronouncing seven sacred words and only the correct pronunciation of these words can make it die.

As the great German novelist Thomas Mann once said, "The right word *hurts*."

So it would appear that electronic technology has retrieved the conditions of ancient myth, in which information is dangerous, and knowledge of it can enable one to inflict massive, asymmetric damage upon one's enemies with instantaneous, speed of light effects.

The world's first Information Cyberwar, furthermore, is actually an immunological war, for the Internet is a gigantic global immune system that connects all of our computers together by a reservoir of collective consciousness that mimics the semiotics of the body's immune system. Julian Assange's WikiLeaks entity is a pathogenic organization that is currently assaulting it, and now the Internet must respond to this assault by changing its structure and developing new antibodies with which to defend itself against any such future attacks. It is very likely that, far from making information less secret, Assange's attacks will actually have the opposite result, ending up with the creation of new, hitherto unprecedented forms of legal control over the Internet that will severely restrict the ability of such global nomads to assault it in future.

Just as 9/11 resulted in the transformation of the United States into a global imperialist aggressor, with a sharp curtailing of the civil liberties and freedoms of its own citizens, so too, Julian Assange's year-long cyberattacks on the United States' informational networks in 2010 may also result in a general loss of access to freedom of information on the Internet. Let's not forget that the Unabomber's postal bombs, in like manner, resulted in tighter security measures at the post office such that individuals can no longer mail packages without being physically present on camera.

Indeed, I suspect that Assange's attacks — and those of others like him — will actually make things *more* difficult in future for the amateur and the average citizen to access the resources of the Internet and to post blogs, sites and videos with quite the same degree of freedom that he or she takes for granted today.

To paraphrase Nietzsche: What does not destroy the Internet will only make it stronger.

6

On the Metaphysics
of Google Earth

Google Earth is the end of the world. All you have to do is press to zoom in, and you can almost see a car's license plate. We need the bigness of the world, the rotundity and immensity of the globe. But we are exhausting that, just as we have exhausted its resources.

— Paul Virilio, *Native Land: Stop Eject*

1.

Google Earth is a type of software than enables you to go anywhere around the planet. You just type in the desired location on the screen and instantly you are zoomed right in to wherever you want to go. If you want to look at the street level, and if the data is available, you just click on the little camera icon and suddenly you are dumped out of the atmosphere to find yourself waking up out of an electronic egg on the ground below, right in front of the location that you wanted to see.

2.

To say that Google Earth is simply a new kind of atlas is a bit like calling the first railroad an iron horse. It is actually nothing of the kind, for it casts *you* the user in the starring role of a narrative in which you take on the omniscience and ubiquity of a god. It *is* a kind of map, as an atlas is a kind of map, but Google Earth is no atlas. It is closer to the narrativities of theater or film than to any kind of old-fashioned printed book like an atlas.

Google Earth is a performance piece. *You* are the actor, the star of the show, the god.

3.

"Transcendence: a specifically European disease," comments Deleuze in *A Thousand Plateaus* and he is right.[1] Google Earth enables you to take on the point of view of a discarnate spirit hovering over the earth, surveying God's creation. Indeed, it is prefigured as far back as Hieronymous Bosch's painting "The Third Day of Creation," which shows the earth enclosed in a giant transparent bubble with a tiny little satisfied Yahweh floating up in the left corner like a Mac icon. You the user *are* that tiny little God, especially since there are no people yet in Bosch's vision of the newborn earth. Google Earth, too, depicts a world without people, for like early photographs whose exposure time took too long to capture people in its images and instead featured ghostly black and white cities shorn of human habitation, the world that Google Earth depicts is similarly void of human presence.

As though you had slipped through the cracks between one second and the next and caught the world blinking.

4.

"We Christians sit at a proper height, not on the ground like animals." Fernand Braudel, in his *Civilization and Capitalism,* quotes this statement from a Spanish text of 1532, by the writer Perez de Chinchon, and it is absolutely symptomatic.[2] Chinchon looking down upon the Muslims of Spain is characteristic of the West's entire way of looking at the world, which unfolded out of the idea of a God separate from his creation looking down upon it from the heavens. On the first page of the Book of Genesis, Yahweh is already a transcendent being who *looks down* upon the earth from his point of view in the heavens above, where clouds of angels swarm about him like locusts. This orientation to the earth as a master craftsman with neck bent looking down on his work — a potter looking down at his pottery, a blacksmith gazing into his forge, the draughtsman bent over his blueprints — is basic to the Western way of approaching things. It is a cultural *style,* the *body language,* as it were, of an entire civilization.

5.

The Easterner, by contrast, looks straight ahead at the earth. His gaze is parallel to it, on a level plane with it: the Japanese, for instance, sleep on *tatami* mats on the floor. The Westerner has his bed up off the ground. The Japanese sits cross-legged for his meals on the floor, as Braudel writes:

> In fact present-day Japanese furniture exactly corresponds to ancient Chinese furniture: low tables, elbow-rests for arms to make the squatting position more comfortable, mats (the Japanese *tatami*) on platforms of varying heights, low storage furniture (cabinets and chests set beside each other), cushions. Everything is adapted to life at floor level.[3]

On the same page, Braudel gives us a picture of a Turkish painter who sits, cross-legged on the ground, as he paints the miniature on his lap. On the facing page, another illustration shows, by contrast, the Westerner seated upon a four-legged chair that raises him up away from the floor to sit at a table that is even higher.[4]

Western man is always surveying the ground as something that is *beneath* him, and in order to get a proper view of it, everything must be adjusted to fit this downward gaze.

6.

This is why he went to the moon: to survey the rest of the earth from the highest possible vantage point overlooking it. The ultimate Panopticon. Caspar David Friedrich's 1818 painting, *Wanderer Above the Sea of Fog*.

7.

There is no one proper way to make a map of the earth, as the history of cartography shows. In the Middle Ages, Arabs oriented their maps with the south at the top, where we currently place the north, since that was the direction of Mecca. Westerners prior to the voyages of the Portuguese navigators placed Jerusalem in the center of the map, with the east at the top. This was how one "oriented" oneself in those days. These were called "T and O maps" because the earth was thought to be composed of precisely three continents, Africa, Europe and Asia, making up a T-shape that was surrounded by the O of the world ocean. With the discovery of America and the addition of a *fourth* continent, the earth became round overnight, and there was no longer any room on it for the gods (i.e., Yahweh and his angels), who were thus banished to the stars. Jerusalem could be the center no longer. On a globe, there *is* no center. Hence, from about 1500 on, no one point upon the earth could be said to be the center about which everything else turned. This is globalization, phase one, as Peter Sloterdijk has somewhere remarked.

The races of the three older continents, Africa, Europe and Asia, were thought to be the descendants of the three sons of Noah: Ham, Japheth and Shem. What to do now about the races of the *fourth* continent, the natives of the Americas? From whom were *they* descended?

To this day, there is a conflict between what Western science says about where the Native Americans came from and what they themselves believe: Western discourse says they were the result of various migrations, whether from across the Bering land bridge or even earlier, from the east during the Solutrean Paleolithic is variously argued.

But *their* myths say that they came from the ground, from the *world below,* from whence they climbed up into this world. Thus, the image of the ladder is basic to their thinking.

Hence, the pueblo style of architecture, in which one is always *ascending* or *descending* from one plane of the world to the next. Inside the depths of the kiva, you are at the bottom of the world, *beneath* the earth in the Primeval dreamtime of the world's archaic dawning.

8.

The gods and peoples of Asiatic myth are always springing into being from somewhere down below: out of watery abysses or rocks or cosmic eggs or mountains of one sort or another. (Indeed, if we were forced to choose which mythic system is closer to what our contemporary scientists tell us, the Biblical one, in which life blew down to the earth from the heavens ["Yahweh" is from the Arabic root *hwy* meaning "to blow"], or the Asiatic myths in which it all came up out of the earth, then we would have to side with the Native Americans, for in the theogony according to science, the earth is a cosmic egg that hatched and gave birth to everything that crawls or flies upon its surface.)

Google Earth, accordingly, *could* have been designed in other ways. It could just as well have been Google Underworld, with the point of view of the software placing the user as a kind of mole burrowing its way through an impossibly complex latticework of subterranean tunnels. In this version, whenever you want a streetview, the bubble would shove its way up out of the ground like the periscope of a submarine in order to peep at its street level surroundings. This would have been a software of Immanence, one designed without an aversion to the earth.

In this scenario, you the user become a kami spirit.

9.

But in actuality, the bubble of the streetview that descends to the earth is an electronic retrieval of the ancient Greek myth of the soul's descent through the spheres for incarnation on earth in the somatic presence of a physical body. In this myth, the soul at birth has already undertaken a long journey through the cosmos, stopping at each of the celestial spheres along the way, where it received the imprint of one or another archetypal quality such as Courage or Eros, as it made its way down toward earth for the birth of its physical body, woven together out of the four elements.

Transcendence again. Our *real* origins are heavenly. The earth is not our true parent, but only the mother of our physical body. Father Sky is the true parent.

10.

There is a science fiction novel by Isaac Asimov, entitled *The End of Eternity,* which is instructive here. The story concerns one Andrew Harlan, who is an Eternal, an elite group of temporal engineers who periodically interfere in human history to make what they call Reality Changes, or slight adjustments that can have large consequences in human affairs. The Eternals are people who were once temporals, or normal human beings, who have since been selected and trained by the Eternals to be one of them. They don't live forever, they age normally, but they live in a Temporal Field that exists outside of all time and space. They use a kind of elevator called a "kettle," to shuttle up and down the centuries, at any point of which they may enter except for the years between the 70,000th and the 150,000th centuries which are, for some mysterious reason, closed to them. When they enter the centuries beyond that date, humanity has disappeared from the cosmos.

Harlan falls in love with a temporal woman named Noys Lambent. When he finds out from another Eternal that a reality change made to her century, the 482nd, will result in creating a new Reality in which she will cease to exist, he decides to commit the crime of abducting her from time and stowing her away in Eternity. He places her in the 111,394th century. Meanwhile, he attempts to sabotage a plan in which the Eternals are trying to ensure the creation of their Eternity by sending a man named Cooper back to the 24th century, when another man named Vikkor Mallansohn was supposed to have invented the mathematics that would make the invention of Eternity possible in the 27th century. Cooper is supposed to teach this man — like an angel — the mathematics that will lead to the invention of Eternity. Just as they are about to send him off via the kettle, however, Harlan smashes the controls of the machine and Cooper is sent back to the wrong century, namely, the 20th. But when Harlan's superior Twissell explains to him that their very existence is now in jeopardy, and that they must save Eternity by rescuing Cooper, otherwise Eternity and Harlan's reality will disappear from existence, then Harlan agrees to travel back to the year 1932 to save Cooper.

He takes his girlfriend Noys Lambent along with him, and when they travel back to a cave in the desert of the Southwest in 1932 to find Cooper, Lambent reveals to him that she is actually a member of a race of supermen living in the forbidden period above the 70,000th century, a race that had put a block on the ability of the Eternals to tamper with their timeline. She tells him that she and her people have realized that Eternity was a mistake, for it coddles the human race by always steering them away from the disasters and catastrophes that would make them venturesome enough to discover interstellar space travel. She points out that in all the timelines managed by the Eternals, every attempt on the part of humanity to discover space travel is short-lived and doesn't take, due to the perpetual interference of the Eternals. Eventually, this leads to the disappearance of humans from the cosmos altogether. She insists that the Eternals must stop interfering in the timelines so that humanity will discover space travel and go on to create the Galactic Empire. She says that all she has to do is send a letter to an Italian physicist (Enrico Fermi) that will instruct him in bombarding uranium with neutrons which will lead to the invention of atomics in 1945 and will eventually set in motion a chain of events that will lead to the radioactive despoliation of the earth, and hence the need for humanity to leave it behind and develop space travel. In the final pages, Harlan chooses her scenario and in making his decision brings about the end of Eternity, which slowly disappears as the novel ends.

Despite its convoluted plot, Asimov's novel is a wonderful, coded description of the evolution of Western civilization, in which the gods who are forever *watching over* the earth from the stars, *looking down* upon humanity and shepherding and protecting it, are eventually left behind so that humanity can become — as in Existentialism — *its own* creative genius. Thus, the gods who once watched over us from the heavens have been displaced and it is *we* Westerners who have taken their place, looking down on our own planetary civilization from the orbital zone around the earth once occupied by *them*.

With the launch of Sputnik in 1957, as McLuhan always loved to point out, the earth was not only contained, for the first time, *inside* of a mechanical environment, but it was shorn of divine intelligences who watched over and protected human beings from their transcendent vantage point among the stars. Now it is humanity that watches over itself via satellite technologies, which have transformed the earth into a single gigantic toy.

We are now the gods we once used to worship, thanks to our miraculous technologies.

11.

So God may be dead, but his shadow still hovers about everything we Westerners do. Google Earth was produced by a society in which Father Sky once held the privileged position. He is gone now, but his shadow looms over the shoulders of the workers who carry on like scribal monks in his stead, producing technological artifacts as miniaturizations of his once mythic production of the earth as an artifact.

12.

Thus, Google Earth is an ideogram, illustrating an *idea* about how to approach the earth. In fact, *all* maps are ideograms. Open a copy of Vesalius, for instance, where you'll find the depiction of the human skeleton as a frame that *supports* the body, keeping it upright and away from the earth. Anatomy texts in the Middle Ages, however, especially Arabic ones, show the skeleton not as a support but rather as a *weight* keeping the soul anchored to the ground and preventing it from floating away back to the heavens, its proper source and origin.

Thus, metaphysics always determines *how* we see *what* we see. Or how anything at all becomes intelligible to us, as Heidegger would put it.

Including Google's version of the Earth.

For it is Google Inc. which is slowly metamorphosing into the role of Asimov's Eternals, watching over us puny humans and everything we do with their satellites, roving cameras, auto-scanned emails, free software, and digitized books. If any organization on this planet can be said to be transforming Asimov's mythology of the Foundation into our daily reality, then it is surely Google, Inc. which may, one day, have as much control over our lives as his Eternals.

His Foundationers, too, began their project as an attempt to create an Encyclopedia Galactica not all that far off from Google's attempt to scan and store all the world's knowledge in its databases. And just as his Foundation eventually became a military-industrial supergiant, so too, we had better watch out how much power we allow Google to arrogate over our lives.

13.

Paul Virilio's comment, with which we began, implies that what Google Earth does to the planet is to transform it into a toy. Google Earth robs the world of its spatial gigantism by shrinking it down to the level of an electronic marble. This gives us Westerners the illusion that we have complete control over the earth, and that the user, while using the software, is at the helm of Spaceship Earth, which he is ready and willing to pilot.

Thus, Google Earth, in shrinking the planet down to a plaything for the average Internet user, conveys the illusion that he has complete mastery over the planet and can therefore do with it as he pleases.

Such a technology is completely incompatible with the idea of the planet as a sacred Being, an Other with which ancient religions have taught us to be in fear, awe and reverence. It is impossible to have reverence for a toy, especially if you're an adult.

And so to perpetuate the illusion that the planet is merely the plaything of Western man — just as it was for his God — is tantamount to a diminishing of the earth and the human relationship to it.

Google Earth *is* the embodiment of an idea, not just some electronic atlas that makes finding things more convenient. Its very design and metaphysics of transcendence asks you the user to believe that Western science, in conquering the planet by mapping out every square inch of it, can dispense with any notions of the earth as a sacred Being within which we humans are actually embedded, like weather patterns. It asks the consumer to believe that we are ontologically separate from the earth, hovering above it like angels or gods, and surveying it like cartographers getting ready to terraform a desert planet.

The Earth, in losing its primordial gigantism, thereby becomes dispensable: a mere throwaway, like an aluminum can that you simply toss over your shoulder.

Google Earth fosters the illusion that we are not *in* the planet like bacteria in the guts of an animal, but rather, *on* it, like spacemen gathered on the moon.

In other words: we no longer need it.

Like designer genes patented by agribusiness corporations, we can simply tailor it to fit the jagged outlines of our convoluted industrial exoskeletons. The Earth has become a designer product; yet another consumer object, like a discarded tire, to be tossed onto the rubbish heap.

After all: who needs it?

Some Concluding Comments to Part I: A Miniature History of Capitalism (or, The Evolution of Aladdin's Cave)

So, to take a step back, as it were, from the foregoing and view it with a single panoramic eye: we have Amazon selling books, toys, electronics, DVDs, etc.; YouTube purveying videos of every sort and kind; Wikipedia pretending to offer us "knowledge," and WikiLeaks giving us intensely classified documents; we have Facebook hawking human relationships as its wares, and Google Earth scaling down the planet and turning it into a toy. Other sites, of course, offer other services: Grooveshark sells access to music downloads; eBay sells all sorts of objects, used and new; priceline.com sells travel tickets; Netflix rents videos, etc. Every site, in other words, is its own store offering some product or service — whether free or not — to a consumer audience.

If we were to cast back, though, to the origins of capitalism, where we would find the markets that were set up in the town squares of every European city from as early as the eleventh century, we would discover the dim and distant forebears of these Internet sites in the stalls of the various vendors lined up in rows out in the open air, which served as the foundations of our consumer society. Each vendor here, too, had a different product or service to sell, as Braudel describes in his magisterial three volume *Civilization and Capitalism:*

Only the wool and cloth halls, [he writes] saltfish and fresh seafood stalls were under covered markets. But all around these buildings, clustering against them, were open-air markets in corn, flour, butter, candles, tow and well-ropes. Near the "pillars" which stood all round, secondhand-clothes dealers, bakers, shoemakers and "other poor masters of the trades of Paris who have the right to the halls" would dispose themselves as best they could.... A collection of different markets one alongside another, surrounded by heaps of rubbish, dirty water and rotten fish....[1]

As Braudel tells us, the earliest markets were entirely open air but many of them were soon covered within a century or two and became Halles, like the Great Halles of Paris at the end of the eighteenth century from which, as Walter Benjamin showed us, the Parisian arcades emerged in the first couple of decades of the 1800s as essentially enclosed streets lined with shops.

The first shops, however, says Braudel, emerged as rivals to the markets, although they came into being at exactly the same time in about the eleventh century. These were the shops of artisans, such as butchers, shoemakers, blacksmiths, tailors, etc., whose situation differed from that of the markets of the town square in that the shops were permanent and open everyday whereas the markets were held, as Farmer's markets still are to this day, only a couple of days out of each week. Thus, the butcher would carve up meat that he would sell at market two or three days a week, since the urban authorities required it, but "before long, the artisan was selling from his own shop 'from the window' as they said, in the *interval* between market days. So this alternating activity made the earlier shops places of intermittent business, rather like markets."[2]

But soon, the artisan's shop gave way to the general store, in which the figure of the middleman arose. The middleman, unlike the artisan, did not produce the goods that he sold in his own shop but bought them from another producer and sold them to the consumer. "The middleman," Braudel says, "was the man of the future," for indeed, his general store, stocked with products drawn from distant geographical centers of production, became the basis for the nineteenth century department store. If we take a glimpse into one of these general stores, that of Abraham Dent of Kirkby Stephen in north England at the end of the eighteenth century, we gain some idea of what these stores offered to consumers:

This grocery and general store, which is known to us because its books of 1756 to 1776 have survived, sold practically everything. One prominent item was tea (both black and green) of different qualities — and at high prices, because Kirkby Stephen was inland and thus unable to take advantage of smuggling; then came sugar, treacle, flour, wine and brandy, beer, cider, barley, hops, soap, Spanish white (a finely powdered chalk used as a pigment), lampblack, pearl ashes, beeswax, tallow, candles, tobacco, lemons, almonds, raisins, vinegar, peas, pepper, "the usual condiments and spices," mace, cloves. And Abraham Dent also sold all kinds of haberdashery: silk, cotton and woolen fabrics, needles, pins, etc. He even stocked books, bound magazines, almanacs, and paper. In fact it is easier to list what he did not sell: viz. salt (which is hard to explain), eggs, butter and cheese (these no doubt were easy to find at market.)[3]

Physical objects, in other words, imported from sites all over north England which, in turn, had imported them from afar: the teas and silk from China; the sugar, cotton and pepper from India; the tobacco from the New World, etc. The general store was a nexus point where economic flows from all the great civilizations of China, India, Japan and Islam, converged to offer the modest European consumer a plethora of goods to choose from, goods which had scarcely been in his grasp a mere three centuries earlier.

The arcades in Paris, meanwhile, came into being during the first few decades of the nineteenth century. The first one, the Passage des Panoramas — still standing — emerged around the year 1800. "After 1800," Benjamin writes, "we must go all the way to 1822 to meet with a new arcade: it is between this date and 1834 that the majority of these singular passageways are constructed."[4] Covered by glass roofs with iron girders, the arcades were simply street level rows of shops encased by a greenhouse. They at once transformed the consumer into a species of hothouse flower, albeit a flower which wandered from shop to shop at a leisurely pace on a Saturday afternoon. Benjamin describes the contents of this first arcade as follows:

Shops in the Passage des Panoramas: Restaurant Veron, reading room, music shop, Marquis, wine merchants, hosier, haberdashers, tailors, bootmakers, hosiers, bookshops, caricaturist, Theatre des Varietes. Compared with this, the Passage Vivienne was the "solid" arcade. There, one found no luxury shops. Dream Houses: arcade as nave with side chapels.[5]

The great heyday of the arcades was, as Benjamin remarks, from about 1800 to 1834, after which date they are superseded by the first department stores. In Paris: Au Bon Marché (1838), Le Louvre and La Belle Jardiniere. In London: Kendal, Milne and Faulkner, located in Manchester. In America: Wanamaker's, Macy's, Carson, Pirrie Scott. The 1850s is the key decade for this new development, arguably made possible by the advent of the railroad which was able to centralize goods by delivering them to the back-doors of these capitalist monstrosities. Wanamaker's, for instance, in Philadelphia, was called "the Great Depot," because it was a converted train depot, a huge flat space on the inside, like a space for exhibition at a World's Fair, only a fair, in this case, in which thousands of goods were on display for purchase.

The department store obsolesced the arcades by essentially swallowing them whole. Siegfried Giedion describes the architecture of Au Bon Marché for us — designed by Eiffel and Boileau — as follows:

> Its area of more than thirty thousand square feet is divided into a series of courts of various shapes, each covered by a large glass skylight. The passage from court to court is simplified by the presence of lofty iron bridges.... Never before had light flowed into a store in such bright streams. A true glass architecture had been erected over the framework of the building. The creative fantasy of the nineteenth century can be felt in its combination of glass skylights, aerial bridges in iron, slim iron columns, and the curious ornamental shapes so characteristic of the period.[6]

Au Bon Marché, then, took up the arcades and simply stacked them, one atop the other — as the first pyramids stacked the mastabas — to create a vertically rising dreamworld of an enormous iron and glass Aladdin's cavern. Thus, the arcades, as the old medium, became the content of the new medium of the department store.

The downtown shopping center, however, where these department store giants thrived, itself began to be obsolesced within a few decades by the coming of the automobile, which had the effect of decentering the city through the creation of the suburb which, though it did not invent — for the electric street car had already done that in the 1880s — it certainly expanded to gargantuan proportions. By the 1950s, many of these suburbs were located far away from downtown shopping districts, and this gave Austrian architect Victor Gruen, then living in Los Angeles, something to think about.

Gruen responded to the situation by creating the first bi-level indoor shopping mall in 1956, the Southdale Mall in Edina, Minnesota as a way of miniaturizing the downtown city center, hermetically sealing it off and dropping it down into the middle of suburbia as a center unto itself. Gruen's intent was actually to banish the automobile by (re)creating a public urban space in which only pedestrians could exist, thus retrieving the vanished pedestrian world of the arcades, of the sidewalks, cafes, benches, gardens, etc, of old Europe, right in the middle of autopolic suburbia. Gruen naively believed that he was preventing urban sprawl in doing so, for what he didn't realize is that such decentralized centers would soon act as centers for new developments all their own, as these miniature cities — which is what malls really are — immediately spawned surrounding strip malls, hotels, restaurants and other commercial and retail properties, thus actually accelerating sprawl rather than halting it.

But now the shopping mall, too, is disappearing from our cityscapes, which are becoming increasingly blighted with boarded up strip malls and the ghostly rotting shipwrecks of indoor malls. With the reappearance of the old market stalls of the vendors in early European town squares in the form of Internet sites, the actual physical stores are being sucked out of our malls one by one, and being replaced by their Internet equivalents. Thus, the physical-economic space constructed by centuries of capitalist evolution is being dismantled and deflated in a matter of decades by the power of the integrated chip.

So the sequence moves from: outdoor markets to covered Halles; individual shops to general stores; the covering of entire streets full of shops with iron and glass arcades; the stacking of arcades into department stores; the chain-linking of department stores with arcades to form indoor shopping malls; and now, finally, to the relocation of vendors to suburban living rooms via the Internet, which retrieves and recreates the entire world as a gigantic cavern made out of light and pixellated images. And now more and more purchases are being made with cellphones and other mobile apps, so that shopping is becoming an increasingly nomadic experience.

"'The market, which is already weak, is dramatically shifting away from stores and toward online,' said Colin A. McGranahan, a senior analyst at Sanford C. Bernstein & Company. 'The online share of the market is now a critical mass....'"[7]

The problem, however, with this latter development is that we are witnessing the shrinkage and collapse of public spaces in our cities, which are becoming infested with economic black holes once occupied by vibrant shopping centers where people used to go to hang out, shop, meet friends, go on dates, etc. With the disappearance of these public spaces, our society is becoming that much more *a*-social: now we don't even have places to go where we can be alone together.

So it is an absolute myth that the Internet increases sociality, brings people together and creates new communities. It only does this as a by-product of the communities and neighborhoods that it is destroying and wiping out with the economic blight and social disintegration that it brings along with it. Sociality on the Internet is only *in lieu* of real physical human interaction. It does not, in any way, *increase* it, as the proponents of the religion of digital progress would have us believe.

Have I gained any new friends as a direct result of the decade or so I've spent on the Internet? I've certainly bumped into a lot more people than I would have in the physical world, but I don't count any of these people as "friends" in any meaningful sense. I've never met any of them; don't really know who they are; and know nothing of their sufferings, a taboo topic, by the way, on the Internet. Whereas real friends are not the least bit afraid to swap tales of their woes, this is something I've noticed that instantly drives such Internet "friends" away and which is the true and telling detail about the real lack of depth concealed by the "virtual reality" of these relationships.

The friends that I have now are precisely the same ones that I had *before* I ever started using the Internet. But maybe I'm old fashioned.

So the Internet's dismantling of centuries of capitalist enterprise is also simultaneously an impoverishing of the social spaces and even non-places of our cities, which are rapidly disappearing beneath its advance.

Perhaps it is the ultimate antidote to urban sprawl: the Internet might be the invisible force field that urban sprawl has finally come up against, and now it is beginning to destructure and dismantle itself as one shopping center after the next collapses and disappears into the penury of economic oblivion.

Soon, there may not be a mercantile world located in physical space left at all. Just an endless horizon of gas stations and convenience stores. In such a society, you can do all your shopping at home, find your friends at home and forget about living in your city at all. There will be no bookstores to go to in order to see authors give readings of their latest books; no record stores to make serendipitous discoveries of new music; no department stores left for Christmas shopping. Hell, there may not, for some inexplicable reason that is beyond me, even be coffee shops left.

Who knows?

PART II

A Collection of Gadgets for a Museum of the Future

1.

First, though, a glance into the museum of ancient history, to which I think we must turn for a moment in order to answer a basic question, namely, why is it that amongst all the civilizations of world history, Western society is the *one* society that is most completely obsessed with innovation?

Indeed, most civilizations throughout human history have had mechanisms in place to squash and discourage innovations from ever seeing the light of day, for precisely the reason I have given in this book's Introduction, namely, that there exists among such societies an intuitive awareness of the culturally destructive consequences that such innovations tend to bring along in their wake. If we were to glance backward into the abysm of Time's past in search of an example of the conflict between the urge to innovate and the urge to conserve, no better one could be found, I think, than that of the contrast between the Mesopotamians and the ancient Egyptians, for it is an interesting point of fact that the ancient Mesopotamians, by contrast with the more conservative Egyptians, loved technological innovations and originated so many of them that it could be said without exaggeration that the Mesopotamians invented the very idea of "civilization" as we have come to know and recognize it. Writing, for instance — as we have seen — was invented there in the middle of the fourth millennium B.C., as was tin-based bronze metallurgy, the first looms, the first wheeled vehicles, the earliest attested use of bee-keeping, the first padlocks, beer and wine, the concept of kingship, even the very idea of the city as a state unto itself. As Fernand Braudel points out in his *Memory and the Mediterranean*,[1] however, the Egyptians resisted many of these same innovations for centuries: bronze working, for instance, did not become common there until about the time of Tutankhamun (1350 B.C.), although the Mesopotamians had been using it as early as the middle of the fourth millennium B.C.; the same goes for the wheel, which the Sumerians had also invented in the fourth millennium and which the Egyptians did not take up until after they were invaded by the Hyksos, who used the two-wheeled chariot together with the compound bow to dismantle the entire structure of the Middle Kingdom; and the Egyptians also resisted the use of the *very* ancient pottery wheel, preferring instead the even more ancient stone bow drill, and so on.[2]

Of the two civilizations, Mesopotamia was by far the more politically unstable, and this may not have been due, as most historians assume, to the fact of Mesopotamia's geographical position being so vulnerable to attack from all sides, by contrast with Egypt's comparative isolation, but rather to Mesopotamia's openness toward innovation, for constant exposure to such innovations tends to create unstable social and political conditions. Mesopotamian mythology is filled with heroes who are forever stealing powerful secrets from the gods, such as elixirs of immortality (Gilgamesh), the Food of Life (Adapa), the power of flight (Etana), etc. And each one of the Sumerian gods, furthermore, was associated — as was *not* the case in Egypt — with a specific form of technology. Enki, for example, was the patron of canals and irrigation; Inanna, of astronomy; Enlil was said to have invented the hoe while his son Ninurta was thought to have invented the plough and also irrigation; Nanna-Sin, the moon god, was the patron of boat builders, and Uttu, the spider goddess, of weaving, etc. etc. In Egypt, few divinities — with the exceptions of Ptah, Thoth and Seshat — were associated with patronage of a specific technology, whereas *all* of the Sumerian divinities were patrons of at least one or another art or craft.

Indeed, one of the strategies by which ancient societies kept technological innovation to a minimum was the institution of *very* forbidding cults of ancestor worship, for it is normally the job of the Ancestors to guard the ancient archetypes of the tribe upon which the world was thought to be patterned at the time of Creation. *No* new ideas were required after that epoch, since the world was envisioned to have been created as perfectly complete from the start, and therefore not in any need of further improvement. Consequently, in societies in which the cult of the dead plays a heavy religious role, such as in ancient Egypt or (early) China, innovation is generally frowned upon, for the Ancestors do not like change and it is their job as a kind of social immune system to conserve the structures of the society from becoming destabilized by new ideas.

In Mesopotamia, however, the West's later preference for innovation is already apparent. Consider the Sumerian Gilgamesh story known as "Gilgamesh and Akka": when Akka, the ruler of Kish is about to march on Uruk, Gilgamesh seeks out the council of Elders in order to get permission to go to war against Akka. They refuse him. So he gathers up all the youths of the city who are of fighting age and asks them if they want to go to war with Akka, which, of course, they do. Thus, Gilgamesh is the first character in the history of literature to override the wishes of the Elders in deference to those of the young. He is literature's first defiant hero.[3]

The West has had its gaze turned away from the Elders ever since, for in the days of Minoan Crete, it was the young and the living who were most fascinating: the Cretans were the first society in the West who chose *not* to bury their dead under the floors of their houses, a custom which had been standard since the days of the Mesolithic Natufians. The dead signify the realm of the past, and along with it, all the weight and burden of tradition, but for the first time in history, in the island world of ancient Crete — and perhaps its isolated geographic position had something to do with this — they were clearly separated from the domus of the living (i.e., the present). Look carefully, museum goer: there *are* no old men depicted in Minoan frescoes, only young men and women, and even children. This is not an accident, either, as the Cretans set the precedent for the West's bias toward novelty, which was then picked up by the Greeks, for whom the cult of the Wonder Child — as evidenced by their Kouros grave statues and the *Iliad* itself (Achilles even had his own cult) — was the primary religious fetish.

Ever since then, the West has been turned toward the future and away from the past; toward the living and away from the dead; toward the young and away from the old. Consequently, innovation has been its rule and conservation its exception.

2.

For an example of the Islamic type of Wonder Child, however, it is instructive to compare with Gilgamesh and *The Iliad* the great epic known as *The Adventures of Amir Hamza,* a text which, like *The Gilgamesh Epic* in Mesopotamian civilization, is climactic, for it is the work with which the civilization of Islam signs off. Islam, by and large, has had its head turned back in the opposite direction to that of the West, looking back toward the founding Elders and *away* from the dizzying pace of innovation that has characterized modernity. This marvellous epic was written down in the middle of the 19th century, by which time Islam had long since passed its heyday, and it is a text that looks back, significantly, to the days of the founding of the religion itself. Though Amir Hamza is the Prophet's paternal uncle, he nevertheless functions in this text as a sort of stand in for the Prophet himself, for he is born in the city of Mecca and sets forth, as a personification of the soul of Islam, to conquer the world. His journeys range over vast tracts of geographical space from India to Greece in imitation of the restless roaming of the evolutionary course of Islam itself. Eventually, he arrives at the opulent city of Ctesiphon on the Tigris, the capital and center of the Persian Sassanids during the final days of their fading glory. There he enters the service of the Persian emperor Naushervan, himself the son of the historical King Chosroe I, whose reign falls in during the years 539–579 A.D.

Now, in the earlier (11th century) Persian epic known as the *Shahnameh,* Naushervan's reign occurs about two thirds of the way through the narrative, at a time when the author, Ferdowsi, is illustrating the decline of the Persian empire, which is beginning to spiral down into an age that is modeled, perhaps, on the Hindu Kali Yuga, in which virtue becomes a rarity and violence and vice the norms. The *Shahnameh* is one long recounting of an age of heroes, the apogee of which had been centered around the exploits of a warrior known as Rostam, who had been the main warrior of Kai Khusrau, a depressed Persian king. By the days of Naushervan, however — who was known as "Naushervan the Just" — Rostam's days are but a memory, and kings are becoming less and less effective and ever more corrupt. One definitely has the feeling of a declining World Age that is cycling down by the time of the Sassanids, who were themselves anxious about which religion to turn to in order to hold their disintegrating empire together.

This forms the setting for *The Adventures of Amir Hamza,* the occurrence of whose birth in a small provincial town in the Arabian desert is evocative of the birth of a World Savior who is about to inaugurate a new World Age (that, namely, of Islam). Hamza is born into the epoch of Persian decadence, that is to say, as a Wonder Child who promises to renew the dying culture with the breath of new life and a new religion. And indeed, the energy and vitality of Hamza's campaigns of conquest is strikingly contrasted with the lassitude and corruption of the scheming courtiers of Naushervan's Sassanid court. Early in the narrative, Hamza bursts forth from Mecca after conquering a warlord named Hishama bin Alqamah, who had been threatening the city of Ctesiphon with war. News reaches Naushervan's ears of the mighty feats of this mere Arabic boy, and soon Hamza is called upon to travel to Ctesiphon along with his two companions, the wily Amar Ayyar and the archer, Muqbil. His adventures of conquest and monster slaying are then recounted in exquisite detail.

Though Hamza is technically born *before* the Prophet, the narrative nevertheless proceeds as though Islam were already up and running and that Amir Hamza was merely its proselytizer. Everyone whom he bests in combat he forces to convert to the religion of Islam and so it soon becomes evident to the reader that Hamza *is* Islam itself and that the narrative recounting his geographical peregrinations and worldly battles is in some way a recapitulation of the history of the conquests of Islamic civilization.

Thus, Islam, in the days of its faded glory in the middle of the 19th century, produces its last great book, which is a story that recounts in allegorical format the conditions that gave rise, once upon a time, to the creation of the world's Last Book, the Koran, for Islam is a culture that claims that the Koran was indeed the Last Book. *Its* Wonder Child, then, is to be contrasted with those of the West which, beginning with Gilgamesh, refuse to bow to the Elders and proceed, instead, to conquer the world with a series of technical innovations.

Islam, on the other hand, has refused the path of such innovations and proceeded instead to attempt to conquer the world with a book.

3.

Turning now toward a museum of the present, in an age of the post–Holocaust horrors of the twentieth century, where we find Joseph Beuys' Auschwitz installation of 1958: this installation provides us with a sort of palimpsest for the second half of our journey through postmodernity, an age characterized rather more by the *dis*continuities and *de*contextualizations of its apparently random and disconnected technological artifacts. Beuys' installation, too, already characterizes the patchwork nature of our current age, in which no object ever quite ... seems ... to ... *fit* in anywhere.

Thus, likewise, Beuys' installation, in which we are confronted by an apparently disparate collection of objects all carefully displayed like the relics of a saint inside of a glass case: a map of the camp; blocks of fat on a rusting hotplate; a clay image of the Crucified Christ on a dish; a mummified rat on a bed of straw; rotten sausages; discarded bottles stopped with old corks; bits of string; a pair of goggles; rusting slices of metal. It is as if the Holocaust were envisioned as a series of partial objects attempting to thrust their way up through the memory as symptoms of a repressed and abandoned trauma that one cannot quite fully forget but that keeps pushing its way up nevertheless in the form of these little archipelagoes of banal, disconnected objects which somehow never seem to connect to form a coherent pattern. An abbreviated vocabulary, in other words, for an entire world, a sinister world to be pieced together only by one with sufficient intrepidity of mind to begin assembling the objects back into their proper contexts: this bit of sausage, here, that's what the guards ate; this bit of string there, that's what the prisoners tied their shoes with; these blocks of fat.... And so on.

In the second half of this book, likewise, I present the reader with a collection of partial objects for a museum of the future, objects torn from their contexts and placed beside one another, as though in a glass display case, with all the connections between them removed: a digital camera, here; a cell phone, there; a laptop over there; a tiny, malfunctioning robot; a video game console; a personal pod. Put them together; they're objects taken from your world, dear reader, objects of a still life for you to assemble as you choose in order to make sense out of the all-encompassing technosphere of the world I have torn them from. A world in which they are not partial objects at all, but rather fragments from a single coherent monstrosity of a living, breathing Megalopolis that has become self-aware and sentient and has turned human beings into its slaves, like the inmates of an electronic Auschwitz whose denizens are forced into acts of bizarre and humiliating servitude. The Mesopotamians and the Egyptians never had any megamachine quite like *this*.

In this post-civilized World-as-Matrix, we are all masochistic victims of a sadistic machine that embeds each one of us inside of its dreaming mind, connecting our neurons to its integrated circuits so that what we see is not what appears on our retinas, but rather *its* visions of a digitized reality which has become the *only* reality we can ever see, even while awake. We no longer look out upon the world with our own eyes (to quote Darth

Vader), but with the eyes of the Vision Machine (to use Paul Virilio's phrase) which does all the seeing for us.

Soon, it will even be doing all the thinking for us, so that we will no longer think our own thoughts, but rather, *its* thoughts. We will dream its dreams and build its world, and one day, some archaeologist will dig up these partial objects and place them inside a glass case in some museum of the future with an enigmatic tag that reads: "From Mesopotamia to America: The Course of Technological Evolution."

Here, right this way, see for yourself how these people lived. In this first case over here is an object that was once known as a personal computer...

7

The Mythology and
Metaphysics of the Macintosh

The Myth

The great myth of Western civilization, then, is not, as Oswald Spengler insisted, that of Faust; neither is it, as the American mythologist Joseph Campbell once suggested, Prometheus, or even the Grail quester of Arthurian legend; it is not even Lewis Mumford's "myth of the machine"; it is none of these. Rather, *the* great myth of Western civilization — and it has been the great myth since the days of Minoan Crete — is that of the Wonder Child's struggle against the Elders.

Its first great literary manifestation was, of course, the *Iliad,* whose protagonist, the twenty-something Achilles, has been suggested by some scholars to have been a late innovation added to the mythos of the Trojan War by Homer himself.[1] His magical powers of invulnerability give Achilles more of the feel of a folk hero than any traditional hero of a literary epic, and the fact that he is absent from most of the book's action implies that he was never necessary to whatever its original structure may have been. Also, he is too young to have been one of Helen's suitors, for the Greeks at the time the epic opens have already been fighting in Troy for ten years. The other heroes — Diomedes, Odysseus, Agamemnon — had all pledged themselves to the rescue of Helen if ever she were abducted; Achilles alone among these heroes is too young ever to have made such a pledge. In short, he may have been an innovation of Homer's to an already traditional epic of war and battle.

Which is important because the conflict between Achilles and Agamemnon is certainly not over a girl; it is, rather, the conflict of youth against age; of reverence for the cult of the Wonder Child with miraculous abilities who will, from henceforth, become *the* central fetish of Greek religiosity from the grave statues of its beautiful young Kouros boys to Alexander the Great himself, the youngest world conqueror in history. There are no old men depicted in Greek art until the Hellenistic Age, and this is not an accident, since the Greek reverence for youth was tantamount to an orientation toward innovation, novelty and all things new that would characterize Classical civilization from Homer on down to the Romans.

In the Medieval period, European art was haunted by the persistent reiteration of the Wonder Child in the form of the Infant Christ and his Virgin Mother at the expense of representations of Yahweh, the old man and the Old God of the bygone age of the Jews, who appears less and less often in this art as it evolves through the centuries. The child represents the future; the old man, the past. And along with an orientation toward the future comes a willingness to experiment and try new things that has been characteristic of the Western attitude toward technology to the present day.

Indeed, in the climactic battle scenes of *Return of the Jedi*, Luke Skywalker's fight against Darth Vader and the Emperor — crippled, deformed old men both — is not just about Freedom vs. Tyranny, or democracy against totalitarianism, but more specifically, it is an echo of the Wonder Child's struggle against the ways and traditions of the Elders that was first announced in the *Iliad* and has been characteristic of the Western mentality ever since.

And it also happens to be the central myth of Apple Computer.

The Commercial

On January 22, 1984, Apple debuted its commercial for the new Macintosh computer on television, a commercial directed by Ridley Scott, who had just then completed *Alien* and *Blade Runner*. The commercial, one of the most famous ever made, begins by showing a single-file line of drab, shaven-headed men marching through a glass tunnel on their way to a meeting with Big Brother who appears before them, as in Orwell's novel, on a gigantic television screen. A woman dressed in a white T-shirt imprinted with a schematic Macintosh computer and wearing red shorts runs, carrying a sledgehammer, while in pursuit behind her is a group of helmeted police, face shields drawn for combat mode. The woman runs down the center aisle of the meeting room where she hurls the sledgehammer at the giant video screen with its talking head spouting ideology, which then explodes into white phosphorescence as the words appear onscreen voiced by a narrator: "On January 24 Apple Computer will introduce Macintosh. And you'll understand why 1984 won't *be* like '1984.'"[2]

Steve Jobs, who co-founded Apple Computer with Steven Wozniak, was a kind of anti-executive executive who refused to hire anybody who showed up for an interview wearing a suit and tie, since he himself never wore one, and often did not even wear deodorant. He and Wozniak created the first affordable personal computer with the Apple II in 1977, and by the end of that year, they had also introduced the first floppy disk drive. They were millionaires by the age of 25.

Jobs identified IBM, Apple's primary rival, with the dragon to be slain. In ancient myth, dragons were often killed by thunderbolts hurled at them in the form of hammers, swords, spears, etc., and in this light it becomes clear that the role of the woman in Ridley Scott's commercial is that of a dragon slayer hurling a thunderbolt at the staid old establishment of IBM, a conservative East Coast corporation with its roots in the Cold War. Big Brother, in the Mac commercial, *is* IBM, which Jobs made clear in the keynote speech that he gave near the end of 1983 when he first unveiled the commercial to a live audience.[3]

The hammer that the woman-as-dragonslayer hurls, furthermore, is a signifier for the Macintosh computer itself, Apple's response to the IBM PC which IBM had put out in 1981, a computer based largely upon the technology of the Apple II. If Apple lost the computer wars then, according to Jobs, a Dark Age would settle over the industry. In his own words:

> If, for some reason we make some big mistake and IBM wins, my personal feeling is that we are going to enter sort of a computer Dark Ages for about twenty years. Once IBM gains control of a market sector, they always stop innovation. They prevent innovations from happening.
>
> If you look at the mainframe marketplace, there's been virtually zero innovation since IBM got dominant control of that marketplace fifteen years ago. The IBM PC fundamentally brought no new technology to the industry at all. It was just a repackaging and slight extension of Apple II technology, and now they want it all.
>
> Apple is providing the alternative.[4]

And that alternative was, of course, the Macintosh computer, the sword drawn from the stone of the Wonder Child's workshop which, once forged, would become the means for the Old Man's undoing.

The Subtle Body of the Text

The first Macintosh computer, known as the 128k, introduced a revolutionary new idea: that of the so-called graphical user interface, in which *images* became simulacra of *things*. This was inspired by the visit of Jobs and some other Apple personnel to the Xerox Palo Alto Research Center in 1979, where they first saw a demonstration of graphical user interface software. As Young and Simon, Jobs' biographers, describe it:

> What Apple saw that day was a display on which the user made selections, not by typing out cryptic commands, but by moving a pointer to designate the desired onscreen object. And individual windows for different documents. And onscreen menus. Today, this is the standard way that most people interact with computers, but then it was extraordinary. Up until that time, computers were controlled by typed commands, and the screens generally displayed nothing but letters and numbers. Here was a graphical user interface (GUI, as it would later become known) unlike anything ever seen on a computer screen before, and better yet, it was working.[5]

The computer's "pointer," furthermore, was called a "mouse," a technology which had been invented by Douglas Englebart at Stanford Research Institute in the 1960s. This was all revolutionary new stuff, but Xerox turned out not to be interested in their own technological innovations. However, Apple was, and so they implemented it with the introduction of their Lisa computer in 1983, which was too expensive for the average user but became affordable with the Macintosh in 1984.

The Macintosh is a machine for the transformation of physical objects into light. The graphical interface overlaid upon the computer screen — hitherto a black screen with commands typed in green characters — a secondary stratum of images of coded flows of information: physical objects such as desktops, manila folders, paintbrushes, file drawers, pens, pencils and typewriters were all encoded in the form of "icons."

Thus, with the creation of desktop publishing — invented with the Mac — one could now *see* a virtual image of a page of text, together with all its graphics, exactly as it would appear before being printed out in physical form. In other words, a *subtle* form of the document or text began now to precede and displace the *visualized idea* of the text held in the mind's eye before it was created as a piece of physical matter.

The Macintosh, then, has a *dematerializing effect* upon the physical world, an effect not all that different from the magical child's abilities in ancient myth to transform physical things into luminous visions. When, for instance, the boy child Krishna — a true Wonder Child, indeed — lifts up Mount Govardana with one hand in order to shield the cows and the *gopis* from the rain, the mountain is no longer a physical *object* at all, but a visionary *image* from the realm of myth and dream.

Luminous Technology

The evolution of the Macintosh taken as a whole, from the 128k in 1984 to the iPad in 2010, is a tale of the gradual victory of forms of *suksma technology* over *sthula technology,* a gradual and inevitable absorption of the physical by the luminous. It is a tale of the transformation and disso-lution of the very *idea* of the computer into something more akin to a piece of electronic stained glass.

If the evolution of Western art from the Medieval period to the nine-teenth century is a tale of the unfolding of the physical and the concrete at the expense of the realm of the subtle and the visionary, then the evo-lution of the computer via the Macintosh is a narrative that reverses the physical back into the world of the subtle, of the realm of ghostly visions and phantom forms.

The One Non-Negotiable Element
of the Personal Computer

The personal computer, as it was invented by Apple in 1981 with the Apple II, was basically a crossing of the typewriter with the television.[6] The phantom realm of the CRT screen, that is to say, was crossed with the linear rows of type arranged on the typewriter (a miniaturized printing press which enabled everyman to be his own printer) in such a way as to begin to dematerialize typed words themselves, which were no longer inscribed upon a sheet of actual paper, but now existed virtually in the form of pixilated bytes on a computer monitor. The words, that is to say, began to attain a new status of virtuality: they *might* exist, but unless they were printed out, they might also just as easily disappear like thoughts in the mind withdrawing into some secret reservoir of consciousness never to be heard from again.

With the advent of the Macintosh computer in 1984 — preceded by the Lisa in 1983, the first to actually feature GUI — the idea was that one could now begin to manipulate *images* with a mouse and a typewriter's keyboard the way one had previously, with a typewriter, manipulated typed words on a page. Images could be typed, moved, fused, dissolved, etc., exactly like thoughts in consciousness.

To draw once again from Indian philosophy: consciousness is known there as *citta,* mind-stuff, which has the spontaneous capacity of moving around in the mind and taking on the shapes of whatever the senses perceive in the outer world. A liquid crystal display does almost the same thing as it takes on the forms of the electrical impulses that pour through it as data. The Macintosh computer, then, comes very close to the technological replication of consciousness — or at least, the consciously controlled thought forms of *waking* consciousness — closer than any other technology hitherto.

As the evolution of the Mac unfolded throughout the 1980s and early 1990s, the computer monitor tended to remain as a separate unit from the hard drive and the keyboard and mouse. The Macintosh was basically a four piece unit.

But when Steve Jobs rejoined Apple in 1997 (after having been forced to leave in the mid 1980s), and created the iMac, the monitor and the CPU were fused together into one unit, while both the keyboard and the mouse still remained separate. The iMac was the first computer to be specifically designed *for* Internet usage, coming equipped with an *internal* modem and the first USB port. The floppy disk drive, which Apple had invented, was now gone, replaced by a CD drive.

Over time, it becomes evident that *the* essential component of the computer, the *one* piece that is non-negotiable, is the *screen* (together, of course, with its CPU). It is to the computer what Goethe's idea of the Leaf was to the archetypal plant: the central informing Idea of which all the other parts are but extensions and transformations.

This is finally proven once and for all with the introduction of the iPad in 2010, in which the computer is stripped down to the screen and everything else is subordinated to it, including the keyboard, which is now transformed into *light* in the form of a digital simulacrum of the keyboard.

Thus, the keyboard, the main element which had survived from the computer's descent from the typewriter, is finally dissolved and etherealized to become an *internal* organ of the computer itself. All that remains of the hybrid of typewriter and television is a flat, luminous screen that glows with the internal self-radiance of a piece of stained glass.

Thus, with the iPad, the destiny of the computer is revealed, as the transformation and etherealization of *all* its component parts into organs made out of light.

A Brief History of Invisible Worlds

The Macintosh computer, then, opens up a window into a luminous, *non-physical* world. And what, then, is the nature of the world that it reveals?

To answer that, we must look back at some earlier windows to alternate realities opened up by ancient cultures. Let us start with the Paleolithic: according to David Lewis-Williams in his book *The Mind in the Cave,* the walls of the painted caves were not conceived of merely as solid surfaces upon which painted animals cavorted like primitive graffiti, but rather as windows opening onto another reality altogether, a world of phantom animal spirits that the painter, using his paints as a medium, was able to break open the rock in order to *see,* a world of ancestral beings and eternal forms upon which the physical world had modeled itself since the beginning of Time.[7]

Upon the walls of Egyptian tombs, likewise, the painted images opened up a world of magical spells and eternal beings, a world that could be manipulated by the dead person's *ka* only if he knew the proper utterances that would unlock its various gates and thresholds and move him past their demon guardians into an eternal Afterlife.

In the world opened up by Greek statuary, a realm of eternal Acts of Men in Motion was visualized, a realm of Platonic essences and archetypes upon which all men in the accidental world were to model their actions. The key to *this* world lay in the mastery of philosophical concepts — not magical spells — which, once known, would gain one entrance into the eternal Academy of Great Men and their Deeds.

For the Christians, as Gilles Deleuze has pointed out, Essence began to be identified for the first time *with* the accidental by way of the myth of the avatar of God, the Being who came down *into* this world.[8] The forms of Byzantine art, then, are concerned more with the earthly, with transitory men like Justinian and the incarnated Christ than with Eternal Forms. This paved the way for the Western preoccupation with the accidental and the ephemeral at the expense of substance and essence.

On the analogy with the metaphysics of these other parallel realities, then, we might say that the world opened up by the luminous window of the Macintosh gives us access to the current Western episteme, which is a realm of coded flows of information and data caught in a flux of perpetual change. You can't step into the same Information river twice in this society, for the subtle realm structured by its software and its Ideas is one that is always subject to revision, in accordance with its dominance by the myth of the Wonder Child who has no reverence for the teachings of his former masters, but wishes only to shape the world in accordance with *his own* mind.

When you are using a Macintosh, you have entered *inside* the mind of Steve Jobs, a realm composed of subtle images and graphics not structured around the power of the Word — Jobs was a college dropout — but around the Image as all-encompassing signifier which has swallowed up the Word, just as his iPad swallowed up the keyboard and turned it into an icon.

Digital Hub

On January 9, 2001, Steve Jobs gave a keynote speech at the Macworld Expo, in which he articulated his vision of the personal computer as the center of a "Digital Hub," in which, far from becoming obsolete, the personal computer was destined to become the nucleus of the digital revolution in which all other digital gadgets could be jacked in like so many drones subordinated to the Queen Bee.[9] The vision Jobs was articulating, then, was an image of the subtle, luminous reality configured by his Macintosh swallowing, absorbing, digesting and engulfing *all* other gadgets and physical components, just as the Mac via the iPad would gobble up all the components of the computer and transform them into organs of light.

With the introduction of the iTunes application at this same Macworld Expo, followed by the iPod in October of that year, the CD as a physical object was effectively eliminated and dissolved, transformed, that is, into an object made out of *light*. With a single stroke, the iPod rendered the portable CD player obsolete. Now one no longer had to carry around one's favorite CDs in order to listen to music. You could, as Jobs pointed out, keep them all, your entire library, in your pocket, *inside* of a gadget the size of a deck of cards.

With the introduction of the iTunes Music Store in April of 2003, furthermore, which Jobs conceived as the first legal rival to illegal music download sites like Napster and Kazaa, and for which he received the blessing of the entire music industry, he further dematerialized the industry by eliminating, not just the CD, but the *music store itself as a physical entity.* It was not long after this — in 2006, to be exact — that Tower Records closed down. "Between 2003 and 2006," as Andrew Keen writes, "800 independent music stores closed their doors for good."[10] Music stores are now a thing of the past, for they have been translated and transformed by the Wonder Child's wizardry into components made out of light and shadow located not in any real physical three dimensional space, but in the subtle realm of the Internet.

And where is the Internet?

Nowhere and everywhere.

Just like the astral plane.

Subtle Matter in Cyberspace

The mythology of Apple Computer, then, is that of the myth of the Wonder Child who befuddles and mystifies the Elders with his magic tricks, just like the Christ child when his parents found him lecturing to an astonished audience of Pharisees in the Temple. The metaphysics, furthermore, is one of the transformation of three dimensional objects located in physical space into the self-radiant images of subtle matter in cyberspace. Light *on* gradually gives way to light *through.*

Consider the iPhone, introduced by Jobs at the Macworld Expo in 2007: this is the first phone to eliminate the keyboard by virtualizing it with touch pad technology. Not only that, but with the iPhone, the cell phone itself is dematerialized and absorbed into the Macintosh computer, for every iPhone is essentially an avatar of a Macintosh computer made small enough to fit into one's pocket. There is very little that a Macintosh computer can do that an iPhone can't. The iPhone absorbs the cell phone, takes it *inside* the virtual reality of the Macintosh, and then extends it out into physical space as an avatar of itself, thus rendering all other cell phones effectively obsolete. At once, the other phone companies begin copying it by introducing their own versions of touch pad phones. (Google's Android is its primary competitor.)

Thus, it is the goal of Apple Computer to absorb and transform all physical electronic objects and turn them into extensions of Mac computers precisely by eliminating their physical components and etherealizing them into phantoms made of so much light and shadow.

What we are witnessing before our very eyes, then, is a technological drama played out upon the capitalist proscenium, of the victory of *suksma* technologies over *sthula* technologies, of the transformation and destructuring of the entire physical world-space created by capitalism during the Newtonian Age into a Manichean economy dominated by technologies of Light.

By the time all of this is over, you can expect to witness not just the disappearance of things like CD players and DVD players, or even record and book stores, but of *the entire mercantile world of capitalism configured by stores located in three dimensional space altogether.*

The victory of *suksma* technologies means the inevitable virtualization of *capitalism taken as a whole.*

The retail store is becoming a fossil soon to be buried deep in the archaeological strata of archaic forms of capitalism. Future Walter Benjamins engaged in Arcades-type projects will write books with titles like: *The Origins and Extinction of the Retail Store* or *The Rise and Fall of the Shopping Mall.*

Mark my words.

8

Digital Photography and the
End of the Visionary Image

The World's First Photograph

Paradoxically, it is only at the moment of their vanishing when things become suddenly visible.

An old Christian legend recounts that just as Christ was about to disappear from the physical world, on his way along the Via Dolorosa, a woman named Veronica wiped the sweat from his brow with a cloth and imprinted upon that cloth was an image of Christ's face, later said to be able to work miracles. This is, as it were, the earliest photograph ever taken, earlier even than Niepce's 1826 photograph, using a pewter plate covered with bitumen, to capture a rooftop view from his window at Le Gras. The myth of Veronica provides photography with its central, hidden myth, namely, that the ability to record permanent images is nothing short of miraculous. Photography is yet another example of the technological restaging of ancient myth.

But now today it is possible for us to *see* traditional photography for what it is, precisely because it is in the act of disappearing.

Thus, like a swimmer coming out of the water who now has a clear vision of the environment he has left behind — a shimmering blue-green pool of undulating waves flecked with gold sunlight — so we too, presently surfacing from our immersion in a century and a half of traditional photography, can now actually perceive the contours of that medium as though it were a topological entity.

Syncopated Images

How, then, *did* the world once appear to these photographers?

Take the photos of Diane Arbus: the one with the strange child on the playground clutching a grenade in his left hand; or the photo of the giant inside the living room, towering over his parents; those murky, slightly out of focus shots of families on the streets of New York or reclining in lounge chairs in their suburban back yards; the scowling twins on the beach; the Tattooed carnival man; a world of dwarves, giants, misfits and fascinating nobodies. A black and white cosmos of grainy images whose lack of detail makes the photos work precisely because they invite the viewer to complete them.

Contrast this world with Richard Avedon's: the cartography of scars lacerating Andy Warhol's post-surgery torso; Marlon Brando, bare chested, shaving; a solitary Bob Dylan, looking like he needs nobody in the world, striding along a glistening, rain-wet street; Audrey Hepburn in profile, half her face swallowed up by shadows; Nastassia Kinski entwined with her boa constrictor; Kennedy and his son; the Beatles; Marilyn; all of them like phantom shapes scrawled in charcoal onto the walls of some strange netherworld.

The sum of the two worlds, then, taken together?

A universe of deep contrasts, at once chiseled and murky, a chiaroscuro of forms only half-revealed to our naked eyes while our minds dream up the missing pieces.

Syncopated images, in other words.

A Confession

Once, many years ago, in my mid twenties, I took a drug called Xtasy. I don't even know if the drug is still around, but I do remember that the onset of its first effects brought a sudden sharpening in my visual acuity. Although it was at night, I was able to see such fine-grained visual detail that I imagined it must be something similar to how a cat sees in the dark. The grain of the leaves on the trees was as startlingly clear as an artwork by Andy Goldsworthy; the stars were chiseled flames burning against the dark blue canvas of the night sky; the Hale-Bopp comet, which happened to be going by at the time, was visible as an intense smear of vanilla paint.

The detailed high resolution of digital photos reminds me of this increase in visual acuity caused by my taking the drug. But this very fact, that the Xtasy increased the quality of my vision, means that our senses *could* be sharper, that they have the capacity to access an even higher resolution version of the external world, but that they normally don't. And for good reason.

Our senses are like transformers which step down the power of the reality current so that our nervous systems don't get overloaded with sensory input. Drugs open up these neural floodgates, allowing in more sensory input, which is why many people who take them on a regular basis often cannot make the trip back. Surreality is much more interesting than quotidian reality.

There is something nauseating, however, about the excess of detail in digital photography, as though one's senses had been worn raw by some traumatic overload and could not bear too much reality, the way one cannot bear too much sunlight when one has just emerged from a dark interior. After looking at too many of these photos, I soon feel the need to counter their effect by digging up some Edward Steichen pictures in order to revel in the soft, grainy focus of the aesthetic universe — still heavily akin to painting — that he created. The photographs of Edward Steichen are true works of art: the Flatiron building glimpsed through naked tree branches in the rain; the Brooklyn bridge arcing toward Manhattan from a vertiginous height in the middle of the afternoon; a silver-limned pond gleaming in the slice of moon drifting up between a copse of skeletal trees; women posing like stars from silent movies. A world of capitalist dreams and visions; Adorno's Culture Industry seen through the gaze of the *camera obscura*.

Digital images, on the other hand, feature clean, crisp pictures that glisten with the aura conferred upon them by technological efficiency.

And therein resides the problem.

The Necessity of the Negative

Traditional darkroom photography is about aesthetics; ways, that is, of seeing, to use John Berger's famous term. Digital photography, however, is about *a* way of seeing, seeing things in only one way: with greater technical efficiency. Americans constantly mistake technical efficiency for artistic improvement. Too often it is assumed that just because a gadget becomes more efficient — as, for example, digital photography has in eliminating the labor intensive step of the darkroom — that it somehow improves the medium overall.

We have the following comments made by Ansel Adams for a BBC documentary to consider:

> Adams: The negative is like the composer's score — all the information's there — and the print is like the performance. So you interpret this score at varying aesthetic, emotional levels but never far enough away to violate the essential concept.
>
> Interviewer: So if somebody were to take your original negative, which is the score, and print it up, one would end up with a totally different photograph because it's a different performance?
>
> Adams: I hope it would be different, after all, when I was a pianist, I was playing music of Bach and Vivaldi and Mozart who were not only long dead, but had never heard a grand piano. So, in a sense, any performance of that music is sort of a transcription, a contemporary composition which is made for the contemporary instruments, which is something else.[1]

The interviewer then goes on to point out three different prints made by Adams from the same negative, decades apart, and all of which, as Adams says, have different emotional values, precisely like different performances of the same musical score.

Much of the artistry of traditional photography, then, lies precisely in the hand's manipulation of the negative in the darkroom. This chemical process is in no way — as technophiles like to assume — an entirely superfluous step in the creation of great photographs. In fact, it is evident from Adams's statements that if you eliminate the darkroom, you eliminate the artistry from the medium, on the mistaken assumption that it is all just a matter of technical efficiency.[2]

Literal Images

Consider Adams's photographs of Yosemite. A comparison of these analogue images with digital images of the same landscape, which are easily available on Flickr or Picasa, is both revealing and instructive, for it shows that what the digital images suffer from is too much detail. They are *too* literal. What makes Adams's photographs great works of art, on the other hand, is the fine sifting of muted softness — not soft focus, for Adams's photos are always in sharp resolution — that has the effect of derealizing the image, thus conferring on it an oneiric quality, as though it were an image that had come floating up from distant memory out of the haze of the past. The digital images of Yosemite — almost always in color — are not art, and can never be art, precisely because there is too much reality engraved into them.

The photographs of Ansel Adams, by the way, are also interesting for another reason: taken in composite, they all add up to the articulation of a single great Vision, that of a world of primordial landscapes void of human beings. Adams's project was to stage the vision of a world abandoned by some great Creator at the dawn of time after carving out his inhuman geographies, satisfied with leaving the newborn world as a realm of endless mutating landscapes evolving over millions of years, moving with its own cosmic pulsations, a world in which no imaginable human presence could affect anything. His pictures, like the works of a great literary artist such as James Joyce or Thomas Pynchon, are thus illustrations of a coherent world view.

Photographic Haiku

Digital photography destroys all of this with the starkness of its over-real images that are far too complete to allow space for the dreaming human imagination. The imagination is absolutely *not* welcome in digital photography. There is no room for it. Reality in these photographs is too harsh, too fully present, like the paintings of the mad which are filled up with so much detail that the margins have disappeared and there is no room left for the play of the viewer's mind.[3] The great masters of Chinese landscape painting understood this, for they left vast tracts of wide open space in their paintings so that the viewer's gaze could help to complete their worlds. And is this not, in fact, the essence of the Haiku? That it is deliberately incomplete, syncopated so that the mind is left to fill in the gaps between glimpses of discontinuous reality?

> By the old temple
> Peach blossoms
> A man treading rice
> — Basho

These few simple lines conjure forth an entire worldscape in the reader's mind. They are simple and economical. They work precisely because they leave information *out*. That is the effect of great art: to open up spaces in the world through which new worlds might come into being, with the assistance of the human mind as midwife.

Edward Weston

If Adams was the master of the panoramic vista, his contemporary Edward Weston was the master of the intimate landscape. Each of *his* photos scales up the tiny and the intimate to the level of a panorama: a woman's back, a toilet, a sand dune, a seashell, a flower; all are close ups that have the non-linear effect of amplifying the small out of all proportion into the power and beauty of an entire landscape unto itself.

Digital images of equivalent forms, though sometimes beautiful, invariably fail to inspire any comparable sense of wonder, for the images of insects and flowers in vivid, airbrush-like detail transform the objects depicted into science textbook illustrations, not works of art. Digital photography is no handmaiden of art, but it *is* a perfect servant of science, for the kinds of IMAX-like detail of which it is capable are merely didactic and invite an inquisitive attitude, not one of reverie. Traditional photography — and here I am not speaking of photo-journalism, which is another matter altogether — is like a photographer's daydream that has been captured and transfixed via silver halogens onto a sheet of paper so that it can be shared with everyone.

Mapplethorpe's Daydream

Robert Mapplethorpe's daydream, for example, is of the human body as a work of art, very much in the style of Greek sculpture: his photographs are alive with fascination for the human physique, especially the *beautiful* human physique that has been sculpted into a rigid state of athletic perfection. Indeed, this is so much the case that every object he photographs is transformed into an analogue of the human body: his close ups of flowers, of irises and lilies, remind one of the various shapes and curves of his close ups of geometries of the human body.

But where he differs from the Greek aesthetic is that his pictures present the body as a series of partial objects, as an image, that is, of the fragmented and disorganized body of the infant prior to its Lacanian mirror stage, at which point the body is suddenly recognized as a coherent whole by the child in the mirror, who then very quickly develops coordination and walking skills. Mapplethorpe's images are bodily fragments: the muscle-hardened torso of a black man; the self-portrait in which only one of Mapplethorpe's arms and part of his face are visible in the frame; a man dressed only in leather chaps who is bent over a marble slab in profile, and whose head we do not see, but whose semi-flaccid penis is displayed on the marble as though it were an art object; a woman bent over and contorted to emphasize the archipelago of her spinal vertebra, her head tucked away from sight.

Mapplethorpe uses the camera to *carve up* the human form, to analyse it, not to synthesize it. For what is important about photography is not so much what is in the frame, as what is *excluded* from the frame. And what Mapplethorpe excludes is any sense of the body as an integrated form. His vision of the human form is pre-mirror stage.

But it *is* a dream, nonetheless, an artist's fantasia of physical *dis*-integration in an age in which the self has been splintered into pieces by technology.

The Luminous Images of Edward Burtynsky

In a way, Edward Burtynsky's color photographs document a world view that is just the opposite of Ansel Adams's, for his is a record of the *damage* which gigantic human industrial engineering projects have wreaked upon the earth, a world in which it is impossible to ignore the human presence. His photographs capture the scars and abrasions left upon the earth by tiny humans with colossal technologies at their disposal: his eye captures the striated marble quarries of Carrara, Italy; or the burning red rivers of nickel tailings in Sudbury, Ontario; or the open pit coal mines of Sparwood, British Columbia; or the concentric layers of copper mines arranged as though by deliberation around a central pool of turquoise-colored water in Bingham Valley, Utah. These photos are a cartography of incisions sliced into the body of the earth, and yet, through the aesthetic gaze of Burtynsky's eye, they are simultaneously transfigured into works of a beauty so luminous that they seem to have been created as the deliberate works of some giant land art project.

Burtynsky's photographs are *so* luminous, in fact, that they appear to radiate their own inner light, as though they were the modern equivalent of stained glass projects built to portray a chapel documenting the heroic epic of modern industrial man's conquest and enslavement of the earth's material resources. In fact, Burtynsky is the poet of Heidegger's idea about the modern technological understanding of Being as Enframing (*Gestell*), and his photos would illustrate Heidegger's essay on "The Question Concerning Technology" better than just about anything else I can think of.

Burtynsky's images have a sculptural quality to them, for he is the type of photographer who sees with his hand. His technoscapes of densified oil drums or ferrous bushlings are highly textured images that function as technological analogues of the action paintings of Jackson Pollock. His walls made out of cubes of compressed, multi-colored scrap metal, or random piles of discarded circuit boards in Chinese scrap yards or chunks of Cankun aluminum in Xiamen City are highly contoured images. Whether he is photographing steel mills in China; oil refineries in Houston or Ontario; or fields of pumping oil rigs in California; his eye has a peculiar flattening effect on the spaces photographed, such that all sense of distance and perspective disappears, and his cityscapes become models the size of train sets. But this is precisely the effect of a tactile, rather than a purely visual, feeling for space, for space as perceived not by the eye but by the hand is peculiarly flat, like an Eskimo carving out of walrus ivory.

Burtynsky's photographs are absolutely unique and if you haven't seen them then you need to. They are a classic example of the kind of visionary way of *seeing* that traditional photography as a medium enables.[4]

The Loss of Visionary Coherence

It is precisely this kind of visionary coherence, though, that is lost in digital photography, for it is too immediate, too *now* in order to function in the kinds of delayed mental spaces that make it possible for an artist to assemble an idiosyncratic vision of the world. Digital photography makes its images available instantly, which is great, if you're a tourist. If you're an artist, it is catastrophic, as catastrophic as the demolition of history is when events are broadcast around the globe in real time, which eliminates the deferred mental space necessary for the processing of events, as Paul Virilio often pointed out.

Let us not forget that with digital photography, the temporal frame of chemical and mechanical processes upon which photography was based is completely dismantled. The image is simply plugged in and turned on, as it were, with electric current immediately shot through it. It can be instantly erased or displayed on a video screen, and hence becomes a useful tool for journalists. But art does not occur at the speed of light. It must be slowed down enough to allow for the intervention of the transformative human hand in order to shape it.

The Elimination of the Hand

But, of course, in eliminating the darkroom, not only is the space of deferred time eliminated, but so also is the human hand. The digital photo is so obscene precisely because it denudes the image of its tactile qualities: the graininess of the traditional photo, for example, the sense of texture that gives to the image its concreteness is gone, and along with it, the invisible yet unmistakable presence of the shaping human hand.

Digital photography steps up the visual sense and divorces it from the other senses, resulting in images that are purely a creation of the mechanics of the eye. This separation reveals just how much and how often we actually *see* with our *hands*. Illuminated manuscripts, for instance, with their iconic fonts and hand-written lines are still highly tactile. But with the advent of the printing press, the reading experience becomes macadamized, as it were, making it an easy affair for the eye to simply glide along, unhindered by input from any of the other senses.

In a similar way, the alphabet, as McLuhan never tired of pointing out, divorced the visual sense from all the other senses, and the printing press even more so. Simultaneously with this stepping up of purely visual qualities around the year 1500, depth perspective was developed in oil painting. What characterizes the geometrical art of perspective is a type of seeing that favors the eye and creates a unified homogeneous space in which all objects are subordinated to a single point of view. The sense of touch, however, is discontinuous. In ancient art, objects tend to occupy and define their own spaces, which is why figures are of varying sizes. In Egyptian art, for instance, pharaoh is always depicted on the battlefield as a giant, completely out of scale in relation to all the other tiny human soldiers engaged in battle on the ground below.

This same shift from haptic to visual takes place alongside developments in European architecture, for whereas Medieval cities are a discontinuous jumble of buildings, all of differing sizes and shapes, each occupying its own space, the cities of the Baroque are streamlined and uniform, with long, perspectival avenues arranged for marching armies, as Lewis Mumford pointed out. Washington, D.C., with its grand vistas and long avenues, is one of the last of the great Baroque cities.[5]

All of which parallels the differences between digital photography and traditional photography, for in the case of the former, the clean, crisp images from which all noise has been purged indicate that the sense of touch has been banished from the image. This becomes even more evident when we consider that the function of the darkroom, as its name implies, was to step down the visual function so that the hand could be brought into play in the shaping of the images. Eliminating the darkroom is tantamount to eliminating the sense of touch from the image. Thus, traditional photographs, like illuminated manuscripts, were produced kinesthetically. The result was a highly textured and very concrete image.

Elegy for Analogue

But now those analogue images are disappearing into a pointillist universe of bytes and pixels. When photographs are plugged in and turned on via digital technology, they become dematerialized. They go directly from reality to take up residence inside the integrated circuits of computer chips, where they are stored as a form of virtual memory. The images attain the status of virtuality, that is to say, they are not *real* images, but computer memories subject, as are all human memories, to erasure, modification, information decay, or simple deletion. In doing so, the ontological status of photography shifts from that of a high art to a graphic art form and becomes capable of producing no more sophisticated images than the nauseating illustrations that are displayed in the glossy pages of graphic design manuals. Real artists with visionary talents will turn to other media as film gradually, and inevitably, disappears.

The end of yet another art form as collateral damage in the tireless march of progress of technology.

9

How Cell Phones
Disrupt the Flows

Derailment

On September 12, 2008, at 4:23 on a Friday afternoon in Chatsworth, California, a Metrolink commuter train carrying 222 people collided head on with a Union Pacific freight train. Both trains were traveling at about 40 miles per hour, and when they hit, the Metrolink engine car was forced backward into the first passenger car, whereupon it caught fire. Seven freight cars and three locomotives — the Union Pacific had been led by two locomotives — were derailed. Twenty-five people were killed and another 135 injured in the worst U.S. train accident since 1993.

The evident cause of the accident was the result of the Metrolink train's failure to heed a red signal and wait for the Union Pacific to pass it along the single track, as it did daily. Cell phone records, however, show that the engineer of the Metrolink, one Robert Sanchez, 46, had received a text message at 4:21:03, to which he responded by texting back at 4:22:01. The accident then occurred precisely 22 seconds later at 4:22:23. Sanchez didn't even have time to apply the brakes, whereas the driver of the Union Pacific only saw the commuter train coming at him four seconds before impact, and had just applied his brakes when the two trains smashed together. The sound of the crash must have been terrifying. Sanchez, needless to say, did not survive it.

He had, furthermore, been texting all day, even though it was against Metrolink policy for him to do so. He had received seven and sent five text messages between 3:00 P.M. and the time of the accident. Earlier that morning — he had worked a split shift on that day — he had received 21 text messages and sent 24 while running a train between 6:44 A.M. and 8:53 A.M. (Supposedly, he had taken a two-hour nap at about noon, and went back on shift at 2 P.M.)

A teenage train enthusiast by the name of Nick Williams told reporters that he had exchanged three text messages with Sanchez, whom he considered a mentor. He claims to have received the engineer's message at 4:22, in which Sanchez said he would be meeting up with another passenger train later that day. A photograph of the teen's phone with the message on it from Sanchez reads:

> Inbox (10/44)
> Date: Sep 12, 04:22 pm
> Yea ... usually @ north
> Camarillo
> From: Rob Sanchez Metr

"I just replied back, 'good deal,' ... and I never got a response back," Williams said.

Revolutions

As French theoretician Paul Virilio has pointed out, there have been two great revolutions in technology since the nineteenth century.[1] The first is the transportation revolution that began somewhere in the early decades of that century with the advent of the railroad and the steam ship, and then later on, with the perfection of the internal combustion engine, came the automobile. In the twentieth century, this was completed with the airplane and the rocket that carried men to the moon in 1969. The essence of this revolution was its ability to move the human physical body about through space, thus traversing vast distances in ever shorter and shorter intervals of time.

The second revolution was the communications revolution inaugurated virtually simultaneously, first with the electric telegraph in 1837 and wire services like the Associated Press in 1846, and then in 1876 the telephone and in the 1920s, radio. In the 1940s came television and in the 1960s the launching of the geosynchronous satellites of Howard Hughes, which wrapped the planet in an invisible sheath of electromagnetic radiation that carried human voices and images through the air at the speed of light.

The first revolution brought about an increase in human mobility and sociability: relatives and friends, hitherto separated by months or even years of traveling time, could now meet up with each other in days or hours. The results were physical, corporeal and concrete. But this is not the case with the communications revolution, in which not people, but *phantoms sent in their stead,* were now beamed around the world in the form of detached voices, flickering low resolution images and liquid crystal ghosts. People were not present, but rather became *telepresent.* Shades and revenants straight out of the underworlds described by ancient myths and epics were, for the first time, made tangible by the media. These were not physical humans, but ghostly excrescences of their physical selves made out of electrons and photons rather than atoms and molecules.

In the case of the Los Angeles Metrolink crash, it becomes possible to see how these two arcs of technological novelty crossed each other's paths with catastrophic consequences. A phantom presence materialized in the form of text messages sent by a teenage train enthusiast managed to capture the engineer's consciousness for just long enough to divert his attention away from the task at hand, namely managing the physical transportation of a trainload full of people, which he carried, as it were, on his back like Saint Christopher bowed over with the weight of Christ as he wades across the river. The telepresence of the thoughts of a teenager, made visible to Sanchez on the liquid crystal display of his cell phone, acted with asymmetric force to bring about the destruction of two mighty trains, weighing hundreds of thousands of pounds each. The phantom thoughts of a teenage boy, in other words, brought about one of the biggest train wrecks in United States history.

There is a Manichean conflict hidden in the smoking ruins of this train wreck, a conflict between technologies of light and transcendence on the one hand, and those involving the manipulation of elemental forces of metal and steel which have been extracted from the earth's mineralogical realm and forged into engines of mass transportation, on the other.

Human Prostheses of the Matrix

Cell phone technology works by overlaying a hive of electromagnetic hexagons — each hexagon complete with its own tower, having a radius of about ten miles — on top of the city like a second, invisible city, creating a further layer of striations. The signal of the driver of an automobile talking on a cell phone is relayed from tower to tower as she travels along the road, enveloped in an etheric bubble of low frequency radiation that bends and warps and elongates with her movements.

The architecture of this network is of a kind that theoretician Peter Sloterdijk would call "foamic" in that foam is a subtle web of cavities and walls with a delicate but structurally sound integrity. In his *Spheres* trilogy, Sloterdijk points out that with the breakdown of our global macrosphere — i.e., the cosmological immune system made out of gods, angels and filaments of myth which once protected the European mind during the so-called metaphysical age — each individual has now, within the post-metaphysical age, to exist within his own private microsphere. The sum total of these microspheres results in the creation of a kind of social foam that resists integration into a single larger macrosphere that would absorb them all, such as was once the case with God, for instance, or Plato's Living Cosmos.

Only in an age in which the private microsphere of the individual has become the basic elementary socio-cosmological unit, could cell phone technology exist. Indeed, the technology itself actually makes the hidden ontology visible. We have cell phones because each of us is now a world-island, a cosmos-in-miniature, unto himself and the cell phone, correspondingly, is a technological outgrowth made possible by this basic ontological fact of the status of the human individual who now exists "outside" of any protective macrosphere.

Each of us *is* a cell whose life now tends to center around cell phones as his point of axial rotation. The phone itself, with its square-shaped liquid crystal display, is an individualized electro-island parceled out from the Matrix, to which the individual nevertheless remains connected by invisible electro-magnetic umbilical cords.

When you press the phone to the side of your head, a microsphere of low frequency radiation erupts with plasma lines that connect you, umbilically, to the nearest cell phone tower which, in turn, cycles your pulse signals through the Matrix to which we are all, nowadays, connected in one way or another. The island of the tiny liquid crystal window in your phone is *your* personal portal to the Matrix, which connects *you* to the Great Hive, the macro–Matrix of pulse signals, electronic grids and glowing microprocessors of which we are all now human prostheses.

The Invasion

The cell phone as it is held up to the side of the head emits a non-ionizing bubble of radiation that swallows half the skull and soaks the brain in ELF radiation. Unlike gamma rays or X-rays, this is non-ionizing radiation, so it is not supposed to be dangerous, yet microwave ovens use exactly the same technology to boil water in just about one minute. The brain is mostly made up of water. It is therefore small wonder that many people believe that the recent rise in incidences of brain cancer is connected with cell phone use.

Apart from the mechanics of cell phone–human tissue interactivity, we have to consider the ontological issue raised by the invasion of one's personal bodily space with radiation technologies. If, as the result of the collapse of our civilizational macrosphere, the only thing each of us has left in the way of a personal immune system is our own microsphere, then cell phones represent a truly invasive presence indeed, for they actually force entry into the physical space occupied by one's own body. The results of this invasion are left behind in the form of a scission: the shadow of ELF radiation cast by the anomalous formation of cancerous cells — sometimes even assuming the very shape of a cell phone antenna — that mark the fatal non-symbiosis of human biology with electronic systems.

Once again, Manichean technologies of light disrupt and overthrow physical matter, in this case, living tissue. Just as the pulse signal of the teenage train enthusiast demonstrated its ability to overturn matter by crashing two trains together, so at the level of human biology, it announces its power by creating a cancerous tumor, the personal equivalent of a train wreck. Thus, technologies of light interfere with the realm of matter on yet another plane.

It is no wonder that movies featuring the scenario of alien invasion have proliferated with alarming frequency precisely during the period in which cell phones came into popularity, from *The Puppet Masters* in 1994, to the recent remake of *Invasion of the Body Snatchers* entitled *The Invasion* in 2007. We *are* being invaded, and our bodies know it, and this invasion is being depicted in imagistic form via the subliminal perceptions of our poets and screenwriters. The capturing of the human head by a halo of pulsing energy finds its dream analogue in Robert Heinlein's novel *The Puppet Masters*— of which the film version was released in 1994 — in which humanity is invaded by small larval slugs which attach themselves to the back of the skull and proceed to hi-jack the individual's central nervous system while communicating through "direct conference" with other slugs. As McLuhan was fond of saying, the artist is the Distant Early Warning System of a society and in *The Puppet Masters,* which was written in 1951, Heinlein seems to have been very prescient indeed regarding our current situation.

Cell phones, in the metaphoric picture language of the psyche, are very much akin to alien invaders from another world who have dropped down out of nowhere in order to seize human brains and hi-jack them by implanting parasites inside them, parasites with their own agendas. Science fictional scenarios are rarely just pure products of human fancy: they are the body's semiotics attempting to communicate the dangers of a very concrete situation which the mind is only peripherally aware of, if at all.

Disembodied Voices

Electronic technologies of communication are little machines designed for the capture of human consciousness, and this is most especially the case with cell phones. When you are talking on a cell phone, or texting with it, your consciousness is momentarily captured and decontextualized from the specific circumstances of the immediate lifeworld into which you have been "thrown" at birth, as Heidegger would put it.

In fact, Heidegger's critique of science is worth pausing for a moment to consider here. According to him, science, in questioning the world from a theoretical point of view, de-vivifies the lifeworld and divorces objects from the particular circumstances of their historical becomings, transforming them into pure "things" which are objectively real, but yet completely decontextualized. Things thus become pure objects. "When I attempt to explain the environing world theoretically," he writes, "it collapses upon itself. It does not signify an intensification of experience, or any superior knowledge of the environment, when I attempt its dissolution and subject it to totally unclarified theories and explanations."[2]

Human selves, likewise, are dehistoricized by the same process. The historical "I" embedded in a particular lifeworld is transformed into a merely theoretical "I" just as it transforms an object into a pure "thing" decontextualized from its particular historical Umwelt. This theoretical "I" is of course the Cartesian *cogito* or the Kantian transcendental self, the subjective correlate of the realm of pure objects existing in a theoretical phase space, the same phase space configured by the Cartesian x and y axes.

Cell phones are avatars of this purely theoretical realm, the realm of data and facts, of numbers and diagrams, for they are tiny units which transform the flow of living experience into the realm of "pure digitized information." They do the same thing to human consciousness, for when you are talking on your cell phone, your consciousness has been captured, divorced from the surroundings of your lifeworld, and taken up into the pure realm of disembodied and digitized information. Meanwhile, your body is left behind, where the lifeworld has continued to unfold as it always does, with or without your mind's participation. There now exists a gap, mediated by an electronic device, between your consciousness and the realm of flowing, unfolding experience. By the time your consciousness has crossed back over this gap, the temporal circumstances have already changed, as Robert Sanchez found out the moment he finished sending his last text message.

Cell phone technology, then, is inherently Gnostic: it is designed for the manipulation of human consciousness, to move it across synaptic clefts and over thresholds into the Matrix with which it then interfaces. It leaves the body completely out of account.

The technologies of mass transportation, meanwhile, are specifically designed to move the body about through space at high speeds. The aims of both technologies, then, are fatally incompatible, for electronic communications technologies are specifically designed to manipulate consciousness while leaving the physical world untouched. When I am on my cell phone, "I" am no longer really "there" at a particular point in spacetime, where my body remains to continue with its activities. This is why people who are talking on cell phones while trying to do other things like make purchases or drive cars are so annoying. They aren't really "there" at all; their minds have been captured into the theoretical realm of 1's and 0's, leaving only their bodies behind devoid of conscious attention, like zombies. Hence, the current popularity of zombies in movies, books and graphic novels like *The Walking Dead*.

Did you ever have the impression that a man talking into his cordless headset while walking around seems very much like a man talking to himself? Thus, modern electronic technology manages to retrieve and recreate the conditions for ancient psychoses — people talking to "voices" inside their heads — or ancient mythic situations.[3] The characters of the *Iliad,* for instance, are often disengaged from the immediate circumstances of the battle by the voices of the gods who are always telling them what to do. When Achilles reaches for his sword to kill Agamemnon early on in the epic, it is Athena who appears, *visible only to him,* and stays his hand. In a society like ours lacking a polytheistic ontology, such an individual will later be captured by Foucault's Great Confinement into the asylums of the 17th century. Nowadays, though, such scenarios are a commonplace, for cell phones have managed to recreate the conditions in which people are seen talking to voices of entities that aren't really "there" at all.

Thus, cell phones have technologized the voices of the gods from ancient myth; they are therefore allied with the realm of the phantasmal. There is something uncanny about the technology which they make possible, which brings down a world of disembodied souls, spirits, voices and avatars into a highly mechanized civilization based on mass transportation, of moving bodies quickly about through space. The intrusion of such phantom presences can only act as a hindrance to such a situation, since the two technologies, the Gnostic one of electronic communications and the materialistic one of rapidly moving heavy machinery, are totally at odds with each other. The one technical system has evolved out of a European consciousness that was based on using heavy equipment to move things about in physical space: windmills to channel energy, printing presses to harness ink and paper, steam engines to extract energy from coal and use it to move machines about, etc. The other technical system of electric communications has nothing to do with this world of Newtonian mechanics, but is rather more closely allied to the Magical consciousness structure of the primitive mentality: the realm of disembodied souls and spirits flitting about the astral plane. It reconfigures a structure of consciousness which is totally at odds with the mechanical one.

So, as I have said, there is a Manichean conflict raging throughout our technical systems right now, a conflict in which the appearance of non-material apparitions, of fragments of bodiless consciousness, can suddenly irrupt into situations in which large populations of physical bodies are being manipulated through space by machines of mass transit, and suddenly derail entire operations.

Our technological "ghosts," as they become more and more sophisticated, are beginning to pose an ever greater danger for the world of rapid transit that we have brought into being. Plane crashes, car crashes, train wrecks: it would be interesting to know exactly what proportion of such catastrophes have resulted from the intrusion of such "ghosts."

My guess would be that, since the rise of cell phones in popularity during the mid 1990s, the figures are steadily climbing, for it is the telos of cell phones to disrupt all flows whatsoever: the flows of traffic, the flows of cellular mitotic reproduction in the brain, the flows of thought, the flows of commerce; indeed, amongst terrorists, they even disrupt the flow of empire.

To say that cell phones, then, are a type of "disruptive" technology, would be an understatement.

10

The Killing Eye: Video Games, Surrogate Violence and the Dismantling of Social Machines

Prophet of the Labyrinth

Kafka was the prophet of the video game. All his stories and novels depict a central protagonist engaged in battling his way through some impossible bureaucratic machine toward an eventual, and usually unattainable, goal. K., for example, the hero of *The Trial,* must navigate his way through a labyrinthine judicial system on a quest to find out what he is accused of. In the end, he loses the game: he is taken out to a back lot and executed without even knowing why. In *The Castle,* likewise, the goal is to wend one's way through the town and its strange social hierarchy in order to find a point of entry into the actual castle itself, but in this case, the novel ends abruptly, with K. having failed to make any headway at all.

Indeed, the labyrinth is *the* structuring archetype of all video games, no matter what their premise: from *Pac-Man* to *Halo,* the goal is always to find a *way,* to trace a path through a striated landscape that twists and turns, confounding the player at every step, as he makes his way toward the ultimate goal of freedom from the overcodings of the system imposed upon him. It should not be forgotten that in ancient myth the labyrinth was always connected with the realm of the dead and was usually built for the purpose of housing monsters or evil spirits that the dead person would have to reckon with before he could enter the Blessed Land proper. Thus, the Cretan labyrinth housed the Minotaur, the misbegotten offspring of King Minos who would later become one of the judges of the dead in Hades, while Theseus could only navigate his way through Daedalus's impossible structure with the aid of Ariadne, just as in *Halo,* the Master Chief battles the alien race known as the Covenant with the aid of Cortana, a female artificial intelligence who serves as his sidekick and guide.

But of course, in today's world, the labyrinth has lost its afterlife connotations for the most part, and now stands in for the impossible complexity of the city-as-monstrosity, the Megalopolis which has swallowed us all up and from which we cannot escape. In J.G. Ballard's short story, "Concentration City," the hero who dreams of reinventing the lost science of flight takes a commuter train in order to find out where the limits of the underground city he inhabits might lie, but to his disappointment, the train's lengthy journey only brings him back to where he started, for the city-as-labyrinth is an enclosed structure from which there is no longer any escape.[1] Ballard's story makes the point precisely: in Modernity, we are all damned to inhabit the confines of the steel and glass behemoths in whose guts we thrive, like bacteria, and which, from birth to death, inscribes us with its vast, endless system of overcodings. The Underworld *is* the city nowadays, and we are all the living dead who inhabit it.

The modern state, to speak in the language of Deleuze and Guattari, is an apparatus of capture which codes everything that moves through it, like the tattooed numbers branded into the flesh of the denizens of Auschwitz. If we are machines of desiring production, as Deleuze and Guattari point out in their *Anti-Oedipus,* then our desires are controlled and repressed by the cold, inhuman processes of inscription which the social machine inflicts upon each and every one of us.[2]

In primitive societies, desires were coded through inscriptions performed upon the body itself. Hence, the significance in such societies of scarification, tattooing, circumcision, the knocking out of teeth, etc. Here, it is the physical body which becomes the primary medium for inscription.[3] Pain, as Nietzsche pointed out, is the best mnemonic device there is. Hence, culture is an elaborate and organized system for inflicting cruelty as a means of social control.

But with the rise of the first states, inscription shifts to such media of communication as clay, papyrus, vellum, stone, and so forth. Writing is aligned with the voice and desires are coded and controlled through transportable media. Laws are inscribed in stone and posted for all to see:

hence the Law Code of Hammurabi or the Ten Commandments. The body is no longer the locus of inscription of such codes, for now it is the memory itself which is inscribed via written media. To be able to read is to inscribe words upon the retina of one's memory, where the new social codes are tattooed from henceforth.[4]

Nowadays, codes are inscribed upon the psyche via technology. Hence, Kafka's story, "In the Penal Colony," in which a giant machine inscribes onto a man's body the nature of his crime, is metaphoric of the process by way of which the modern human being is coded and controlled by the vast machine of the state. From cradle to grave, we are marked, scarred and psychologically damaged by vast, impersonal institutions that seek to code our every step: from schools to corporations, hospitals, prisons, nursing homes and the various governmental tentacles of bureaucracy — the department of this, the department of that — the modern individual is a hapless and ineffectual pawn of impersonal bureaucracies that seek to constrain and corral him like a Pachinko ball into one of the slots. The human individual once again, as in the days of primitive societies, has become the tablet to be written upon with social codes, although in this case it is his mind and not his body that is inscribed.

Hence, the function of video games: they are attempts to provide the modern human individual with a means for inscribing his own line of flight that will allow him to evade the system's overcodings. The archetypal video game persona is engaged in an attempt to trace a line of flight through an apparatus of capture which is always metaphoric, in one way or another, of the modern social machine which scars his existence with a nearly unmanageable system of overcoding. The specifics of the system which the protagonist battles do not matter, be it a castle (in *Final Fantasy*), a science fiction world of floating interstellar rings (as in *Halo*), a ghost-infected astral plane *(Silent Hill),* or even the metropolis itself *(Grand Theft Auto)*; it is always an apparatus of capture which the game avatar must combat in order to clear a path that will lead to a singularity in his life trajectory: the attainment of freedom from the coded flows imposed upon him by the social machine.

The media, then, actually have it backward: video games are not the problem, they are an attempt at a solution, for they are designed to provide the beleaguered individual with a map and a set of tools for freeing himself from a social machine that has him cornered. They are populist therapy, a solution to a generalized problem that everyone living in today's world, whether he knows it or not, is plagued with, namely, a technocratic system that is so heavily burdened with taboos that it makes life barely tolerable in an age in which we in the West are supposed to have attained the highest degree of freedom yet imagined by any society anywhere in the world, past or present.

The popularity of video games, however — for they make even more money than Hollywood — tells an altogether different story.

Decoding the Flows

Sticking with the language of Deleuze and Guattari a little while longer, we may say that a coded flow means that something is allowed to *pass through* while something else is *restricted*. In all civilizations, the flow of water, for instance, is regulated by the codes imposed by dams and dykes; in contemporary society, the material flows of utilities such as electricity are coded by the grid that regulates them; in social flows, particularly in the age of globalization, the passage of immigrants across borders must be coded with passports and legal documentation; flows of thought are controlled by advertising and the media; and then there is the always ubiquitous problem of coding the somatic flows of menstrual blood, urine, feces, and other bodily effluvia which have to be carefully controlled with taboos and proper sanitation.

Thus, Deleuze and Guttari's theory of society is a generalized theory of flows. It is the business of society, then, to code these flows. And it is the business of video games — whether the game makers know it or not — to provide the consumer with the means for their undoing.

Decoded flows are a society's worst nightmare because they are anarchic. In a primitive society, for instance, the economy is coded as barter: the transaction is purely one of physical objects between two people. But the quickest way to destroy such an economy is to decode it by introducing money, as in the case of colonization: money is a decoded flow that destroys barter by introducing a generalized abstract equivalent for the transaction, a transaction that can be taxed by the state and kept track of. One is always and forever indebted to the state in such an economy, because one always owes the state in one way or another, from taxes to military conscription.

It is only in the Golden Ages of ancient myth that *all* the flows are decoded, for in the beginning, everyone and everything is running around free. Adam and Eve before the Fall exist in a decoded state of uninhibited flows. It is precisely such a state that video games help the modern individual to retrieve. They are therefore inherently mythic, for they supply narrativized scenarios designed to allow the individual to figure a way back to the state before the Fall, a state of freedom in which the overcodings of the social machine cease to function.

In *Pac-Man,* for instance, the desire is to trace an endless line of consumption while avoiding the codes imposed upon one by the ghosts, which represent the traces of the ancient Japanese cult of the revered ancestors. The goal is to avoid them and the attendant sting of conscience which they represent while following a specifically modern path of consumption traced out on the Western economic model. The semiotics are Japanese, yet the ghosts are sufficiently generic to stand in for any kind of social coding whatsoever. Hence, the game's worldwide popularity.

The specific semiotics may differ from game to game, but the video game as a medium represents the creation of a micro-environment designed to allow the individual to *undo* the codes which the socius has inscribed upon him. Take *Space Invaders,* for instance, which was produced by a Japanese company in 1978 and represents the birth of the semiotically coded video game: the scenario of death from above, raining down instruments of destruction upon cities is of course a narrativization of the bombing of Hiroshima and Nagasaki. But the scenario of death from above is also an archetypal one: in ancient myth, for example, it was the gods who rained down death and destruction from the heavens, as in the case of Yahweh's savaging of Sodom and Gomorrah. However, in the age of the Cold War, this specifically Japanese scenario took on universal resonance with its connotations of the fear of nuclear missiles destroying all the world's cities, which Atari made lucidly clear when they transformed *Space Invaders* into *Missile Command* in 1980, a much more naked and literal statement of the Cold War scenario haunting the apocalyptic imagination of the 1980s. In either case, the task at hand was to undo the coding of the nuclear fear inscribed into the contemporary socius.

In 1982, Williams's *Robotron* anticipated the release of James Cameron's first *Terminator* film in 1984, with its scenario of swarms of homicidal robots converging on the game avatar from all directions, intent on wiping him out. This, in turn, was a reworking of Atari's premise in 1979 of *Asteroids,* in which the persona took on the form of a tiny spaceship under assault by space debris hurtling at it from all directions at once. In both cases, the arcade games pictured the contemporary individual in situations in which he was under assault from huge impersonal systems that were metaphoric of the overcodings of the state bureaucracy converging on him with its demands no matter which way he turned.

Destroy the machine and you undo its ability to impose the codes.

The Individual as Epic Hero

The desires of the human individual in today's society are simply passed over as meaningless by comparison with the needs of its great institutions: the human being now exists to serve the megamachine, either as a cyber-soldier in some far flung desert battlefield, or else he mortgages away his soul in servitude to one or another transnational corporation that holds him in its keep like the clichéd image of a Medieval slave working in a dungeon. With such monstrous mechanical behemoths astride the landscape, the human individual is scaled down to the size of an ant and robbed of all his power and capacity to do anything except become a bystander as the behemoths rip each other to pieces.

Thus, from *Don Quixote* to Kafka's *Metamorphosis,* the history of Western literature is largely a chronicle of the gradual disempowerment of the human being, stripped of his world-shaping potency and reduced to the level of a bug lying on its back, wriggling its legs in a desperate effort to right itself, an effort that is ultimately doomed to failure.

But now enter the video game: the means for his salvation is the activation of a private electronic puppet theater which confers upon him— as does all electronic technology—an asymmetric importance that is out of all scale to his social insignificance. With the might of the video game, the human being is scaled up in power and importance, just like Alice after taking the pill that makes her grow, and finds himself suddenly equal to the impersonal powers of the megamachine that victimizes him on a daily basis. Now the odds are even, and with the asymmetric power conferred on him by electronics, it is a fair fight.

Through video games, the human being is scaled back up to properly human status. He isn't a bug anymore. Instead, he finds himself availed of powers and abilities equal to the heroes out of ancient myth and legend who fought great battles against dragons, ogres and giants, and more often than not, won the battle. The video game restores to the contemporary individual the mythic significance and dignity that the human being once possessed in the days of the old great epics of world literature. While playing a game like *World of Warcraft,* he finds himself in the role of a character out of the *Volsunga Saga* or the *Kalevala,* capable of holding himself with dignity and of being addressed by his peers as a force to be reckoned with.

Thus, the video game is actually a disguised myth machine which envisions epic scenarios that allow the human individual to personally participate in the creation and defense of civilizations, a role absolutely denied to him nowadays by the colossal structure of the industrial state within which he is embedded, and which is completely indifferent to his existence.

Grand Theft Auto *and J.G. Ballard*

In the case of a video game like *Grand Theft Auto,* however — which was originally released in 1997 for Sony PlayStation, but which has gone through several incarnations since — the game avatar is not a defender of civilization, but rather has become its primary threat. In this game, the player becomes a criminal on the loose, able to run around a fictionalized city, terrorizing its inhabitants: he can steal a car from anyone, shoot and kill anyone with no consequences, including policemen who try to stop him. He can start fights, which are depicted with extremely graphic detail in the later versions of the game; blood spurts everywhere, as he runs through the city from carjacking to carjacking, robbing, raping, stealing and killing. So *this* is what it's like to be a criminal, the player thinks. How fun!

Grand Theft Auto is an extremely popular game (it has sold over 70 million copies worldwide). PlayStation, back in the mid–1990s, reinvented the home video game console by transforming the old two-dimensional graphics of SEGA and Nintendo into vivid, Hollywood-like three dimensional game-universes. At first, *Grand Theft Auto* was only two-dimensional, providing the player with a top-down, bird's eye view of the city, thereby distancing him from the action. But with *Grand Theft Auto III,* released in 2001, all this changed, for the point of view descended to the street level down below, where everything takes place as though a real human being were running amok through a vivid, three-dimensional cityscape.

I am afraid it is not easy to explain the popularity of *Grand Theft Auto* and other games like it which assume a shooter's point of view, such as *Halo* or *Doom* (this latter game was a favorite of the Columbine killers) unless we assume that there is a rather deep and fundamental need in the human psyche to experience violence, even if only in surrogate form. The standard assumption is that peacefulness is the normal human "default" psychological mode and that violence is merely an aberration, an interruption, caused by various pathogenic circumstances — such as class struggle, social unrest, etc. — in what would otherwise remain a psychological steady state of cooperation and altruism. (All you have to do is remove the pathogen in order to get back to this state.) I cannot avoid the overwhelming suspicion, however, that the truth is exactly the other way around, as argued, for example, by J.G. Ballard in his last four novels.

In his masterpieces, *Cocaine Nights* (1996), *Super-Cannes* (2000), *Millennium People* (2003) and *Kingdom Come* (2006), Ballard worked out a complex theory of violence that is as fresh and original as anything out of Nietzsche. Take, for example, the plot of *Super-Cannes,* in which an aviation magazine editor named Paul Sinclair and his wife Jane, a doctor, are invited to a utopian office business park called Eden-Olympia located near Cannes and overlooking the French Riviera (it is based on a real office park known as Sophia-Antipolis, located in France to the northwest of Antibes). Jane has been invited to take over the position of the resident pediatrician, formerly occupied by one David Greenwood, a man she knew. But Greenwood, just a few months earlier, had gone on a murder spree at the office park, shooting and killing seven of its executives and three hostages before turning the rifle on himself. No one knows why.

Sinclair, who has been suffering from bad knees due to a recent plane crash, finds himself with a lot of time on his hands and so decides to find out what happened to Greenwood. During the course of his investigations, he witnesses some acts of apparently racially motivated violence in and around Cannes: in a car garage, he watches some security men from Eden-Olympia beat an Arab and a Senegalese trinket salesman nearly to death, while executives look on; in a red-light district one night, these same leather-jacketed security men show up to club prostitutes and their pimps with truncheons; later, the same men raid a posh party in a Cannes mansion where Japanese ad executives involved in making a commercial are beaten and nearly killed.

In conversation one morning with Eden-Olympia's resident psychiatrist, one Wilder Penrose, Sinclair finds out the reason for these acts of violence: Penrose has invented a new form of therapy for the park's overworked and stressed out executives who, upon his arrival at the park four years earlier, had collectively suffered from lowered immune systems and non-existent sex lives. Penrose discovered, by chance, that when these executives were treated to acts of random brutality, such as attacking the local Arabs or Russian prostitutes — whether performed by themselves, or else on their behalf by Eden-Olympia's rugged security men — their immune systems started functioning perfectly. Their sex lives with their wives improved, and the various clouds of depression that had hovered over them vanished. As Penrose explains to Sinclair:

> Homo sapiens is a reformed hunter-killer of depraved appetites, which once helped him to survive. He was partly rehabilitated in an open prison called the first agricultural societies, and now finds himself on parole in the polite suburbs of the city state. The deviant impulses coded into his central nervous system have been switched off. He can no longer harm himself or anyone else. But nature sensibly endowed him with a taste for cruelty and an intense curiosity about pain and death. Without them, he's trapped in the afternoon shopping malls of a limitless mediocrity. We need to revive him, give him back the killing eye and the dreams of death.[5]

Paul eventually discovers that Greenwood's murder spree had not been random at all, but an attempt to kill Penrose and the chief executives responsible for putting this violence therapy into action, and for converting Greenwood himself to its degrading ethos, for Greenwood had been running a child prostitution ring for the executives, and, fed up with self-loathing, had set about to put a stop to it.

Notice how similar Penrose's therapy program is to the theory I have proposed about video games: both involve an attempt at decoding repressive flows that have been inscribed upon the individual by the socius, and both use violence as the means of (re)achieving this primordial state of originally uninhibited and decoded flows.

I would argue further that it is precisely video games that have given contemporary humanity back this "killing eye," even if only in surrogate form. After all, are not video game style combat simulators used by the military more and more often to train soldiers going into battle? When the tanks invaded Iraq, the drivers were described as listening to heavy metal music with songs such as "Kill, motherfucker, kill!" And they shot at targets as if they were playing a video game. How many people will a 16 year old adolescent have killed from the angle of his shooter perspective games before he is an adult? There *is* a connection between virtual violence and actual violence, however loath we may be to admit it to ourselves.

The reader should not think that I am concluding that people who play violent video games go on to commit violent acts, but precisely the opposite: that it is largely because so many people play these games that they find an outlet for ancient aggressions which modernity has coded them to repress, and perhaps then channel what would otherwise manifest itself in the form of even *worse* depression, suicide, homicide, etc., than what already exists.

Video games, then, are depth probes sent down into the deepest abysses of the human psyche where they access long buried and repressed desires — to overturn the machines, harm the Other, save civilization, win the girl, etc. — and create bridges to "outer" them in the form of vivid bytes and colored pixels. Video games are desiring machines specifically designed to disrupt, dismantle and scramble social machines. They are, in other words, direct extensions of the amoral Id, whose contents they siphon off like canals built to harness dangerous waters so they won't flood the villages.

Once again, play the game and you undo the codes.

World of Warcraft: *Hell Is Other People*

There is one other dysfunction of which I believe video games to be symptomatic, and that is the breakdown of social relations. *World of Warcraft,* which is currently one of the most popular online social interactive games being played, is the archetypal example of this. The people who play this game log onto a website and communicate with each other using headsets; they interact with each other, however, in the form of avatars, that is, a chosen Medieval-type image of a warrior, troll, dwarf, wizard or what have you, by means of which they manifest themselves in the game universe. Few of these people ever actually meet each other in the real world unless they attend one of the annual conventions sponsored by the game's manufacturer, Blizzard. On *Frontline*'s documentary show entitled "Digital Nation," we see what social interaction at one of these conventions looks like: a huge convention room that is occupied by rows and rows of computer terminals where individuals wear headsets and "interact" with each other by proxy via the video game. It is like something out of a dystopian science fiction film.

One of the girls at the convention rather soberingly reveals the extent to which playing this game can consume one's life: "I got so into *World of*

Warcraft," she says enthusiastically, "that I was getting up at about nine or ten in the morning and I would play straight through the day and I wouldn't log off until about one or two in the morning. I even kind of quit my job because I didn't want to do anything other than play *World of Warcraft*."[6]

This is, to say the least, a disturbing vision of human sociality, a sociality that has gone severely awry. We have fallen so far down into the depths of the machine that we have almost completely eliminated the Other from our lives, substituting him instead for a video monitor screen in which he is safely distanced from us by the numbing mask of an avatar. No wonder James Cameron's *Avatar* was so popular: it dramatized the replacement of the Other with a CGI avatar that is becoming a commonplace in our society. Human relations have been traded out for relations via machines at every level of this society, and moreover, what is so troubling is that few people seem to find anything wrong with this. To me, it is a nightmare come true.

Nowadays, the Other has vanished inside the matrix and been replaced by his digitized equivalent, just as money as an abstract generalized value once upon a time replaced physical objects in the economic transactions of a primitive barter economy. Now we have the generalized abstract equivalents of human beings: digital avatars which act as social bumpers cushioning the increasingly abrasive effects of social interaction in a society in which civility has all but vanished and in which social relations are becoming increasingly more and more unpleasant. Contact with the Other is no longer necessary or even desirable. If, as Sarte said, "Hell is other people," then video games like *World of Warcraft*— and virtual worlds like *Second Life*— are here to ensure that the Other never comes too close to us. The Other is not my neighbor, the Other is my enemy and so he must be defeated in the game. Society is entirely superfluous and may be dispensed with. Only the self matters.

We are becoming a nation of frighteningly self-preoccupied individuals interested only in themselves and their own private microverses. Gated communities and walls keep out the suffering of others which we do not wish to be burdened by, and if it troubles us too much we can always vacuum clean our guilt by buying a Starbucks coffee which donates part of the proceeds to one or another charity. And if we really feel the need to interact, we can always turn on the computer.

Turn on, plug in and say hello to our "neighbors."

"Social community" in the twenty-first century.

11

Robots, Drones and the Disappearance of the Human Being

How Drones Retrieve Aristotelian Physics

When Paleolithic man used an atlatl to send a spear hurling through the air — at, say, a mammoth — he was trying to increase the velocity of the spear by paving, as it were, an invisible pathway for the projectile to follow through space. Thus, as in Newton's First Law of Motion, the object stays in motion precisely because friction and air resistance are minimized. If you could eliminate them altogether, the object would travel through space with an inertial force such that it would never stop moving. Paleolithic man, then, was unconsciously applying Newtonian physics toward smoothing out the pathways of his projectiles.

With the technology of drones, on the other hand, the United States military is retrieving Aristotelian physics, which says that an object stays in motion only so long as it remains in contact with a motive force. Remove the force, and the object comes to a stop. Thus, when the spear leaves my hand, its motion dissipates because it no longer has any force applied to it.

But a drone is a projectile that always stays in motion precisely because it never loses contact with its motive force. The mover is an electronic pulse signal that is relayed to it from a satellite in outer space which, in turn, receives its signal from an air base in Nevada. The motive force may be invisible, but it is there, real and tangible, and *never* loses contact with the drone, which is precisely why the drone can stay in motion for so long. The Predator drone, after all, can remain in the air for up to twenty-four hours, although Boeing is already at work on a glider powered by solar energy and liquid hydrogen that will be able to stay aloft for seven to ten days. Future monstrosities, however, such as the VULTURE drone, will be able to stay aloft for *five years.*[1]

Newtonian physics need no longer apply.

Video Game Training

Video games are now becoming the training camps for contemporary warfare. The killing eye of the video game becomes, in modern warfare, transportable into remote space with the use of drones, which are basically flying cameras. As one Marines project manager says: "We modeled the controller after the PlayStation because that's what these 18-, 19-year-old Marines have been playing with all of their lives."[2]

The basic situation, then, is that of two guys sitting in a bunker in Nevada controlling drones with joysticks, while the Predators or Global Hawks, thousands of miles away in Iraq or Afghanistan, hover in the air, restlessly scanning the ground below for targets.

Says one of these "pilots": "You see Americans killed in front of your eyes and then have to go to a PTA meeting."[3]

First, we had the domestication of plants and animals during the early Neolithic: the teeth and horns of wild animals, such as the mouflon sheep, were selected for less and less dangerous traits, until the animals became relatively harmless and thus a permanent place was made for them *inside* the domestic space of the village compound. Then, elements such as earth (in the form of mudbricks at Jericho c.9500 B.C.), fire (in ceramics and metallurgy c. 6500 B.C.) and water (as Mesopotamian irrigation c.4500 B.C.) were domesticated and made a permanent part of the flows of high civilization.

Nowadays, we are removing the teeth and claws from warfare by extracting physical human beings from the mechanical projectiles that we have spent two or three centuries constructing around them like metallic exoskeletons. Remove the human from the projectile, and you have removed him from harm's way. You have also extracted the toxic element — i.e., the possibility of death or maiming — from war, just like removing caffeine from Coke or alcohol from beer.

Thus, war, too, is finally becoming domesticated, ground up into the gears of the 9 to 5 office world that is the ultimate descendant of the monkish environment structured originally by the mechanical clock, a point which Lewis Mumford once made so many decades ago.[4]

The Eye of Horus

The ancient Egyptian Eye of Horus, like the unmanned aerial vehicles drifting through the skies of the Middle East, was a flying eye, too, just as the drones are flying cameras. Horus, furthermore, as a hawk deity, was also a god of the hunt, whose prey was normally personified by the god Seth in the form of a donkey or hippo, etc. Thus, the flying eye of the drones is a retrieval not only of Aristotelian physics, but also of the Paleolithic hunter searching for his prey, only in this case, the prey happens to be human rather than animal.

Once again, technology is caught in the act of restaging plays from the theater of ancient mythology.

Heroic Age

The great Heroic Age of the humanist aviator — such as the filmmaker Howard Hughes, or the writer Saint-Exupéry, or Beryl Markham, another writer — ended on a very precise date: October 14, 1947, to be exact, the day when Chuck Yeager became the first man to break the sound barrier by achieving the phenomenally outrageous speed of Mach 1 — over 600 mph — in his rocket powered XF-1 plane. Yeager had inaugurated the age of Roland Barthes' *jet-man*, another species of aviator entirely, as Barthes pointed out in his famous essay in *Mythologies*, a more inhuman priest of the god of speed who, with his helmet and silvery outfit, tended to blur together with his machinery.[5]

With the advent of the age of drones, however — which began immediately after 9/11 with the wars in Afghanistan and Iraq — the twilight of Barthes' *jet-man* has now arrived. "Indeed, with UAV's becoming easier to fly and more lethal, 'Maybe you don't need fighter pilots at all,' says retired marine major general Tom Wilkerson,'" a Top Gun fighter pilot himself.[6]

With the Predator or the Reaper, then, the pilot disappears from the machine altogether, having become as superfluous as the old elevator operator who disappeared long ago from elevators. Indeed, the only way we know he was once there at all is that he keeps turning up in old movies (although he does still survive as a vestigial social structure in some department stores in Japan).

One day, our only evidence that the fighter pilot ever actually piloted air vehicles will be the proof furnished by old movies like *Top Gun* or *The Right Stuff*, with their celluloid archaeology showing that he was there once, sure enough, part of these machines, from which he has been surgically extracted like a tumor in order that the machine may run more efficiently without the friction caused by his presence.

The Two Revolutions Become One

With the rise of drones, then, we can begin to see the crossing of the two revolutions which we have discussed in the essay on cell phones, where I pointed out that the technologies of the communications revolution — telegraph, radio, telephone, etc.— are inherently incompatible (or at least *other* than) the technologies of the transport revolution, i.e., trains, cars, jets, etc. A drone, though, is basically a computerized transport vehicle, and so represents the beginnings of a cross-pollination between the technologies of communication and those of transport. When you eliminate the human being from the transport vehicle and replace him with a computer, then we are moving into the beginnings of a substitution of the human nervous system with an artificial one.

The junction of the two revolutions is now beginning to give rise to an explosion in robotics technologies, not only on the battlefield, but in the home as well, where we will soon be seeing robots doing all our chores for us. iRobot, the same company that builds many of these robots for the military, also makes the now very popular robotic vacuum cleaner known as the Roomba, a small disc-shaped robot that knows how to vacuum your entire house for you; Japanese companies such as Honda and Sony, meanwhile, are busy constructing humanoid robot servants like Asimo, a robot that can walk up and down stairs, fetch food for you, and indeed even run, very convincingly. On the horizon, we are about to be invaded by robot pool cleaners, robot brooms, robot mops, robot dusters, robot ditch diggers, robot gutter cleaners, robot guard dogs, etc.

It is a revolution that is analogous to that described by Siegfried Giedion in *Mechanization Takes Command*, where he points out how the modern kitchen as we know it today was invented during the 1920s with the invasion of a whole armada of appliances — electric stoves, refrigerators, fans, freezers, etc.— that rendered the household servant obsolete.[7]

The current invasion of robotic appliances will soon render the human being obsolete within his own home. We are about to witness the disappearance into utter superfluity of the human being.

The Equation

"The robot is our answer to the suicide bomber," says U.S. Navy researcher Brad Everett.[8]

An interesting equation. One worth drawing on the black board:

On one side of the equation, we have the suicide bomber, an individual who risks absolutely *everything* in order to gain his desired effect. We may term his an "eschatological technology." It is a technology, as Paul Virilio points out, that is actually foreign to Islam, but was imported into it from the Japanese Red Army, a terrorist faction run by Lady Fusako Shigenobu back in the 1970s. Shigenobu had an affair with a member of the Popular Front for the Liberation of Palestine (PFLP) and lived in the Middle East for 30 years. She is generally credited, therefore, with the introduction of kamikaze tactics into Islam.[9]

On the other side of the equation, we have the drone, the unmanned aerial vehicle (or land vehicle) from which the pilot has been completely removed. In this case, *nothing* is risked, not even the possibility of injury. It is a *zero casualty* technology in which not humans, but machines, are sent on their behalf to do battle in their stead.

And the results of the equation?

$x = 0.$

In other words, Death, that mysterious, unknown quantity is, for radical Islamists, *everything*, whereas for us, it is, precisely, *nothing*. And since it is nothing, it is not worth risking for *anything*. For us, the Afterlife is a zero, a blank, a simple cessation of existence. For Islamists, it is Paradise, and it is precisely *this* world that amounts to nothing, by comparison.

Facts and Figures

When the U.S. went into Iraq, it had no robots at all. By the end of 2004, it had 150. By the end of 2005, it had 2,400. By 2006, the number had reached 5,000. By the end of 2008, it was somewhere near 12,000.

At a congressional hearing in 2000, Senator John Warner from Virginia stipulated that for the Pentagon's budget by the year 2010, one third of all battlefield aircraft be unmanned, and that by 2015, one third of all ground combat vehicles be driverless.[10]

Autonomous robots on the battlefield, moreover (robots, that is, which are not remote-controlled but rather make their own decisions) are projected by the Army to be the norm in 20 years. Humanoid robots are to take over the role of the infantry by 2025.

This is a sobering thought.

But it is yet another situation which Goethe foresaw, for in *Faust Part II*, he has Mephistopheles and Faust help the German Emperor win a war by constructing an entire army for him out of empty suits of armor which fight in place of real soldiers. The Emperor wins the war, but by spurious means.

Once again, myth becomes reality by means of technological transformations.

The Superfluous Human

What is happening out in our battlefields provides us with a caricatured or exaggerated scenario which can serve to illuminate otherwise hidden or invisible structures that are going on in our everyday world. For instance, consider this interesting quote from Singer's *Wired for War*:

> The more the military used unmanned systems, the more people came to believe that machines brought certain advantages to the battlefield. "They don't get hungry," says Gordon Johnson of the Pentagon's Joint Forces Command. "They're not afraid. They don't forget their orders. They don't care if the guy next to them has just been shot. Will they do a better job than humans? Yes."[11]

Really?

The underlying assumption here is that the human being is totally superfluous, an unnecessary element on the battlefield that merely gums up the efficiency of the operation. But this does not just apply to battlefields, rather it is a syndrome of thought that is currently infecting American society as a whole and is eating away at it like a cancer. Everywhere we look nowadays, we find the same worship of the machine at the expense of the human being, who always comes out of the equation looking like an inconvenient, leftover remainder: instead of librarians to check out your books for you, a machine will do it better; instead of clerks to ring up your groceries for you, a self-checkout will do it better; instead of a real live DJ on the radio, an electronic one will do the job better; instead of a policeman to write you a traffic ticket, a camera (connected to a computer) will do it better. In other words, in accordance with Virilio's aesthetics of disappearance, the human being is actually disappearing from his own society, just as the automobile long ago caused him to disappear from the streets of his cities.

And the problem with this?

Nothing, except that our society is increasingly coming to be run and operated by machines instead of people. Machines are making more and more of our decisions for us; soon, they will be making *all* of them.

The Hive Society

We are not just in danger of dehumanizing ourselves. That, I think, is evident enough. But as things progress, or rather, worsen, we are actually in danger of *deanimalizing* ourselves, for machines are much more like insects than they are like mammals. And their politics, accordingly — as David Cronenberg remarks in his film *The Fly*—are similarly brutal: no mercy, no compassion, no analysis of the subtle nuances of a situation, simply a pre-programmed struggle for survival. We are slowly becoming an insectoid society, a great hive mind run by insect politicians who are in the process of deanimalizing the human being and stripping him of his hard won mammalian traits of emotional warmth and nurturing that are the characteristic traits of all mammals.

A society run by machines is a hive run by insect technologies. We are witnessing the deanimalization of the human being, stripping him not only of the higher, cultural mind (the Greek stratum, you might say) but even of millions of years of mammalian evolution, regressing him back to the level of a seaborne arthropod or crustacean from whence insects are directly descended.

With research into genetic engineering, for instance, soon we will even have eliminated the uniquely mammalian act of giving birth by womb, replacing it with a simulated act of birth by egg through artificial insemination or some even more bizarre act of laboratory genesis.

A more insect-like society will also mean a society that is colder, more cruel, violent and brutal than any other. We will be that much quicker, for example, to go to war, when we have distanced human death and suffering by dislocating it away from those who pull the trigger thousands of miles from the actual scene of combat. Suffering will be distanced by the video screen and will accordingly seem as unreal and ineffectual as it does in video games. Nobody will even shrug their shoulders about it, much less those joystick operators who will come, increasingly as the years go by, to replace actual soldiers on the battlefield, thus numbing their human sensibilities.

Just imagine the sorts of humanitarian catastrophes that will emerge when human beings have been replaced on the battlefield by machines who will fight in their stead, brutally failing to discern between civilians and the enemy proper.

If we had had the availability of such sophisticated drones during the Vietnam war, do you think we could've entrusted a drone — even with a human being at the other end of it — to discern the difference between a South Vietnamese peasant farmer and a Viet Cong? How could a machine possibly tell the difference? Or a human being using only a grainy, low-resolution video monitor?

Indeed, the advent of drones in the military may be the single most sinister development in the entire history of warfare (with the possible exception of the atom bomb), since it will not only eliminate casualties from "our" side, but also such aspects of war which are essential to it (and which Homer well knew) such as compassion, sensitivity and generosity (sometimes appropriate even for the enemy). Indeed, incidents such as occurred at Haditha in Iraq or My Lai in Vietnam, I believe, will become *more* rather than *less* common, for the use of drones in place of the subtleties of judgment made possible by the flesh and blood presence of real soldiers will simply no longer be possible. Civilians will be crushed along with real enemies and no one will show any kind of remorse for these actions whatsoever, since the video game combatants back at the air bases in Nevada will be able to say: "It was the drone who did it, not I."

He will just shrug his shoulders and go to his PTA meeting without giving the matter another thought.

Even war will become inhuman, something which I am afraid that it cannot be allowed to do. Soldiers *must* have consciences about their actions; it *must* bother them that they pulled the trigger on the wrong person at the wrong place at the wrong time; these are the only kinds of things which put checks and balances on their reluctance to pull the trigger in the first place.

Just as in the case of video games, the replacement of soldiers by drones — which, as we have seen, the military fully intends to make happen — will only lead to more trigger happy "soldiers," or rather, joystick controllers, once consequences for the wrong actions have been removed or minimized by distance.

Remember: road rage on the highway is a function of the numbing of human sensibilities by separating individuals into private metal boxes that are moving too fast relative to one another for anyone to guage the nature of the Other's presence. Remove the cars and put everyone back on the streets as pedestrians and I can assure you that road rage will vanish instantly.

The use of drones, in other words, will have a numbing effect on human sensibilities because it will remove the physical human being from the actual GPS coordinates of the horrors of war that are so horrible precisely because *war is costly.* And the greater the cost in human casualties, or in such side effects as post-traumatic stress, the greater will be the reluctance to engage in it in the first place.

If we transform war into a video game, then it will be played like a video game and taken just about as seriously.

12

A Few Words on the Ovei Pod and the End of History

Electronic Isolation Tank

Though they are not well-known at the current time, I foresee a big future for the Ovei Pod. This gadget is a sort of personal electronic isolation chamber made by a UK company known as The Oculas Group, which sells for about $100,000 each at this point, so they are very, very expensive. But then, this is the way almost all new technologies begin, starting as playthings for the rich, like the automobile and the cell phone did, and then becoming gradually democratized and made affordable with popularity. It is a universal economic morphology, extending all the way back to ancient Egypt: Pharaoh gets first privileges for burial accoutrements, then later they are made available to anyone who can afford them.

The Ovei Pod is a kind of electronic sarcophagus which, as its name implies, is an egg-shaped personal isolation unit that comes in black, white, gold or gunmetal gray and is currently custom made to suit the specifications of the consumer. They are sleek and smooth, looking as though they'd been designed by Apple during its iMac period, and would fit unobtrusively into the background of the big public transport ship in the Journey to the Moon sequence of *2001: A Space Odyssey*. It's about the size of one of those video arcade games where you sit in the driver's seat of a car speeding along a racetrack, but in this case, it seats only one person. You climb inside of it and grab an electronic tablet, then click the door shut behind you by pressing the stylus to the proper icon on the tablet. You then find yourself in a *very* comfortable chair, while a video monitor then swings out from the wall in front of you. Lighting can be adjusted to your comfort while you decide whether you want to play video games, listen to music, surf the Net or watch one of the many movies stored in your hard drive. Or maybe you would just — this might require some imagination — prefer to adjust the lights so that you can actually sit back and read a book — on your e-reader, of course — having securely isolated yourself from all external distractions.

In any case, it is an inherently solipsistic technology, one based upon a retrieval of the isolation tank of the 1970s, only here, instead of being immersed in a primordial womb-*welt* of saline solution, you find yourself floating in an electronic ether, just you and your liquid crystal window that looks out into the landscape of the Matrix, that Otherworld of Eternal Forms that has come to displace the delicate figures of Biblical myth that once adorned the stained glass of churches, or the ancient, archaic Animal Beings that once upon a time opened up a vista into the Paleolithic realm of the Ancestors. Those sacred figures are all gone now; instead, they have been replaced by luminous figures from the banal world of virtual malls and Hollywood movies, or else the folkloric warriors of video games. *This* is your mythology now.

It's all you have left.

The Bygone Age of the Macrosphere

It wasn't always this way, though.

Once, only a few centuries ago, you were encased inside of a cosmo-logical macrosphere — to borrow Peter Sloterdijk's term — a protective world womb made out of myth and meaning that enclosed and contained you inside of a *world*, a world defined by the contours of a Three Act myth of Creation, Crucifixion and Apocalypse. No matter what took place around you, be it Black Death or Hundred Years' War, everything made sense because everything was part of a grand macronarrative that put every-thing — including you — in its place like the saints in the niches of a Gothic cathedral. Nothing happened that could not be explained either in terms of the will of God or the more ancient pagan mental fossil of an inscrutable Fate that shattered men's lives whenever it wished. The crises that befell a King Lear or a Hamlet, a Don Quixote or a Wilhelm Meister, were unfoldings of a mythology of meaning and purpose from out of which the individual's life was thought to unfold and take its place amongst the stories of the ancients like new constellations joining those of the Argo or the Lyre in the nighttime sky. A place for everything and everything in its place.

Consider Dante's journey, for example, through a cosmos bounded and encompassed by a universe of spheres within spheres, with a luminous, though fallen, Earth, carefully watched over by divine beings whose project it was to supervise Creation. In response to the anguish of Dante's depression when he is driven from the comforting civic womb of the Medieval walled fortress city of Florence in 1302, Beatrice, hearing his cry, sends Virgil up from the Infernal depths to go into the dark woods of exile and fish Dante from the clutches of the three animals that have confronted him, snarling, outside his city's gates. Virgil then guides him down through the concentrically — and obstetrically — narrowing circles of Hell — earthly mirrors of the concentric spheres of the planets — describing to him, like a museum guide, and in rich detail, the origin and purpose of the fate of every one of Hell's denizens. No one is there without good reason, and this is evidenced by the fact that the dead, who have never seen a living man in the Afterlife before, demand to know the reason for Dante's presence, making the then firm assumption, of course, that there was one. Virgil explains, explains, explains; he explains to Dante the meanings and purpose of God's judgments, and to the dead, the meaning and purpose of Dante's guided tour.

In the process, Dante — the real life Dante — manages to make sense out of the misfortune of being exiled from the city in which he had grown up, i.e., Florence, by seeing it all as part of a larger plan for him to create a literary masterpiece as a second, alternate womb, a cosmic womb, to replace the physical one that had sheltered him as a child growing up in Fiorenza. If he had not been exiled from the first sphere, the civic sphere, it is very likely that he would never have needed to create this second sphere, the literary macrosphere mapping out God's cosmos and explaining it all to his entire Medieval audience in vernacular Italian.

That was in 1300, but by 1500, the world had changed considerably — the printing press, for one thing, had arrived and along with it visual space and depth perspective in painting, as well as new ways of doing things — but nonetheless, the world is still safely ensconced within the sphere(s) of its Christian cosmos in which everything makes sense. We have, as evidence of this, Bosch's famous painting, *The Garden of Earthly Delights*, a sort of visual equivalent of Dante's theology, although containing some very different connotations, for Bosch, according to art historian Wilhelm Fraenger, was a member of a strange and heretical sect known as the Adamites.[1]

Let's take a look at his triptych for a moment and see what it says, through Fraenger's eyes: with the panels closed, Bosch gives us a vision of the cosmos as a giant translucent sphere containing the flat disc of the earth with a tiny Yahweh up in the left hand corner observing with satisfaction his own handiwork. When the panels are opened, we are treated to yet another tri-level vision of the world, this time laid out, however, in terms of the chronology of Joachim of Floris's three ages: the Age of the Father (left panel)—the Son (middle panel)–and the Holy Spirit (right panel). The left panel shows the Garden of Eden just after Yahweh has created Eve by pulling her out of Adam's side. The middle panel gives us the famous (and heretical) vision of earthly delights as a series of erotic encounters, while the third and final panel shows us an image of Hell.

In the left panel, notably, there is a small pool shown in the foreground from which all sorts of strange hybrid creatures are emerging: winged fish, a three headed pelican, lizards, a strange half-fish half-duck-billed creature in the water that is reading a book as symbolic of the fact that even the creatures at the bottom of God's creation benefit from the resonance of His Word. These creatures are all caught up in the process of metamorphosing into something else; they are like alchemical salamanders that symbolize the process of personal psychological evolution. In the middle panel, the myriads of people engaged in one or another amorous encounter are not, as is commonly assumed, on their way to being damned and sent off to Hell in the right panel, for the Adamites had some strange sexual rituals which they practiced as part of their vision of a sexuality taking place during the prelapsarian innocence before the Fall, *before* the act was cursed with shame.

On the right panel, we see Satan sitting on a kind of toilet, devouring humans and shitting them out into a small pool that is the entropic counterpart of the evolutionary pool of the left panel, with the Fountain of Life in the center panel balancing them both. Thus, in Bosch's vision of creation, all aspects of it are in process of evolution and decomposition; everything is in motion through his cosmos, moving from sin and depravity toward redemption and spiritual illumination, for unlike Dante, *his* Hell implies no permanent residence, but is rather a state from which one can be redeemed if one sees the Light and changes one's ways.

In *both* visions of the world, however, Dante's as well as Bosch's, the universe is a place of meaning. No action, however wayward, sinful or banal, goes unpunished or unrewarded. Man's actions, under the dome of this macrosphere, *matter*. Everything is accounted for and all of life is embedded within a womb of *meaning* and *consequence*. A life lived badly will wind you up in Hell. A life lived with proper regard for ethical consequences will create a paradise out of its own momentum. The world itself is a revelation of divine powers which are at work everywhere, in every little detail.

Now, of course, with the various scientific revolutions that followed — from Copernicus to Darwin — this macrosphere of myth and meaning within which the universe was encased, like a protected jewel, and which took the needs of human beings and their concerns seriously, was completely shattered and dismantled, especially when Darwin in 1859 provided his alternate creation myth to that recounted in the Book of Genesis: living forms, he points out, arrived on earth as the result of *competition*, not as the *command* of any divine fiat. There *are* no gods involved in the process of evolution, at any point.

The results of the collapse of this Western macrosphere, however, were utterly catastrophic, for the subsequent events of the 20th century may be regarded as the direct consequence of the destruction of this idea of man situated inside of a world egg of protective spirits and divine (or evil) presences involved in the working out of his fate. The annihilation wars of the 20th century were tantamount to a series of competing master narratives that attempted to rush in and fill this void of meaninglessness with one grand metanarrative or another — such as the myth of Aryan supremacy or the myth of the proletarian worker's oppression and comeuppance — that would seek to replace the deflated Christian meta-narrative, as Alain Badiou has described in his book *The Century*.[2] When the world wars ended, however, it was the democratic and capitalist narrative that won out, a narrative which, unfortunately, has no idea what to make of man *as* man or what to do with him except turn him into an archetypal shopper. Beyond that, the Allied victory offered no larger narratives of meaning whatsoever, and in fact, very soon, with French postmodern philosophy, began to deconstruct the very possibility of the Western mind ever again building such narratives which would situate the human being in a context of world sense and meaning. There has remained, ever since, a gap in our cosmology, in which gigantic and mysterious processes of cosmogenesis take place seemingly without ever acknowledging its great jewel of the entire process: the creation of the human mind.

For a contemporary window into our current world picture analogous to that provided for us by Bosch and Dante, consider a text like Cormac McCarthy's novel *No Country For Old Men*, which shows us the resulting world that we now find ourselves living in, a world bereft of meaning, consequence, justice, ethics or values of any kind, a world in which there is no encompassing protective macrosphere to make sense out of events for us. The serial killer, Chigurh, leaves the fates of his victims to the toss of a coin, for they are random, pointless acts of crude and purposeless violence. Chigurh manages to kill everyone in the story with one (significant) exception — a man whose existence he is not even aware of and played in the movie by Tommy Lee Jones — which is a direct consequence of the meaninglessness of a world in which the hero no longer triumphs over the bad guy precisely because there is nothing left for the hero to stand *for*. *There are no worthwhile values anymore*, McCarthy tells us, in this postmodern world which we have made: *we* are responsible for it and so *we* are responsible for the resulting view of human life as brutal, random and senseless. Hence, the purpose of framing the narrative from the point of view of an old sheriff who remembers the bygone days of conservative small town values during which such acts of brutality were rare and isolated occurrences, precisely because such values tended to prevent such acts from ever happening.

The Personal (and Very Private) Microsphere

But what does any of this have to do with a technological gadget like the Ovei?

Well, it tells us about the type of world whose ontological conditions have made the existence of such a gadget possible in the first place, for one thing. The Ovei clearly illustrates the status of the individual in a world in which there is no longer any protective overarching macrosphere. The individual has become a world-island unto himself and can only protect himself with a technological microsphere like the Ovei, a gadget which has come to replace the ethical-theogonic macrosphere that once made sense out of his life. With the Ovei, the individual can cut himself off completely from the world outside, numbing his body and his mind with comfort while distracting his brain's quest for meaning and questions of value and significance by paralyzing it with the drug of electronic satiety. The very existence of the Ovei is a tacit admission that the *only* thing that matters in our society anymore is entertainment, which the individual may just as well soak himself in, since all other social and ontological systems that once took him into account have failed. Education has failed, the schools have broken down; the state is destructuring; the family is crumbling; the arts and sciences have splintered into a thousand useless and contradictory ideas that no longer add up to any sort of coherent or meaningful world picture whatsoever. The individual, wrapped in his cozy womb of electronic pleasure, is all that is left of a once great civilization.

The Ovei Pod is a monkish cell of nihilism which disavows anything in the world worth living for beyond the state of entertainment. It is, indeed, a physical materialization of the electronic world cavern inside of which the individual currently finds himself a shipwrecked wash-up on the shores of his own world-island, severed from all socially intercommunicative spheres whatsoever.

Indeed, the existence of the Ovei Pod is a confession that Western civilization has failed in its mission of protecting and shaping the individual's cognitive development with a compelling and all-explanatory macronarrative that has a shaping power to inform and educate his mind to think for itself. The Ovei Pod, at the End of History, confesses that an intellectually bankrupt and morally impoverished universe of entertainment is all that Western Civilization has left to offer its citizens in the way of *paideia*. It is the ultimate end result of the digital revolution and perfectly sums up all our previous chapters discussing the various technologies in the foregoing pages, for it shows us, very clearly, where the modern individual, surrounded and encompassed by all these gadgets, is finally ending up (inside of a masturbatory electronic closet).

It is the technology of tomorrow, perhaps, offering us a gleaming, disguised cavern of a civilization in total epistemological-ontological ruins. The cosmic macrosphere has indeed contracted to the point of a private electronic microsphere inside of which the individual can hide while civilization burns all around him.

Some Concluding Comments to Part II: A Miniature History of War and Technology (Since 1815)

Goods do not spring from nowhere. Every new gadget presupposes a long history of technological development which makes the existence of that gadget possible, just as an atmosphere enables a flame to burn. In this chapter, I want to look back, in the spirit of yet another "miniature" history, at the development of this very technological atmosphere, at least since the Industrial Revolution at the turn of the nineteenth century, which made the existence of new media like the Ovei Pod and the Macintosh possible in the first place. I also want to draw the evolution of technology since the ending of the Napoleonic Wars in 1815 as a series of five distinct, structurally stable epochs.

Too often, the cosmological effects of new technologies are overlooked by historians, and in the following sketch, I would like to emphasize some of these effects, for technologies — as we have seen with the Ovei Pod — actually create their own self-enclosed worlds with their own laws and their own possibilities. Every technology is also tantamount to the defining and encompassing — in the sense of a draughtsman's compass — of a technological horizon. Captured and taken up inside of our technologies, we are transformed into passengers looking out the windows of these conveyances at the world speeding past, which is always seen in relation to *a moving window* of technology that frames it via the principle of relativity in the classical Galilean sense: am I stationary on the ship while the terrain moves past me, or is the land stationary while I am moving past it? The nature of the technology determines the nature of nature and also the nature of the answer.

Here, then, is a glimpse of five such moving horizons of technological development since 1815:

I. The Age of Steam, 1815–1861

Interregnum War: Napoleonic Wars
Primary Medium for Documenting War: Oil painting
Archetypal Machine: Steam Engine
Communications Media: Telegraph
Key Text: *Reflections on the Motive Power of Fire* (1824) by Sadi Carnot
Paradigmatic Painting: *Rain, Steam and Speed: The Great Western Railway* (1844) by J.M.W. Turner
Axial Work of Literature: *The Red and the Black* (1830) by Stendahl

Each of these epochs is preceded by a major war (in the case of geological eras, this corresponds to the cataclysm that precedes and clears the stage for the arrival of new species). In this first Age, the Napoleonic Wars, which extended from 1793 to 1815, were an epoch of almost incessant warfare in which Napoleon tried, and failed, to create a universal state by welding Europe together on the political plane. Wars are often great periods of accelerated technological evolution, but in the case of Napoleon's wars, there were not many new technologies, only his new method of all-out warfare respecting no traditional rules of conduct (i.e., no fighting at night, or in winter, periods of sufficient rest in between battles, etc.). Napoleon violated *all* of these rules and shocked Europe — including Egypt — thereby.

But Napoleon's failure to unify Europe on the political plane seems to have been a kind of rehearsal for its unification on the technological plane which immediately followed, as both the new technologies of the railroad and the telegraph embodied mechanizations that crossed national borders just as he had tried to do, and succeeded where he had failed, by uniting all of Europe — including America this time — on the plane of communications.

This first Age, differing from subsequent epochs, was primarily an age of mechanical technologies, steam-driven and centralizing in their impact. The era begins on the plane of theoretics with Sadi Carnot's foundational work on thermodynamics, entitled *Reflections on the Motive Power of Fire,* published in 1824, just before the rise of the railroad (Turner's 1844 painting, *Rain, Steam and Speed* is archetypal for this era).

In 1818, the Black Bull Line had begun regular steamboat service between New York and Liverpool, which had the effect of cutting the time necessary for crossing the Atlantic from three weeks to a mere ten days. This new acceleration of the human body through physical space was followed in 1830 by the first public railroad services: the Liverpool and Manchester railway in England and, in the same year, the Baltimore and Ohio railroad in the eastern United States. By 1851, the New York and Erie railroads were completed and in 1869, the first transcontinental railroad between American coastlines.

One of the economic effects brought about by these railroads was the rise of the department store, for it is not an accident that London's first great department store, Kendal, Milne & Faulkner, opened in Manchester in 1836, just after the railroad had begun operation there. Wanamaker's Great Depot department store in Philadelphia, furthermore, was a converted train depot.

Structurally speaking, this era is an age of centralization, of the building — especially in America — of roads, canals and railroads (the Erie canal, connecting New York and Chicago, was completed in 1825); of the storing and sorting of capitalist goods in huge, warehouse-like stores; but it also begins to exhibit the first signs of the coming decentralization of the cities with the creation of the first suburbs, which were, initially, isolated houses built by the rich across the Hudson and East Rivers in New York. As Dolores Hayden in her book *Building Suburbia* describes, this is the time of Alexander Jackson Downing, who was the first to emphasize in his writings the importance of having huge front and back yards with curvilinear pathways and lots of additional space for gardens.[1] (Downing's sentiments are thus embedded in the American Romanticism of nature of this period.) This development of the suburb was soon followed by a second phase of "enclaves" when whole neighborhoods and communities for the wealthy were constructed. Commuting across the water to the city, however, remained both expensive and dangerous: Downing himself died in an accident while commuting when his passenger ship caught fire and sank.

A key technological development during this epoch foreshadows what will become a major structural feature of the next with the first practical application of electricity in the 1844 invention of the telegraph. Whereas prior to this period, all human communications — whether spoken or written — were embedded in a material substrate — stored in books in libraries or carried by human messengers through space using conventional means of transport — the telegraph was the first technology to begin to divorce human thought from the world of physical matter and to open up a *separate* world running parallel to the physical one, a world made up of electrical phantoms, ghosts and human telepresence. This is the origins of what I have termed "*sukshma* technology," and it is the first step taken toward what will eventually become the present epoch's characteristic of domination by such luminous gadgets of human communication.

Another important development of this period was the birth of what Paul Virilio has called "the vision machine" with Nicephore Niepce's invention of photography in France around 1826. This was a chemically-based technology — descendant, therefore, of the traditions of alchemy — which, when crossed with electricity, will give birth to the motion picture during the next epoch. Once photography is "plugged in and turned on," as it were, it will become another technology of phantoms, a means of chemically processing and constructing eidolons, just as in Goethe's *Faust Part II*, the shades of Helen and Paris are resurrected from the Underworld of antiquity by alchemical means. Goethe, in this great prophetic work, was already foreseeing the coming of the cult of the movie star.

II. The Age of Electricity (1), 1865–1914

Archetypal War(s): American Civil War; Franco-Prussian War
Primary Medium for Documenting War: Photography
Archetypal Machine: the Dynamo
Communications Media: Wireless Telegraph; Telephone
Key Text: "The Virgin and the Dynamo" in *The Education of Henry Adams*
Paradigmatic Painting(s): *Boating* (1874); *Le Dejeuner sur L'Herbe* (1863) by Eduard Manet
Axial Work(s) of Literature: *Buddenbrooks* (1901) by Thomas Mann; *Remembrance of Things Past* (1913–1927) by Marcel Proust

This age begins with the Civil War (1861-65) in America and the Franco-Prussian War (1870-71) on the European continent. In both of these wars, new technologies played decisive roles in their outcomes: the use of a superior railroad, for instance, helped the Prussians move their troops about much more quickly and efficiently than the French and together with brilliant strategizing (as well as superior artillery) became a decisive factor in the Prussians winning that War.

The Civil War was, however, the first rail war, and set the precedent for the Franco-Prussian war in its demonstrated ability to move troops about more quickly through space with the use of the railroad. The Civil War was also the first telegraph war: the telegraph enabled Lincoln, for instance, to keep in touch with the movements of his generals in a way that had hitherto never before been possible; and it was also the first photography war in the sense that it was the first war ever to be documented by the camera in such intimate detail. Indeed, Mathew Brady's exhibition in 1862 of Alexander Gardner's photographs of the mangled dead on the field of Antietam shocked the general public, for it was the first time it had ever been so intimately exposed to the horrors of the battlefield.

New technologies of destruction were spawned by the Civil War, as well: the use of the first landmines, the first rail artillery, the birth of the battleship (called "Ironclads"), the Gatling gun and new kinds of repeating rifles that enabled the soldier to fire off fifteen shots before reloading; all were created during this war.

Washington Roebling, a soldier who had fought in the Civil War on the side of the north, became chief engineer of his father John Roebling's great engineering project, the building of the Brooklyn Bridge, which took place over more than a decade (1869–1883). The bridge towers, at 275 feet tall, became, in essence, the world's first skyscrapers — they were seven times higher than the tallest of New York City's four-story skyline — and represent the birth of its rise as a vertical city. In Chicago, meanwhile, the steel-framed skyscraper itself was invented by William LeBaron Jenney in 1885, with the construction of the Home Insurance Building, ten storeys high (at 138 feet, however, it was still dwarfed by Roebling's Gothic towers). This was followed by Bradford Lee Gilbert's Tower Building in New York in 1888, which rose to 11 storeys; Post's New York World Building in 1889 (309 feet) at 18 storeys; in 1897, by the Gillender Building (20 storeys; 273 feet); and, in 1902, by Daniel Burnham's Flatiron Building at 21 storeys (285 feet).

And, as though to compensate for these Towers of Babel storming the heavens, between 1900—1904, the New York subway system was constructed as another world *beneath* the city.

Now the prevailing characteristic of this epoch was that of *plugging everything in and turning it "on."* When the Brooklyn Bridge, for instance, opened in 1883, it was fully illuminated by electric light. It is the first bridge in history to be plugged in and turned "on." Indeed, cities began to be illuminated with electric light in the 1880s, after Edison's 1879 invention of the first light bulb.

When you apply electricity to human conversation — that is, "plug it in" — the result is the telephone, introduced by Alexander Graham Bell in 1876 as an offshoot of the telegraph; when you apply electric current to photography, the result is the motion picture, developed in Paris in the 1880s and in America in the 1890s by Thomas Edison; when you apply electricity to the rail, the result is the electric street car, also developed in the 1880s.

One of the primary *effects* of electricity is to decentralize wherever and whatever it touches: thus, the advent of the electric street car and the trolley decentralizes the city by making it possible, for the first time, for the working classes to own houses out in the suburbs, since the new suburbs are built precisely along these trolley car lines. The lighting of cities helps transform night into a perpetual day, thus reversing and decentralizing the domestic realm by making it safer for women and children to go out at night and hence, providing the new entertainment industry of vaudeville theaters, penny arcades and amusement parks with their own built-in audiences. The old opposition of daytime activities vs. nighttime activities begins now, for the first time in history, to disintegrate. The custom of going to the movies or the theater at night — the Greeks, by contrast, performed their plays in the middle of the day — stems from this period.

With the introduction of the Ferris Wheel at the World's Columbian Exposition in Chicago in 1893, the amusement park was provided with its core attraction, which leads to the founding of Steeplechase Park on Coney Island in 1897 — a park directly inspired by the World's Fair — and Luna Park in 1903. These parks were always located at the very edges of the city, at the end of the trolley car lines, which carried their audience out to them from the suburbs and are therefore a structural feature of the decentralization process begun by the application of electricity to the city.

Thus, though the Civil War had the effect of uniting America politically, one of its unforeseen by-products was that the North's electrification of its cities led to the disunification of these cities as, with the rise of suburbs and their associated worlds of amusement parks, arcades and nickelodeons, the splintering and fragmentation of cities into multiple worlds within worlds was set in motion, thus *dis*-unifying cities on the infrastructural plane.

Electricity has the unintended and unforeseeable effect of rapidly generating microcosms within microcosms which tend to proliferate like swarms of Lebnizian monads, creating a kind of social and infrastructural "foam" in opposition to the monospheric worlds that mechanization tends to support and reinforce. Mechanization, through centralization, creates domed, self-enclosed cities as gigantic macrospheres: this effect is one that Walt Disney, for instance, much later on with the building of Disneyland — surrounded originally by a railroad — and EPCOT city — in which the decentralizing automobile was banished — would nostalgically try to revive with his idea of domed worlds ringed round by monorails, railroads, etc. Electricity, though, destroys such worlds with its rapid proliferation of swarms of communities, each supplied with its own civic centers.

Thus, as this first epoch of electricity shows, when you plug a city in and turn it "on," the effect is to destroy it as a city and to recreate it as a swarm of self-contained neighborhoods and communities.

The chapter on "The Dynamo and the Virgin" in Henry Adams' 1906 autobiography, *The Education of Henry Adams*, is the primary cultural studies document which attempts to understand the implications of this epoch.

Edouard Manet's 1874 painting, entitled *Boating*, is constitutive for this epoch because it exhibits the beginnings of the *effects* of electricity on the human sensorium, since it is during this epoch that traditional Euclidean space begins to Balkanize and break apart into multiple spaces, multiple worlds, multiple times. The disappearance of the horizon line in Manet's painting is disorienting — it signifies that the world of this boater and his girlfriend has *broken off* from the macroworld and become its own self-contained microcosm — and intentionally so, since the dissolution of Euclidean space is tantamount to a collapsing of the world as neatly defined, mapped and graphed along the Cartesian x and y axes. *That* age, from here on out, is over, and only non–Euclidean geometries, such as those associated with Gauss, Cauchy, Riemann and Lobachevski, will be adequate to grasp the new multi-body complexities of the dawning Aperspectival Age.

Thomas Mann, in his novel *Buddenbrooks*, and Marcel Proust, in *Remembrance of Things Past* are the great works of literature for this epoch which chronicle the last days of the great European aristocracies and the decline of their empires with the onset of World War I, which destructured the Austro-Hungarian and Ottoman Empires.

III. The Age of Electricity (2), 1914–1945

Interregnum War: First World War
Primary Medium for Documenting War: Cinema
Archetypal Machine: Internal combustion engine
Communications Media: Radio
Key Text: *Mechanization Takes Command* (1948) by Siegfried Giedion
Paradigmatic Painting: *Moonrise and Sunset* (1919) by Paul Klee
Axial Work(s) of Literature: *Ulysses* (1922) and *Finnegans Wake* (1939) by
   James Joyce

This epoch begins with the First World War, the first truly *global* war, another war associated with major technological upheavals. Whereas submarines, battleships, airplanes and dirigibles pre-existed this war, it was nonetheless the first war to make extensive — and cosmological — use of *all* these new machines of transportation. The Germans, for instance, were the first to begin the practice of the aerial bombardment of cities when on September 18, 1915, they bombed London with the use of three dirigibles under the command of Heinrich Mathy. The British response to the German assaults from the air and from beneath the sea with the first U-boats was to invent the tank in November of 1917 at the battle of Cambrai, which was an attempt to solve the problem of mobility over a battlefield gridlocked by trench warfare.

The German navy, largely destroyed by the British early on in the war, was kept in communication by the use of the wireless radio, an invention by Marconi in the decade or so prior to the outbreak of the war. And whereas the Civil War had been the first photography war, so the Great War was the first one to be largely chronicled by the use of the silent motion picture camera. It is the first *cinema* war.

Whereas the vast majority of troops, upon entering the war — as the silent films clearly show — were still riding horses and using oxen to tow cannons and artillery, by the war's conclusion, they were mostly driving trucks, lorries and other gas-powered automobiles.

The automobile, then, becomes *the* archetypal machine of this epoch, for in 1914, there had been about 125,000 New Yorkers who had owned cars, whereas by 1918, when the war was over, there were more than 300,000 of them.

Thus, the essence of the war structurally was its invasion of the three worlds which had composed the fabric of cosmic space in ancient mythology: the upper world (airplanes and dirigibles); the underworld (submarines); and the mid-world (tanks, trucks, etc.). The invasion of these three worlds by the gas-powered engine would thus set the stage for the coming architecture of the cities of this epoch, which would similarly invade all corners of ancient cosmic space with internal combustion engines of every sort. In Russian mythology, for example, we find the story of the shamanic hero Volga of whom it is said:

> Volga grew in strength and stature,
> Eagerly Volga sought wisdom.
> He could swim as a pike in the deep seas,
> Fly as a falcon under the clouds,
> Race as a grey wolf on the open plains.
> All the fish sped away in the blue sea,
> All the birds flew away beyond the clouds,
> All the wild beasts fled away into the dark forest.[2]

In other words, Volga's mastery over the three realms of land, sea and air are meant to demonstrate his powers as a shaman over the entire cartography of ancient myth, just as submarines, airplanes and tanks replace these mythic transformations with mechanized ones as the basis for the creation of the modern global cosmopolis.

On the plane of communications, though, this epoch was pre-eminently that of radio. Whereas the wireless had evolved out of the telegraph, radio evolved out of wireless communications technology — which had enabled the sending of Morse code through the air — and so shortly after the conclusion of World War I, GE created the Radio Corporation of America (RCA) in 1919. The first commercial radio station, KDKA, went on the air in November of 1920, broadcasting the results of the presidential election of Warren Harding. By the following year, there were eight commercial radio stations on the air, and in 1922, there were more than 600. By 1927, more than a quarter of American households owned radios.

Thus, whereas the various transport technologies of the Great War had appropriated the mythological realms of land, air and sea, radio as a *suksma* technology ("radio" means "to radiate") began to retrieve and reappropriate the realm of the dead, transforming human physical presence into discarnate voices that came pouring in through the ether from everywhere all at once, like the shades and revenants of ancient myth. The 1920s was the decade that saw the invasion of the domestic sphere by the underworld of Greek mythology in the form of a radio world of disembodied voices and shadowy beings.

But the 1920s, as Siegfried Giedion pointed out in his *Mechanization Takes Command*—*the* primary cultural studies text, by the way, for understanding this epoch — was also the decade when the suburban home — particularly the kitchen — was invaded by all sorts of new electrical gadgets: the first refrigerators were available by 1922; the first dishwashers in 1924; the first pop-up electric toaster by 1925; the first garbage disposal in 1927; and the first electric fans and electric ovens by the end of that decade. Thus, the 1920s, like the decade between 1995–2005, was a period of massive proliferation of technological gadgets that invaded the home and restructured the domestic sphere entirely, thus causing the domestic servant to disappear. It is no surprise that this decade of rapid technological acceleration ended with the onset of a Great Depression, for too many innovations at once tends to have a destabilizing effect upon economies.

I have chosen Paul Klee's *Moonrise and Sunset* as the constitutive painting of this epoch for its wonderful capturing of the ways in which electricity erodes the distinction between night and day and transforms cities at night into cathedrals of glowing radiance. Also, the sense which the painting conveys of tiny little worlds emerging and sprouting into other worlds reflects the decentralizing effects of electricity on the modern megalopolis. The city, in this painting, is transformed into a ubiquitous presence on land and sea, precisely the effects of radio broadcasting which renders the city omnipresent via the ether. Thus, to spin off one of McLuhan's aphorisms, any truck stop café with a radio becomes as metropolitan as New York or Paris.

And, of course, James Joyce's *Ulysses* is *the* great literary synopsis of the transformation of the city by electricity into a living urban organism all unto itself, in which human beings become merely appendages and bodily organs of the city, just as the chapters of the book function as analogues to the organs of the body of Ulysses himself.

IV. The Age of Electronics, 1945–1995

Interregnum War: Second World War
Primary Medium Used in War: Radio; radar electronics

Archetypal Machine: Jet engine; rocket
Communications Media: Television
Key Text: *Understanding Media* (1964) by Marshall McLuhan
Paradigmatic Painting: *Lavender Mist* (1950) by Jackson Pollock
Axial Work of Literature: *Gravity's Rainbow* (1973) by Thomas Pynchon

    Hitler's attempt, during World War II, to retrieve the Medieval fortress city by surrounding Europe with the Atlantic wall was doomed to failure because it did not take into account the use of a type of new technology that the Medieval fortress mentality had never been designed to defend itself against, namely, aerial bombing raids which, as we have seen, the Germans had themselves invented during the Great War. The fire bombing of German cities proved to be Hitler's undoing in spite of such clever new inventions as the jet engine and the V2 rocket.

    World War II is the first electronics war, however, since it was during this conflict that the science of electronics was born out of the technologies of jamming and counter-jamming of radar defense systems. The German 'Himmelbelt' was a local air defense network composed of an integrated system of radars, antiaircraft guns, fighters and searchlights. The allies made it their primary task to disrupt and dismantle this system so that they could proceed to firebomb German cities.

    The organization in charge of this task was the Harvard Radio Research Laboratory, which was run by Fred Terman, the dean of engineering at Stanford University. It was as a direct result of Terman's work for the military that Stanford became one of the defense department's primary research facilities in electronic warfare. And so it is as a direct result of World War II that Stanford University became the nucleus of Silicon Valley.[3]

    The radar screen is the first true example of *suksma technology*, for it is the first time that an electronic screen substitutes physical objects for self-luminous phantoms of light made out of electrons and photons. The computer, furthermore, was also conceived during this war as part of its code breaking system.

    World War II was also the first radio war, for both FDR and Hitler exploited this medium for sounding the respective tribal drums of their societies.

    After the war was over, the world of the suburbs erupted as though the ashphalt streets themselves were laying houses like eggs. Levittown in

Long Island, New York is, of course, the charismatic example, constructed during the years 1947–51 as the first truly mass-produced cookie cutter suburb. And to go along with the cheap new tract housing, cheap new food was invented with the advent of McDonald's in 1948, created by Dick and Mac McDonald in San Bernardino, California. Jack in the Box was founded in San Diego in 1951 and Kentucky Fried Chicken in the following year in Louisville, Kentucky. Burger King, in turn, was founded in Miami, Florida, in 1954.

The passing of the Federal Interstate Highway Act in 1956 laid down the infrastructural transport system for the creation of the world's largest and most complicated freeway network. Fast food joints, as well as indoor shopping malls, were located near the entrance and exit ramps of these freeways, as they still are to this day.

Television is the archetypal technology of this age: the cathode ray tube had been developed in 1897 by Braun, but television as a technology began to emerge in the 1920s. The Nazis had begun the first regular television service in Berlin in 1935 and the BBC in 1936. In America, public television services began in 1939, although the growth of the broadcasting industry did not take place until the late 1940s, when television began to displace radio in consumer popularity. There is perhaps, as Raymond Williams has remarked, an inward relationship between television as the favored medium for an age that was newly mobile: television displaces, decenters and transforms the local into the Everywhere all at once.[4] Later, during the 1960s and early 1970s, the Vietnam War will become the first television war.

Jackson Pollock's painting *Lavender Mist* is from his abstract expressionist period and, as Paul Virilio has pointed out, the way in which Pollock painted these works, by dismissing the easel and laying them on the ground and walking around them, already foreshadows the coming view of satellites looking down at the earth with their abstract countryscapes visible from space looking more or less like an abstract painting.

Thomas Pynchon's masterpiece *Gravity's Rainbow,* meanwhile, performs a cultural archaeology on the space age by going back to its origins with the Nazi invention of the V-2 rocket. He reminds us that there is a direct continuity from the Nazi *Vergeltunswaffe* ('revenge weapons') to White Sands, New Mexico and the birth of the Space Age, since many Nazi scientists captured by the Allies were imported to America to become founding architects of its space program.

V. The Age of Digital Technologies; 1995–present

Interregnum War: First Gulf War
Primary Medium for Documenting War: Cable Television
Archetypal Machine: the Personal Computer
Communications Media: Internet
Key Text: *Pacific Shift* by William Irwin Thompson
Paradigmatic Painting: *In Limbo* (2005) by Odd Nerdrum
Films: *The Matrix* (1999) by the Wachowski brothers; *Existenz* (1999) by
    David Cronenberg

The First Gulf War in 1990–91 was, as Paul Virilio pointed out, the first *total* electronic war, in which ancient weapons of obstruction and Late Medieval weapons of destruction were obsolesced by weapons of communication.[5] It is a war in which the horizons of the battlefield have shifted to the orbital space of the heavens about the earth, in which the eyes and mirrors of satellites act as GPS systems which track the enemy's communications infrastructure. With the use of Stealth bombers, in which their images are erased from radar screens; to the use of U2 spyplanes, AWACS and Nighthawks; to the fact that the first objectives of the invasion of Baghdad were not so much to attack the city as to take out its communications infrastructure and to jam its electronic frequencies while the Stealth bombers went in and delivered their laser-guided missiles. It is a war in which human beings first begin to become bystanders to a technological opera of automated weapons systems like Cruise and Tomahawk missiles. The surrender of Iraqi soldiers in Saddam Hussein's army to a Pioneer drone at the war's climax is a turning point in the history of warfare.

This war clears the way for the present epoch in which we now find ourselves, an age of global electronics technologies prolonging an endless nightmare version of the same Gulf War extended across the Middle East and splashed across the video monitors of our ubiquitous screens. The Gulf War is the first war to take place live, in real time, on cable television.

The personal computer is, of course, the archetypal machine for this epoch, opening up the etheric universe of the Internet inside which we currently find ourselves surrounded and cocooned.

Thus, the gadgets which have composed the architecture of this age, from the personal computer to the digital camera to the handheld palm pilot, are all direct descendants of the technology of warfare which has brought us to this stage of world history, a stage in which history itself has been transformed into a global video arena. If the Romans had their gladiatorial spectacles and their hippodromes, then we have transformed the earthly globe itself into a vast blue orbital Colosseum flickering with the tiny scintillae of videonic spectacles glittering across its surface as it drifts through the yawning darknesses of cold, interstellar space.

With the disappearance of deferred time, in which history is processed via the intellect through the application of the written word toward reflection upon events, the age of literacy and of the human mind becomes a thing of the past. When everything takes place instantaneously in real time, there is no longer any time for the use of the human mind's reflective capacities and any kind of outmoded Gutenbergian technology, such as the printed page, that cannot keep up is in process of being left behind.

The archetypal painting which best captures the sense of this epoch is Norwegian artist Odd Nerdrum's *In Limbo,* which he completed in 2005: in it, we see a group of disembodied human spirits floating on their backs in a black, formless ether. The image is a perfect metaphor for the surrounding of the earth with a pulsing field of electromagnetic human phantoms, which are sent beaming around the globe like the ancient spheres of the Greeks. We are indeed surrounded with disembodied, telepresent humans that are traveling at the speed of light, in the very air in which and from which we draw breath. We have created a technologized equivalent of the ancient world's vision of the ubiquitous presence of the dead hovering about the earth like a second, disembodied realm, and Nerdrum's painting perfectly brings out the isomorphism shared by these two cosmologies, ancient and modern.

David Cronenberg's film *Existenz,* furthermore, perfectly captures the sense of ontological disorientation that these technologies inflict upon our senses. *The Matrix* by the Wachowski brothers does the same thing, although with less grace and more vulgarity than Cronenberg, who happens to be a displaced literary artist, whereas the Wachowskis are displaced comicbook writers. *The Matrix* is therefore a celluloid graphic novel, but *Existenz* is a kind of literary celluloid masterpiece. Both films raise the issue that in the electronic building of simulated worlds, we are confronted with a crisis of world-making, for the virtual realities that these technologies are capable of generating are so confusing to the human psyche that they can be mistaken for the Real itself. But the Real, as Lacan well knew, is precisely that which can never be encompassed by the Symbolic, and always exists just outside of, and beyond it, ever threatening to shatter these fragile bubble worlds with the trauma induced by its impact. The Real is the enemy of all human-cultural Symbolic systems, and it is always a source of paranoia within such systems. Never have our symbolic worlds been so convincing, these films suggest, and at the same time so fragile.

William Irwin Thompson, in his book *Pacific Shift*, was the prophet of this whole epoch and for a full understanding of its significance, the reader could no better for himself than to go back and study this text. Thompson understood that the Pacific basin, with its electronics industries spread out from Tokyo to Silicon Valley, has become the new Mediterranean basin for the epoch in which we are situated.

The full elucidation of this new epoch is, of course, what this book has been about, but for a more detailed chronology, see the timeline of Key Events in Appendix I.

Postscript on the Dialectic of Art and Technology

What's the world like these days, the old man with the black eyepatch had asked, and the doctor's wife replied, There's no difference between inside and outside, between here and there, between the many and the few.... And the people, how are they coping, asked the girl with dark glasses, They go around like ghosts, this must be what it means to be a ghost....

— José Saramago
Blindness

The Internet, as we have seen, is recasting the world as an acoustically resonant cavern — or sphere — in which all linear-biased spatio-temporal orientations are being scrapped. Three dimensional location in physical space and the temporal sequencing of processes via past-present-future are vanishing into a pure present of ubiquitous all-at-onceness. Linear processes are disappearing, and so now there are no longer any goals, points of view or places to get *to*, as all of us are already everywhere on the planet simultaneously. Where would we go? *Where* is already *here*.

Such values are, of course, profoundly upsetting to a world still clinging to hierarchies and center-periphery models of all kinds. The clash between WikiLeaks and the United States government illustrates this, as does also Microsoft's failing attempts to remain relevant in a world of open source networking such as that articulated by Google and Amazon.

Whenever a new medium comes along, it often happens that there is a period of overlap and struggle between the old values that the new

187

medium is obsolescing and the new values that are constitutive of the world being shaped by it. The sixteenth century, for example, was such a period of overlap and clash between the profoundly visual values of the printing press and the old Medieval scriptorial culture, which was still highly tactile and oral-acoustic in nature. Thus, the apocalyptic imagery in the paintings of Hieronymous Bosch, with all the burning buildings in the *Temptations of Saint Anthony* or in the Hell panel of *The Garden of Earthly Delights,* is not really about Last Things, for these images are, rather, visionary depictions of the state of disorientation inflicted upon the Renaissance psyche by the new values of visually connected space and lineal organization. As Marshall McLuhan comments:

> To the sixteenth century person, this new world was an outrage because it destroyed every known human value. What we now think of as the basis of our whole civilization — namely uniform, connected, and continuous space, rational space, rational order — was, in the sixteenth century, a barbaric intruder into their order. Visual space was considered the destroyer of all human order. Now we think of it as the basis of all human order.[1]

Hence, the assault of the army of skeletons in Brueghel's 1562 painting, *The Triumph of Death,* which are running around slicing off the heads of the living, cutting their throats and herding them into cages, is not so much a personification of the plague or the Black Death as an embodiment of the assault of the new visual and linear values upon the psyche of Renaissance man, for whenever a society is destabilized by the advent of major new media — such as the printing press — it is experienced as a trauma of apocalyptic magnitudes. The imagery as it appears in the arts, though exaggerated, is nevertheless an indicator of how such a society *feels* about what is happening to it, just as when you get sick with a virus, you might have absurdly caricatured dreams of fighting off armies of demons and devils.

Thus, the impact of the new digital technologies is having an absolutely catastrophic effect upon our Western psyche. The society is currently reeling with the effects of an economic crash while the psyche, besieged with the new gadgets and their new demands upon the collective sensorium, is registering its state of confusion and disorientation in films and literature like Cormac McCarthy's novel *The Road,* or Don DeLillo's *Cosmopolis,* or José Saramago's *Blindness.*

The film version of McCarthy's novel, released in 2009 (the novel came out in 2006), is worth pausing for a moment to discuss in this regard. The story is set in a post-apocalyptic future when civilization has been decimated by some unnamed catastrophe, a nuclear war, perhaps, or a bolide collision with the earth. We are never told, and it doesn't matter, because the import of the crumbling bridges and ruptured highways, the ashy gray skies and the spindly trees is an image of the current condition that the Western psyche finds itself in: it is so badly disoriented that is *as though* it has been hit by a catastrophe of such magnitude.

We follow the peregrinations of a man and his eight-year-old son across a landscape of devastation as they traverse a road leading south to the coast. Along the way, they barely escape notice by bands of roving cannibals who have had to resort to eating people because there are no longer any animals or plants left alive. The man and the child must forage for whatever they can find — at one point, they luck out and stumble across a cellar full of canned provisions — but they always manage to just barely escape notice by these savages. *The Road* is a sort of contemporary reworking of Brueghel's *The Triumph of Death*, a work of art which was also produced during another epoch of profound shifting in cultural sensibilities. The dead, as in Brueghel's painting, are also ubiquitous in McCarthy's narrative: "The mummied dead everywhere. The flesh cloven along the bones, the ligaments dried to tug and taut as wires. Shriveled and drawn like latterday bogfolk, their faces of boiled sheeting, the yellowed palings of their teeth."[2] What's dying is, of course, the old centralist values of physical location in geographic space and orientation to the cardinal points.

In an age in which journeys and pilgrimages — along with all such center-periphery models — have been rendered obsolete, *The Road* is a perfect example of the new kind of abolition of spatial and geographical orientations that the Internet has inflicted upon us, for *The Road* is a journey that leads nowhere, has no particular goals and orients us to no particular landscape. It is purely incidental that McCarthy's protagonists are following the road south, because it could just as well lead in any direction with equally indifferent results for the narrative. The man and the boy do reach the ocean, but nothing much happens when they get there beyond the father's getting sick with a fever and dying. And the narrative itself, in avoiding all the clichés of the traditional journey story, consistently confounds the reader's expectations of such narratives, for the man and the boy never fall into captivity or indeed even encounter much in the way of dramatic conflict at all. It is strictly a tale of survival in a world without horizons or cardinal directions, truly a story of streets with no names (the novel, appropriately, has no chapter breaks or titles). Contrast this with a narrative like *The Wizard of Oz* in which the yellow brick road leads to a very specific goal, for Baum's narrative was still heavily visual and lineal in nature.

Don DeLillo's novel *Cosmopolis* is like this, too, for it tells the story of a single day in the life of multi-billionaire Eric Packer who sets out from his posh Manhattan apartment one morning in April of 2000 — the very month in which the dot-com bubble burst — in his stretch limousine in order to get a haircut at a barber shop on the other side of town. His journey is hampered by the fact that the president of the United States is in town, thus jamming the traffic, and there is also the funeral of a famous Sufi rap artist named Brutha Fez. These slow-downs give Eric all the time he needs to exit the limo to eat meals with his girlfriends, go to their apartments for sexual escapades and then return to his limousine, where his hi-tech wired gadgetry enables him to do some very giddy market trading. In fact, by the end of the day, he has lost all his billions as the result of betting against the rise of the yen. And he does get that haircut — sort of — before having to meet up with a stalker who has been carefully monitoring his every move via video screens that have tracked and made Eric's life thoroughly public down to its minutest details.

But *Cosmopolis*, despite its journey to the specific location of a barbershop, is really a novel without goals like *The Road*, for Eric's day meanders pointlessly from one episode to the next as he conducts business from his office on wheels. In the age of the Internet, offices, too, are now obsolete, since business can be conducted from anywhere at all, for location in physical space no longer matters online. A lifetime's fortunes can be scrapped in a New York minute, while the individual finds himself drifting out of all socio-historical context in cyberspace, where center-periphery models have ceased to be relevant.

Cosmopolis and *The Road* are modern journey narratives in an age which has rendered all such journeys obsolete, for there is now no place to get *to*. Compare the goal-oriented journeys of Dante or the typical Arthurian Grail quester, for whom the attainment of the goal provides the narrative with its very *raison d'etre*. Packer's haircut, by contrast, is virtually a non-event: it is not the real goal of the story at all, which turns out to be his confrontation with the stalker that comes in the novel's final pages.

Like *The Road*, *Cosmopolis* is a journey without goal, destination or purpose, for in the new digital world in which these events take place, there is no point in going anywhere since at the speed of light one already *is* where the action is *at*.

The artist makes visible what is taking place in a society beneath the threshold of conscious perception. As Heidegger put it in his essay "On the Essence of Truth," science takes a particular stance or attitude toward the world such that the specific questions it solicits of beings make certain facets of existence come forth into unconcealment in the open region of the dialogue between subjects and beings (truth as *aletheia*); simultaneously, though, the process causes other facets of beings to *withdraw* into concealment. Thus, no theory of truth can ever be complete, since every proposition directed at nature causes it to *reveal* as well to *conceal* certain aspects of its total mystery. Science believes that it is the only valid mode of solicitation of beings, whereas in reality, its particular type of questioning causes all sorts of aspects of the totality of *ek-sistence* to withdraw from view. It is precisely the artist, however, who brings out of concealment those aspects of the world that science has caused to fall off the radar. He or she makes visible what science has made invisible to conscious perception.

This is very similar to McLuhan's idea that the job of the artist is to make invisible environments created by new technologies visible; the artist, that is to say, attempts to redress the balance which technology has knocked off kilter by providing these new environments with *counter* environments that have the effect of readjusting the sensory ratios which the new technologies have knocked out of whack. Thus, the damage that new media inflict upon a society's sensorium is reset and repaired precisely by the artist, who thus finds himself in the role of a society's immune system, rushing like white blood cells to the wound inflicted by the weapon in order to suture it up.

Consider José Saramago's 1995 novel *Blindness*, which tells the tale of a sudden mysterious blindness which descends upon the population of a city — a stand in for Lisbon — and which strikes at random. Since it is thought by the government that the disease is contagious, all those who are afflicted with the blindness are rounded up into concentration camps, one of which is created out of the ruins of an abandoned mental hospital, where our protagonists are holed up in an increasingly crowded situation of the blind, while the supply of food becomes evermore scarce. The resulting conditions lead to the formation of rival tribal groups, one of which is a sort of matriarchy that forms in response to sexual brutalities by the men.

Blindness not only shows us how the old visual values of the Gutenbergian world are being stepped down in the electronic sensorium which favors more acoustic-tactile ones, but it also makes visible the current shrinking of space caused by light speed technologies which demolish privacy and thrust everyone into everyone else's space. One of the by-products of individuals floating — detached and yet omnipresent (like the figures in Odd Nerdrum's painting *In Limbo*) — in the acoustically resonant world-space of the new electronic cavern is that it is a very crowded, disorganized space indeed. Individuals slam into each other as a daily consequence of this new world of dislocated and decontextualized individuals cut free from the containing boundaries of their antique geographically specific macrospheres. Indeed, *all* of the late paintings of Norwegian artist Odd Nerdrum are specific explorations of this worldless world we are now captured inside of, for these paintings are filled with images of pale skinned, naked human beings floating in the obscure, murky darknesses of a nowhere that *might* be the astral plane but could also be the orbital region surrounding the earth.

Saramago's hospital as prison, likewise, is metaphoric of the echoing cavern world in which acoustic and tactile values predominate over the old values of visually connected space and linear social organization of the world that was the norm prior to the twentieth century. The nation state, with its ordered rows of troops marching in straight lines, is now disintegrating into tribal warfare and every man for himself, guerilla-style modes of social relation that no longer follow typographic linearity. Joyce indeed had it right: all the Finns are again awakening in the neo–Paleolithic world-as-cavern in which each individual becomes a new kind of hunter foraging in the global blogosphere for whatever scraps of civilization might be relevant to his particular world-island habitation. We are all now Robinson Crusoes washed ashore outside the collapsed walls of the nation state macrospheres which, once upon a time, we could rely upon to sustain and protect us.

So, when a new technology comes along that is of such profoundly disturbing nature as the printing press, let's say, or electric technology, it disturbs and disrupts all the sense ratios of the society. This disequilibrium, once inflicted, is expressed by the society in its works of art as narratives depicting an invasion or massive social disturbance of some kind. Hence, science fiction came into being in the nineteenth century as a response to the industrial invasion of society by factories, steam engines, gears, wheels and pulleys of all kinds. This invasion was dramatized in narratives like H.G. Wells' *War of the Worlds*— the *Triumph of Death* of its time — or in the short stories of Edgar Allan Poe.

It is in the work of the artist, then, that the disturbed sensory ratios are worked out through dramatized scenarios over the decades until the ratios are compensated, balanced and reset through the various modes of increased awareness made possible by the artist. Art is therefore not a luxury, but a necessity, for it is intimately interinvolved with technological evolution. Where technology disrupts and disturbs, art heals and repairs. And it does this, moreover, homeostatically, as though society were a living organism to which technology acts as the pathogen, while art functions as the immune system which performs the social and psychic reparation that allows the organism to function smoothly again.

The crisis ends when the new technology finds its place, smoothly enmeshed within the interstices of the social machine wherever it will fit, and the technology ceases to be a threat. Hence, the current fears regarding the Internet that we hear often articulated — that it is corrupting the attention spans of our children, monopolizing their time, etc.— are nothing at all new, for the same concerns — now forgotten — were once leveled at silent movies when they first came out (in 1908, the mayor of New York ordered all 600 of its Nickelodeons to close and refile for new licenses that sought to control their content with a firmer grip[3]), comic books in the 1950s and inevitably also television. Fernand Braudel even recounts objections that were made in sixteenth century Europe to the advent of the fork! "A German preacher," he says, "condemned it as a diabolical luxury: God would not have given us fingers if he had wished us to use such an instrument."[4]

These kinds of concerns, though, are always worked out as part of the dialectical evolution of technology and art — disease and cure — and once that happens, the new environment will come to seem like a matter of course.

Thus, an entire world of Gutenbergian media is in process of becoming extinct — and this is currently experienced by literate types like myself as a major trauma — but the cognitive dialectic of art and technology is such that art will eventually heal the trauma inflicted upon our present psyches by these new technologies. It is a cultural healing process that is very much analogous to the grieving process of the human psyche when dealing with a major loss: eventually the psyche forgets, and in forgetting, ceases to hurt.

One day, we will wake up and wonder what it was we were ever worried about.

Appendix: Chronology
of Key Events

So much of what's going on now can be traced back to 1995 (or there-abouts), that it requires a separate Appendix just to keep track of it all. Here are some further significant events covering the period from 1990 to 2011:

1990
February: Adobe's Photoshop 1.0 software for Macintosh is released.

1991
February 23: Iraqi forces in the Gulf War surrender to an unmanned aerial vehicle, or Pioneer drone, the first time in history that troops have surrendered to a robot.

March 27: First GSM (Global System for Mobile Communications) mobile phone call ever made by Radiolinja, a Finnish GSM operator. This began to make possible the shift from analog to digital cell phone use for second generation cell phones, which now became ever smaller and smaller.

December 2: Apple releases Quick Time software.

1992
December 3: First text message (SMS) ever sent by Neil Papworth to Richard Jarvis, which was simply "Merry Christmas."

1993
February 26: The current terrorist wars are foreshadowed with Ramzi Yousef's bombing of the World Trade Center.

June 11: CGI technology begins to take cinema hostage — which has been in steady decline ever since — with the release of Steven Spielberg's *Jurassic Park*.

December 10: The first person shooter videogame called *Doom* released, which would later go on to influence the Columbine killers.

By the end of 1993, over a million subscribers are using GSM cell phone networks. Also in this year, the MP3 audio format was first introduced.

1994

January 1: NAFTA goes into effect, forcing U.S.–Mexican border patrols to tighten up, while the value of the peso is driven down.

December 3: PlayStation introduced by Sony. It revolutionizes the home video game industry, which will eventually influence the military's use of drone technology.

Also in this year: the Swedish telecommunications company Ericsson releases Bluetooth software.

1995

January 1: World Trade Organization founded, beginning current epoch of globalization.

March 1: Yahoo! is founded in Santa Clara, California.

April 30: NSFNet decommissioned; Internet is turned over to the private sector.

July 16: Amazon.com website launched by Jeff Bezos. The death of the Gutenbergian phase of the publishing industry and the end of the days of the printed book are beginning.

August 9: Netscape goes public and the dot-com boom, which will lead to the crash of 2000–02, is under way.

September 4: eBay is founded.

December: The DVD is first introduced to the public.

1995 was, according to P.W. Singer, the key year when modern drone technology became what it is today, for this was the year when unmanned vehicles were crossed with GPS.

Also, early in 1995, Craig Newmark launched craigslist.

Also in this year, the first digital camera to feature a liquid crystal display on the back was the Casio QV-10.

Wal-mart pulls itself out of its slump after the death of Sam Walton by shifting to Asian imports for its products.

1997

March 10: The first Palm Pilots are released.

October: *Grand Theft Auto* for PlayStation released.

December: Macromedia's Dreamweaver 1.0 software released.

1998

January: first HDTVs made available to the public.

Emusic.com launched

April: Priceline.com launched.

August 15: Apple releases their iMac G3 computer.

September 7: Larry Page and Sergey Brin formally launch Google as a website.

September 28: ArtsandLettersDaily.com founded by Denis Dutton.

1999

June: Shawn Fanning founds the illegal music sharing site Napster.

August 23: Blogger founded by Pyra Labs.

October 5: Apple releases iMovie application.

Bookstores that closed in this year: Gaia Bookstore in Berkeley, California.

Also, in this year: The online shoe store Zappos.com, founded by Nick Swinmurn.

2000
March 4: PlayStation 2 launched in Japan.
April: *Mirabella* magazine folds.

2001
January 9: Apple's iTunes and iDVD are made available to the public.
January 15: Wikipedia founded by Jimmy Wales and Larry Sanger.
March: Kazaa introduced by the Dutch company Consumer Empowerment.
March 24: Apple releases its Mac OS X operating system.
July: Napster is shut down.
September: *Mode* magazine folds.
October: *Mademoiselle* magazine folds.
October: *Lingua franca* magazine folds.
October 22: *Grand Theft Auto III* released.
October 23: Apple releases their first iPod.
November: StumbleUpon search engine founded by Garrett Camp and Geoff Smith.
November 15: Microsoft Xbox released, and on the same day its *Halo* videogame.
December 3: Rhapsody.com launched (subscription music site).
Bookstore closures this year: Printers Inc. Bookstore in Palo Alto, California.

2002
February 19: Blu-Ray Disc founded.
March 22: Friendster founded by Jonathan Abrams and Cris Emmanuel.
March: Google releases Google News to the public.

2003
January 7: Apple's Safari browser first released.
February: Google buys Blogger for an undisclosed sum.
April: *Partisan Review* folds.
April 28: Apple introduces the iTunes Music Store online.
May: LinkedIn founded by Reid Hoffman.
August: MySpace launched by Brad Greenspan, Tom Anderson, Chris DeWolfe and Josh Berman.
October: *Book* magazine folds.

2004
February: Flickr launched.
February: Facebook launched by Mark Zuckerberg, Chris Hughes, Dustin Moskovitz, and Eduardo Saverin.
July: Google acquires Picasa.
November 9: Mozilla releases Firefox web browser.
Bookstore closures: Midnight Special in Santa Monica, California.

2005
January 22: Apple's Mac Mini is released.
January 25: Google launches Google Videos.
February 14: YouTube founded by Jawed Karim, Chad Hurley and Steve Chen.
May: TheHuffingtonPost.com founded by Arianna Huffington.

June: Walt Mossberg and Kara Swisher found allthingsdigital.com.
June 28: Google releases Google Earth software.
July: Rupert Murdoch buys MySpace for $580 million.
July: Google acquires Android, Inc.

2006

March 31: Toshiba releases first HD DVD player in Japan.
April 18: first HD DVD titles released by Toshiba.
May: *Circus* magazine (the old rock and roll magazine) folds.
October 9: Google buys YouTube.
October 10: Microsoft's Flight Simulator X released.
July 15: Twitter founded by Jack Dorsey, Evan Williams and Biz Stone.
December: WikiLeaks founded by Julian Assange.
December 22: the last Tower Records closes down.
Bookstores that closed in this year: Cody's Books in Berkeley, Califronia; A Clean Well-Lighted Place for Books in San Francisco.

2007

January 9: Apple's iPhone released.
February 7: Google releases gmail to the general public.
March: *Premiere* magazine folds.
March: Hulu.com founded.
Life magazine folds.
November 19: Amazon.com releases its first Kindle.
December: *House and Garden* magazine, in business for 106 years, folds.
December 13: Rupert Murdoch buys Dow Jones & Co., the owner and publisher of *The Wall Street Journal,* for reportedly $5 billion.
December 31: *The Cincinnati Post,* founded in 1881, folds.
Also, in this year: The cloud computing site known as Grooveshark was launched by Sam Tarantino, Josh Greenberg and Andres Barreto. And Tumblr., a microblogging platform, was founded by David Karp.
Bookstores that closed in this year: Cody's Books in San Francisco, California; Gotham Book Mart and Coliseum Books in New York City.

2008

February 11: The *Halifax Daily News* folds.
February 19: Toshiba concedes to Blu-Ray and discontinues its HD DVDs.
February 23: The *Albuquerque Tribune,* founded in 1922, folds.
August: The *South Idaho Press* ceases publication.
August 29: *The San Juan Star,* founded in 1959, a Pulitzer Prize winning paper, ceases publication.
September: The social networking site Yammer is founded by David O. Sacks.
December 8: Tribune Company, the owner of the *Los Angeles Times* and the *Chicago Tribune,* files for bankruptcy.
December 11: Google releases Google Chrome browser to the public.
December: *Teen* magazine (since 1954) folds up.
Bookstore closures: Dutton's Brentwood Books in Los Angeles.

2009

January: *PC Magazine* ceases publication (in business since 1982), as does *Country Home.*

January 15: *The Minneapolis Star Tribune* files for bankruptcy.

February 9: Amazon releases its second generation Kindle.

February: *Playgirl* magazine folds (running since 1973).

February 22: *The Philadelphia Daily News* files for bankruptcy.

February 27: *The Rocky Mountain News,* which had been in business for 150 years, folds.

March 2: It is announced that all Virgin Megastores in the U.S. will close.

March 16: the last issue of the *Seattle Post Intelligencer* (founded in 1863) rolls off the press.

March 27: *The Christian Science Monitor* publishes its last daily paper, then shifts to publishing a weekly paper.

May 16: *The Tucson Citizen,* Arizona's oldest newspaper (founded 1870), folds.

June: *Vibe* magazine folds (in print since 1992).

July 23: The *Ann Arbor News,* founded in 1835, folds.

November: *Gourmet* magazine (since 1941) folds, due to a decline in advertising revenue.

Also, in the same month, *The Washington Post* announces the closure of three of its regional bureaus in New York, Chicago and Los Angeles.

Bookstores that closed in this year: Black Oak Books in Berkeley, California; Stacey's Bookstore in San Francisco; Abandoned Planet in San Francisco.

2010

January 13: Google releases Google Docs.

February: Hollywood Video declares bankruptcy.

February 9: Google releases Google Buzz, a social networking tool.

April 3: Apple's iPad is unveiled.

May 20: Google officially announces Google TV.

June 6: *The Honolulu Advertiser,* a daily newspaper founded in 1856, ceases publication.

August 3: The music subscription service Rdio.com launched.

August 24: Spotify.com, another emusic site, launched.

August 27: Amazon releases its third generation Kindle, its most popular yet.

September 23: FCC approves proposal to free up unused television airwaves for high speed wireless broadband networks.

October 26: Barnes and Noble releases its Nook Color.

November: Path.com, a social networking service for mobile devices, is launched by Shawn Fanning and Dave Morin.

2011

May 26: Google announces the Google Wallet app for making payments.

June 28: Google launches Google+ in order to compete with Facebook.

July 22: Borders Books begins liquidating its remaining stores.

Notes

Introduction

1. Elizabeth L. Eisenstein, *The Printing Press as an Agent of Change* (Cambridge, UK: Cambridge University Press, 1997).

2. Paul Starr, *The Creation of the Media: Political Origins of Modern Communications* (New York: Basic Books, 2004), 338.

3. Ibid., 355.

4. Ibid., 339.

5. Harold Innis, *Empire and Communications* (Toronto: University of Toronto Press, 1972), 162.

6. Harold Innis, *The Bias of Communication* (Toronto: University of Toronto Press, 1971), 59.

7. Bernard Stiegler, *Technics and Time, 1: The Fault of Epimetheus* (Stanford, CA: Stanford University Press, 1998), 32.

8. P.W. Singer, *Wired for War: The Robotics Revolution and Conflict in the 21st Century* (New York: Penguin, 2009), 101.

9. Derek Thompson, "The iPod Is Dead to Me": http://www.theatlantic.com/business/archive/2010/10/the-ipod-is-dead-to-me/65148/.

10. This quote comes from McLuhan's interview with Edwin Newman: http://www.youtube.com/watch?v=z9Eq3sDgl9o.

First, a Brief Note ...

1. Joseph Campbell, *The Mythic Image* (Princeton, NJ: Princeton University Press, 1990), 361.

2. Marshall McLuhan, *The Gutenberg Galaxy* (Toronto: University of Toronto Press, 2002), 105.

3. Ibid., 107.

Part I

1. Bernard Stiegler, *Technics and Time, 1: The Fault of Epimetheus* (Stanford, CA: Stanford University Press, 1998), 43.

2. See the documentary, *The Virtual Revolution,* Episode 2: http://www.youtube.com/watch?v=8sH4HHiMNko&NR=1.

Chapter 1

1. Alain Danielou, *Gods of Love and Ecstacy: The Traditions of Shiva and Dionysus* (Rochester, VT: Inner Traditions, 1984), 68.
2. Robert Spector, *Amazon.com: Get Big Fast* (New York: HarperBusiness, 2000), 168.
3. Ibid., 6.
4. See John David Ebert, *Celluloid Heroes & Mechanical Dragons: Film as the Mythology of Electronic Society* (Christchurch, New Zealand: Cybereditions, 2005), 54–56.
5. This quote by Striphas comes from this video: http://www.youtube.com/watch?v=g3oZLpeueWg.
6. Elizabeth L. Eisenstein, *The Printing Press as an Agent of Change* (Cambridge, UK: Cambridge University Press, 1997), 49.
7. Ibid., 49.

Chapter 2

1. A YouTube video of Hirst's exhibit at the Met can be found here: http://www.youtube.com/watch?v=sWQGa-EBxzk.
2. Randall Stross, *Planet Google: One Company's Audacious Plan to Organize Everything We Know* (New York: Free Press, 2008), 114.
3. Elizabeth L. Eisenstein, *The Printing Press as an Agent of Change* (Cambridge, UK: Cambridge University Press, 1997), 120–21.
4. Paul Starr, *The Creation of the Media: Political Origins of Modern Communications* (New York: Basic Books, 2004), 122.
5. See, for instance, his chapter, "The Neoplatonic Movement and Michelangelo" in *Studies in Iconology* (New York: Oxford University Press, 1972), 171.
6. Benedict Anderson, *Imagined Communities* (London: Verso Books, 1991), 18.
7. See Wendy Brown, *Walled States, Waning Sovereignty* (Boston: Zone Books, 2010).
8. Slavoj Žižek, *Living in the End Times* (London: Verso Books, 2010), 171.
9. Arjun Appadurai, *Modernity at Large* (Minneapolis: University of Minnesota Press, 1996), 22.

Chapter 3

1. Gilles Deleuze and Felix Guattari, *A Thousand Plateaus* (London: Continuum, 2004), 196.
2. Kierkegaard, in *The Concept of Dread,* remarks: "It is noteworthy that Greek art culminates in statuary, in which it is precisely the glance that is lacking. This, however, has its deep reason in the fact that the Greeks did not in the profounder sense comprehend the concept of spirit, and therefore did not in the profoundest sense comprehend the sensuous and the temporal. How striking is the contrast that in Christianity God is pictorially represented as an eye!" (p. 78).
3. Michel de Certeau, *The Practice of Everyday Life* (Berkeley: University of California Press, 2002), 99.
4. Franz Borkenau, *End and Beginning* (New York: Columbia University Press, 1981), 133.

Chapter 4

1. Hans Nissen, *The Early History of the Ancient Near East, 9000–2000 B.C.* (Chicago: University of Chicago Press, 1984), 138.

2. Joan Aruz and Ronald Wallenfels, eds., *Art of the First Cities* (New York: Yale University Press, 2003), 473.

3. By contrast with the Sumerian messenger's back and forth movements horizontally across the landscape, with Moses we have another originator of writing, in this case, one who descends *vertically* with a brand new language, namely, written Hebrew, from the top of a mountain. Enmerkar's clay tablets, made from riverrine mud and silt, furthermore, should be contrasted with the tomb-like stone of the Mosaic tablets. The clay seems bound up with the river-like ephemerality of the Sumerian city-states, which come and go with phallic, temporal rhythmicity; the stone tablets of Moses, on the other hand, are permanent, identified with the geological riverbed *across which* rivers pour. In other words, writing for the one society is associated with earthly affairs, while for the other it is inherently sacred and concerned with Eternal Things.

4. Frederick G. Kilgour, *The Evolution of the Book* (New York: Oxford University Press, 1998), 21.

5. Harold Innis, *Empire and Communications* (Toronto: University of Toronto Press, 1972), 16.

6. Zahi Hawass, *The Treasures of the Pyramids* (New York: Barnes & Noble Books, 2003), 64-65.

7. Mohamed A. Hussein, *Origins of the Book: From Papyrus to Codex* (Greenwich, CT: New York Graphic Society, 1970), 13.

8. Jan Assmann, *The Mind of Egypt* (Cambridge, MA: Harvard University Press, 2003), 68–69.

9. Nicholas Basbanes, *A Gentle Madness: Bibliophiles, Bibliomanes, and the Eternal Passion for Books* (New York: Henry Holt, 1995), 65.

10. Marc-Alain Ouaknin, *Mysteries of the Alphabet* (New York: Abbeville Press, 1999), 42-44.

11. Kilgour, 49.

12. Hussein, 51.

13. Kilgour, 55.

14. The sixth century, incidentally, was the same century in which the reed pen was displaced and gave way to the quill pen.

15. Kilgour, 56.

16. Innis, 60.

17. Ibid., 137-38.

18. Walter Ong, *The Presence of the Word: Some Prolegomena for Cultural and Religious History* (New Haven: Yale University Press, 1967), 47-48.

19. Christopher De Hamel, *A History of Illuminated Manuscripts* (London: Phaidon Press, 1994), 256.

20. Harold Innis, *The Bias of Communication* (Toronto: University of Toronto Press, 1971), 127-128.

21. Eisenstein remarks that the Roman goddess Minerva "was also singled out for special honor as patron of the printing trades." See Elizabeth L. Eisenstein, *The Printing Press as an Agent of Change* (New York: Cambridge University Press, 1997), 143.

22. Heinrich Zimmer, *Philosophies of India* (Princeton, NJ: Princeton University Press, 1989), 59.

23. Zygmunt Bauman, *Does Ethics Have a Chance in a World of Consumers?* (Cambridge, MA: Harvard University Press, 2009), 1.

Chapter 5

1. The New Yorker essay "No Secrets" by Raffi Khatchadourian can be found here: http://www.newyorker.com/reporting/2010/06/07/100607fa_fact_khatchadourian.

2. Mark Landler and Scott Shane, "U.S. Sends Warning to People Named in Cable Leaks," *The New York Times,* January 6, 2011. http://www.nytimes.com/2011/01/07/world/07 wiki.html?_r=1&nl=todaysheadlines&emc=tha2

3. Massimo Calabresi, "The War on Secrecy," *Time* magazine, December 13, 2010, 37.

4. Ibid., 8.

5. Regis Debray, *Transmitting Culture* (New York: Columbia University Press, 2000), 3.

6. See Alain Badiou and Slavoj Žižek, *Philosophy in the Present* (Cambridge, UK: Polity, 2009), 1-48.

7. This program can be found here: http://www.pbs.org/wgbh/pages/frontline/tankman/view.

8. Ravi Somaiya, "Hundreds of WikiLeaks Mirror Sites Appear," *The New York Times,* December 5, 2010. http://www.nytimes.com/2010/12/06/world/europe/06wiki.html?scp=1&sq=wikileaks%20mirrored%20sites&st=cse.

Chapter 6

1. Gilles Deleuze and Felix Guattari, *A Thousand Plateaus* (London: Continuum Books, 2004), 20.

2. Fernand Braudel, *Civilization and Capitalism, 15th–18th Century,* Volume 1, *The Structures of Everyday Life* (New York: Harper & Row, 1985), 285.

3. Ibid., 288.

4. Ibid., 288–89.

Some Concluding Comments to Part I

1. Fernand Braudel, *Civilization and Capitalism, 15th–18th Century,* Volume 2 (London: Phoenix Press, 2002), 36.

2. Ibid., 62.

3. Ibid., 64, 66.

4. Walter Benjamin, *The Arcades Project* (Cambridge, MA: Belknap Press of Harvard University Press, 2002), 36.

5. Ibid., 37.

6. Siegfried Giedion, *Space, Time and Architecture* (Cambridge, MA: Harvard University Press, 2008), 239.

7. Christine Hauser, "Best Buy Feels the Pressure of Rivals on the Web," *The New York Times,* December 17, 2010, http://www.nytimes.com/2010/12/18/business/18bestbuy.html?pagewanted=1&src=un&feedurl=http://json8.ntimes.com/pages/technology/index.jsonp.

Part II

1. Fernand Braudel, *Memory and the Mediterranean* (New York: Alfred A. Knopf, 2001), 97.

2. According to Frederick Kilgour, Mesopotamian mathematics were much more sophisticated than Egyptian mathematics, for by 1650 B.C., the Mesopotamians were already solving quadratic equations, whereas the Egyptians, as indicated by the Rhind Papyrus or the Golonishev Papyrus, were lagging behind. See Frederick G. Kilgour, *The Evolution of the Book* (New York: Oxford University Press, 1998), 32.

3. Andrew George, ed., *The Epic of Gilgamesh* (New York: Barnes and Noble Books, 1999), 143-48.

Chapter 7

1. Caroline Alexander, *The War That Killed Achilles* (New York: Viking, 2009), 95-96.
2. Ridley Scott's Macintosh commercial can be found here: http://www.youtube.com/watch?v=vNy-7jv0XSc.
3. Jobs' keynote 1983 speech in which he first unveiled Scott's commercial and slammed IBM in the process can be found here: http://www.youtube.com/watch?v=lSiQA6KKyJo.
4. Jeffrey S. Young and William L. Simon, *iCon Steve Jobs: The Greatest Second Act in the History of Show Business* (Hoboken, NJ: Wiley, 2005), 81.
5. Ibid., 61.
6. The first personal computer was actually the Altair 8800, introduced in 1975 by MITS. The difference was that Apple's was the first personal computer that came pre-assembled and was not marketed primarily to hobbyists.
7. David Lewis-Williams, *The Mind in the Cave* (London: Thames & Hudson, 2004)
8. Gilles Deleuze, *Francis Bacon: The Logic of Sensation* (London: Continuum, 2005), 87.
9. Jobs' "Digital Hub" keynote speech from January 2001 can be seen here: http://www.youtube.com/watch?v=9046oXrm7f8&p=ABCB88A18BFCEE5B&playnext=1&index=18
10. Andrew Keen, *The Cult of the Amateur: How Today's Internet Is Killing Our Culture*, (New York: Doubleday/Currency, 2007), 100.

Chapter 8

1. The interview can be found here: http://www.youtube.com/watch?v=ZND3eczqoIA.
2. Of course, with the Polaroid, the negative is also eliminated, but the Polaroid — which has mostly disappeared now, anyway — is photography's equivalent of Super 8 film, a niche specialty that is rarely used by visual artists. Despite what a talented photographer like Andre Kertesz has achieved with Polaroids, it is rare for anyone to attempt to use the medium in order to make an artistic statement.
3. See, for example, the paintings of the mad artist Adolf Wolfli, some of which can be found here: http://www.adolfwoelfli.ch/index.php?c=e&level=17&sublevel=0.
4. Burtynsky's website can be found here: http://www.edwardburtynsky.com/.
5. Lewis Mumford, *The City in History* (New York: Harcourt, 1989), 403.

Chapter 9

1. See Paul Virilio, *Negative Horizon* (New York: Continuum, 2006), 154–55.
2. Martin Heidegger, *Towards the Definition of Philosophy* (London and New York: Continuum, 2008), 68.
3. William Irwin Thompson, *Coming into Being: Artifacts and Texts in the Evolution of Consciousness* (New York: Palgrave Macmillan, 1998), 306.

Chapter 10

1. J.G. Ballard, *The Complete Short Stories of J.G. Ballard* (New York: W. W. Norton, 2009), 22-38.
2. Gilles Deleuze and Felix Guattari, *Anti-Oedipus: Capitalism and Schizophrenia* (New York: Penguin Classics, 2009), 139–145.
3. Ibid., 188.
4. Ibid., 205–06.

5. J.G. Ballard, *Super-Cannes* (New York: Picador, 2002), 263.

6. This quote can be found on PBS's *Frontline* show entitled "Digital Nation," http://www.pbs.org/wgbh/pages/frontline/digitalnation/view/.

Chapter 11

1. P. W. Singer, *Wired for War: The Robotics Revolution and Conflict in the 21st Century* (New York: Penguin, 2009), 117.

2. Ibid., 68.

3. Ibid., caption for seventh photo.

4. Lewis Mumford, *Technics and Civilization* (New York: Harcourt Brace, 1963), 12–17.

5. Roland Barthes, *Mythologies* (New York: Hill and Wang, 1972), 71.

6. Ibid., Singer, 130.

7. Siegfried Giedion, *Mechanization Takes Command* (New York: Oxford University Press, 1948), 42.

8. Singer, 62.

9. Paul Virilio, *Grey Ecology* (New York: Atropos Press, 2009), 36.

10. Singer, 59.

11. Ibid., 62-63.

Chapter 12

1. Wilhelm Fraenger, *Bosch* (New York: Prestel, 2003).

2. Alain Badiou, *The Century* (Cambridge, UK: Polity, 2007).

Some Concluding Comments to Part II

1. Dolores Hayden, *Building Suburbia: Green Fields and Urban Growth, 1820–2000* (New York: Vintage, 2004), 26–27.

2. N. Kershaw Chadwick, *Russian Heroic Poetry* (Cambridge University Press, 1932), 45.

3. This information comes from a lecture by Steve Blank on "The Secret History of Silicon Valley," which can be found here: http://www.youtube.com/watch?v=ZTC_RxWN_xo.

4. Raymond Williams, *Television* (London and New York: Routledge Classics, 2003), 13.

5. Paul Virilio, *Desert Screen* (London and New York: Continuum, 2002).

Postscript

1. Marshall McLuhan, "Television in a New Light," *The Meaning of Commercial Television*, The Texas Stanford Seminar 1966, edited by Stanley T. Donner (Austin: University of Texas Press, 1967), 88.

2. Cormac McCarthy, *The Road* (New York: Vintage International 2007), 24.

3. Paul Starr, *The Creation of the Media: Political Origins of Modern Communication* (New York: Basic Books, 2004), 306.

4. Fernand Braudel, *Civilization and Capitalism, 15th–18th Century*, Volume 1 (New York: Harper & Row, 1981), 205.

Bibliography

Alexander, Caroline. *The War That Killed Achilles*. New York: Viking, 2009.

Anderson, Benedict. *Imagined Communities*. London: Verso Books, 1991.

Appadurai, Arjun. *Modernity at Large*. Minneapolis: University of Minnesota Press, 1996.

Aruz, Joan, and Robert Wallenfels, eds. *Art of the First Cities*. New York: Yale University Press, 2003.

Assmann, Jan. *The Mind of Egypt*. Cambridge, MA: Harvard University Press, 2003.

Badiou, Alain. *The Century*. Cambridge, UK: Polity 2007.

_____, and Slavoj Žižek. *Philosophy in the Present*. Cambridge, UK: Polity 2009.

Ballard, J.G. *The Complete Short Stories of J.G. Ballard*. New York: W.W. Norton, 2009.

_____. *Super-Cannes*. New York: Picador, 2002.

Barthes, Roland. *Mythologies*. New York: Hill and Wang, 1972.

Basbanes, Nicholas. *A Gentle Madness: Bibliophiles, Bibliomanes, and the Eternal Passion for Books*. New York: Henry Holt, 1995.

Bauman, Zygmunt. *Does Ethics Have a Chance in a World of Consumers?* Cambridge, MA: Harvard University Press, 2009.

Benjamin, Walter. *The Arcades Project*. Cambridge, MA: Belknap Press of Harvard University Press, 2002.

Borkenau, Franz. *End and Beginning*. New York: Columbia University Press, 1981.

Braudel, Fernand. *Civilization and Capitalism, 15th–18th Century*, 3 Vols. New York: Harper & Row, 1981–1985.

_____. *Civilization and Capitalism, 15th-18th Century*, 3 Vols. London: Phoenix Press, 2001–2002.

_____. *Memory and the Mediterranean*. New York: Alfred A. Knopf, 2001.

Brown, Wendy. *Walled States, Waning Sovereignty*. Boston: Zone Books, 2010.

Calabresi, Massimo. "The War on Secrecy." *Time*, December 13, 2010.

Campbell, Joseph. *The Mythic Image*. Princeton, NJ: Princeton University Press, 1990.

Chadwick, N. Kershaw. *Russian Heroic Poetry*. Cambridge, UK: Cambridge University Press, 1932.

Danielou, Alain. *Gods of Love and Ecstasy: The Traditions of Shiva and Dionysus*. Rochester, VT: Inner Traditions, 1984.

Debray, Regis. *Transmitting Culture*. New York: Columbia University Press, 2000.

de Certeau, Michel. *The Practice of Everyday Life*. Berkeley: University of California Press, 2002.

De Hamel, Christopher. *A History of Illuminated Manuscripts*. London: Phaidon Press, 1994.

Deleuze, Gilles. *Francis Bacon: The Logic of Sensation*. London and New York: Continuum, 2005.

_____, and Felix Guattari. *Anti-Oedipus: Capitalism and Schizophrenia*. New York: Penguin Classics, 2009.

_____ and _____. *A Thousand Plateaus*. London: Continuum, 2004.

Ebert, John David. *Celluloid Heroes & Mechanical Dragons: Film as the Mythology of Electronic Society*. Christchurch, New Zealand: Cybereditions, 2005.

_____. *Dead Celebrities, Living Icons: Tragedy & Fame in the Age of the Multimedia Superstar*. NY: Praeger/Greenwood, 2010.

Eisenstein, Elizabeth L. *The Printing Press as an Agent of Change*. Cambridge, UK: Cambridge University Press, 1997.

Fraenger, Wilhelm. *Bosch*. New York: Prestel, 2003.

George, Andrew, ed., *The Epic of Gilgamesh*. New York: Barnes & Noble Books, 1999.

Giedion, Siegfried. *Mechanization Takes Command*. New York: Oxford University Press, 1948.

_____. *Space, Time and Architecture*. Cambridge, MA: Harvard University Press, 2008.

Hauser, Christine. "Best Buy Feels the Pressure of Rivals on the Web." *The New York Times,* December 17, 2010.

Hawass, Zahi. *The Treasures of the Pyramids*. New York: Barnes & Noble Books, 2003.

Hayden, Dolores. *Building Suburbia: Green Fields and Urban Growth, 1820–2000*. New York: Vintage Books, 2004.

Heidegger, Martin. *Towards the Definition of Philosophy*. London and New York: Continuum, 2008.

Hussein, Mohammed A. *Origins of the Book: From Papyrus to Codex*. Greenwich, CT: New York Graphic Society, 1970.

Innis, Harold. *The Bias of Communication*. Toronto: University of Toronto Press, 1971.

_____. *Empire and Communications*. Toronto: University of Toronto Press, 1972.

Keen, Andrew. *The Cult of the Amateur: How Today's Internet Is Killing Our Culture*. New York: Doubleday/Currency, 2007.

Kierkegaard, Soren. *The Concept of Dread*. Princeton, NJ: Princeton University Press, 1957.

Kilgour, Fredrick G. *The Evolution of the Book*. New York: Oxford University Press, 1998.

Landler, Mark, and Scott Shane. "U.S. Sends Warning to People Named in Cable Leaks." *The New York Times,* January 6, 2011.

Lewis-Williams, David. *The Mind in the Cave*. London: Thames & Hudson, 2004.

McCarthy, Cormac. *The Road*. New York: Vintage International, 2007.

McLuhan, Marshall. *The Gutenberg Galaxy*. Toronto: University of Toronto Press, 2002.

_____. "Television in a New Light." In *The Meaning of Commercial Television*. Edited by Stanley T. Donner. The Texas Stanford Seminar 1966. Austin: University of Texas Press, 1967.

Mumford, Lewis. *The City in History*. New York: Harcourt, 1989.

_____. *Technics and Civilization*. New York: Harcourt Brace, 1963.

Nissen, Hans. *The Early History of the Ancient Near East, 9000–2000 B.C.* Chicago: University of Chicago Press, 1984.

Ong, Walter. *The Presence of the Word: Some Prolegomena for Cultural and Religious History*. New Haven: Yale University Press, 1967.

Ouaknin, Marc-Alain. *Mysteries of the Alphabet*. New York: Abbeville Press, 1999.

Panofsky, Erwin. *Studies in Iconology*. New York: Oxford University Press, 1972.

Singer, P.W. *Wired for War: The Robotics Revolution and Conflict in the 21st Century*. New York: Penguin, 2009.

Somaiya, Ravi. "Hundreds of WikiLeaks Mirror Sites Appear." *The New York Times,* December 5, 2010.

Spector, Rober. *Amazon.com: Get Big Fast*. New York: HarperBusiness, 2000.

Starr, Paul. *The Creation of the Media: Political Origins of Modern Communications.* New York: Basic Books, 2004.

Stiegler, Bernard. *Technics and Time, 1: The Fault of Epimetheus.* Stanford, CA: Stanford University Press, 1998.

Stross, Randall. *Planet Google: One Company's Audacious Plan to Organize Everything We Know.* New York: Free Press, 2008.

Thompson, Derek. "The iPod Is Dead to Me." *http://www.theatlantic.com/business/archive/2010/10/the-ipod-is-dead-to-me/65148/.*

Thompson, William Irwin. *Coming into Being: Artifacts and Texts in the Evolution of Consciousness.* New York: Palgrave Macmillan, 1998.

Virilio, Paul. *Desert Screen.* London: Continuum, 2002.

_____. *Grey Ecology.* New York: Atropos Press, 2009.

_____. *Negative Horizon.* New York: Continuum, 2006.

Williams, Raymond. *Television.* London and New York: Routledge Classics, 2003.

Young, Jeffrey S., and William L. Simon. *iCon Steve Jobs: The Greatest Second Act in the History of Show Business.* Hoboken, NJ: Wiley, 2005.

Zimmer, Heinrich. *Philosophies of India.* Princeton, NJ: Princeton University Press, 1989.

Žižek, Slavoj. *Living in the End Times.* London: Verso Books, 2010.

Index